THE RADICAL WRONG

LIES OUR FOUNDING FATHERS NEVER TOLD US

Victor Daniels, Ph.D.

WASHINGTON, JEFFERSON, LINCOLN, AND OTHERS REFUTE RIGHT-WING EXTREMISTS

THE RADICAL WRONG:
LIES OUR FOUNDING FATHERS NEVER TOLD US

WASHINGTON, JEFFERSON, LINCOLN, & OTHERS REFUTE RIGHT-WING EXTREMISTS

Victor Daniels

ISBN: 9781479165803

Cover drawing by Griffin Barnes

For further information see <www.radicalwrong.com>

TABLE OF CONTENTS

PART III: HEAL YOURSELF, HEAL THE NATION, HEAL THE WORLD

For free downloads of choice quotes and selections to send others,
see **<http://radicalwrong.com>**

"Half a truth is often a great lie." Benjamin Franklin

"A lie gets halfway around the world before the truth has a chance to get its pants on." Winston Churchill

DEDICATION

This book is dedicated to *Occupy Wall Street!,* to the broader *Occupy!* movements, and to the many who have been living in tents, standing in the rain, facing dictators' guns in Arab countries, and helping all the citizens of our nation and the world become people of conscience once again.

It is time to take back the government from government bureaucracy, big business corpocracy, and other entrenched interests. And it is time to give the People a true voice at every level of government. Millions now see that few in power truly hear our wishes and complaints. Many of us resent sending young people to fight and die in unnecessary wars; paying heavy taxes to support such wars; the effects of corporate money machines on elections and government policy; and specific religions trying to enshrine their sectarian beliefs in laws that that bind us all. Men, women, and children of all colors, races, and backgrounds make up the 99%. Some live in comfortable homes and some are homeless. By contrast, the 1% is largely a white male club dedicated to domination rather than democracy. *Occupy!* inspired me to write this book to show that **the wisdom of our founding fathers belongs to all our people – not to a misguided, misquoting privileged minority who simply do not understand or speak for our nation's deepest values.**

Prologue

Recently I was chatting with a woman from another country who said, 'I have encountered a strange phenomenon here. At home someone else and I can disagree about a political question and have a thoughtful dialogue. But you Americans seldom seem to talk about politics with the goal of trying to deepen your insight.'"

"What do we do instead?" I asked

"You act like fans at a sporting event. When someone on your side says something, no matter how stupid or inane, you cheer as if you were yelling for your home team. And when someone who holds a different view makes a statement, even if it's a valid point, you boo as if you were yelling insults at the referee. You don't care about finding out what's true—you just want to win. It is as if you've agreed that it's all right to be mistaken, ignorant and stupid as long as your side scores a goal, or as long as you and your fellow true believers agree that you're right, no matter how wrong you may actually be."

In politics, it is often implied that we are acceptable human beings only if we think and act like our fellow "conservatives" or "liberals," drool like Pavlov's dog when someone on our side slobbers their canned phrases or images for the thousandth time, and for heaven's sake, don't question the trance in which we and others dance. (Meanwhile, be sure to mouth platitudes about individualism.)

Such attitudes are the opposite of the thoughtful dialogue that deepens our understanding that Thomas Paine, George Washington, Benjamin Franklin, Thomas Jefferson, James Madison, and Abraham Lincoln advocated. Mark Twain offers a key insight: "All generalizations are false, including this one." We may believe in some general principle, but have to look carefully at each unique situation if we hope to act wisely.

You can apply that attitude with this book. As soon as you see whom a quotation is from, be aware of whether you have a positive or negative response, and whether you're cheering or booing. Notice yourself reacting with your old program--in your mind, your emotions, and even your body. Then read the passage and truly reflect on it. As you do, you might find that some statements from people who evoke your knee-jerk negative reactions make good sense to you. And some from people you admire may be nonsense. As you rethink some of what you thought you believed, you will have moved out of cheerleading into true critical and creative thinking.

Introduction: Whatever Happened to "Liberty and Justice for All"?

"These are the times that try men's souls. The summer soldier and the sunshine patriot will, in the crisis, shrink from the service of his country; but he that stands it NOW, deserves the love and thanks of man and woman."
Thomas Paine

This is such a time. It is a watershed moment. We can save what is left of our democracy or lose it. If we lose it now, we may lose it forever, for there are those who are trying to enthrone themselves as permanent overlords. Today they are on the attack like sharks that smell blood in the water, prattling about democracy even as they dismantle it.

In recent years right wing extremists have exerted an influence on American politics far out of proportion to their numbers and far from the consensus of most Americans. They are right in about fifteen percent of their program and perspective. The rest is just plain wrong.

Yet like wolves in sheep's clothing, they proclaim loudly that *they* are the ones who are trying to preserve the nation's vital traditions even as they sabotage them from within. Bizarre as it may seem, this movement's haywire honchos actually dare to assert that their rigid, dogmatic ideology reflects the ideas and intentions of the American republic's visionary founding fathers.

In reality, they have just plain lost touch with most of the ideals of our nation's founders. Ironically, anyone who examines their words and platforms with an unbiased eye will surely conclude that if today's right wing radicals had been alive in 1776, many –perhaps even most-- would have been cheering loudly for the Redcoats, hoping for the continued rule of the British Crown, and opposing the American Revolution with all their might.

Although politics is no more the essence of life itself than a vase is the essence of the flowers it holds, it is a container for our lives and fortunes. For a few people it becomes the center of their universe. In recent decades our shared understandings about our government's central tasks have broken down. These days that perennial question from the pollsters, "Do you think our country is moving in the right direction or the wrong direction," gets more "wrong direction" than "right direction" answers regardless of which party holds power.

America is in trouble. It is in trouble because people cannot find jobs. It is in trouble because too many of the 1% who own 20% of the nation's assets show no sign that they care about the well-being of anyone else, or the good health of our air, land and waters. Right wing fanatics have developed a bizarrely distorted belief system that causes them and others to sink ever deeper into ideological quicksands that are diametrically opposed to the thoughts and intentions of our founding fathers.

Lacking understanding of what Paine, Washington, Jefferson and their companions intended, today's political celebrities of the far right have pasted together a self-serving ideology that directs them to impose their misguided agenda on all citizens of the Republic.

Let me be clear. By "right wing fanatics" I do not mean mainstream Republicans such as Dwight D.

Eisenhower, Everett Dirksen, Gerald Ford, Bob Dole, and other such reasonable men and women. Today's right wing extremists call Republicans who are capable of independent thought, and who show respect and mutual courtesy toward their political opponents RINOS – "Republican in name only." Blinded by ideology, such hard-line zealots have it backwards. As I see it, *they themselves are the RINOS.* They wrap themselves in a cloak of ultra patriotic, pseudo-democratic rhetoric and then try to impose their own sectarian political and religious agendas on the nation. Dwight D. Eisenhower did not support that. Barry Goldwater did not support that. And today's Republicans who think for themselves, draw their own conclusions, and make their own decisions do not support it either. But they have been so cowed into submission by the sledgehammer tactics wielded by the militant me-too political bullies of the far right that they are timid about speaking against the latter's agendas. I suggest that when you hear someone use the term "RINO," make a mental note that *he or she is actually talking about himself or herself. The right wing extremists are the real RINOs.* They are not Republicans as I have known them for most of my adult lifetime. Those right wing radicals who want to dictate how the rest of us are supposed to think and act are way out on a limb. It's time to saw it off.

I have no complaint about the rip-roaring right's haywire honchos and their followers *as people.* In many ways they're a lot like you and me. Some are among my friends and relatives. I say hello when I meet them on the sidewalk, and nod or wave when I pass them on the road. And if my radically right-wing neighbor and I are both pruning or grafting our fruit trees, we'll probably do it pretty much the same way. For the most part it is not them as people, but their *misguided political actions, beliefs, and attitudes* that need to be confronted and transformed to avoid catastrophic domino effects of future problems. In the pages of this book, I will use the terms "right-wing extremists," "ultra-right wingers," "radical rightists" and "the Radical Wrong"—as synonyms. They mean the same thing. You know who they are. Maybe you're among them. But even if so, you just might find enough of value here to keep you reading.

There was a time, after the Declaration of Independence, the Revolutionary War, and the writing of the Constitution, when the United States was an inspiration for the world. During World War II, from Europe to Asia and the Pacific it played a key role in defending liberty. Later, America played a key role in rebuilding countries that had been our enemies in that vast war. A friend of mine tells this story: "In 1968 I was in Czechoslovakia as the publicist for a United Artists film crew that was shooting the movie, *The Bridge at Remagen.* In those days Czechoslovakia was still under a Communist regime. Just as a gesture we converted some of our pay into Kennedy silver half dollars and spread them around among the local people we were working with. They *treasured* those coins! Just holding something from America, which they saw as the land of freedom, was like an amulet or talisman to them. We couldn't have given them a finer gift."

In this anonymous modern world where it's easy to be overlooked, forgotten, stepped-on, and exploited, it's no wonder many people feel alienated, angry, depressed, or hopeless.

Recent decades and events have dimmed the glow of America's lamp of liberty. Yet much as we might like to ignore the dark forces in our midst, they are real, and can grow even larger if they are not addressed. Many people are bewildered. Some feel like Michael Moore, who wrote, *Dude, Where's My Country?* Many believe that no political party speaks for them because those who run big business are calling so many of the shots and are paying off so many of the politicians.

What a turn-about! In 1774 Thomas Paine, one of the great writers and patriots of the day, penned a pamphlet titled *Common Sense.* Although today's right wing ideologues would have you believe that they follow in his footsteps, as you soon will see, most of their views are *the very opposite* of Paine's and those of his distinguished colleagues. The time has come to put things right.

Why have so many people been so misled? Because these days few read the actual words of our founding fathers and other great figures in American history. Leaders of the far right may report what those visionaries said, but often they report it incorrectly, in ways that serve their own agendas. If you listen carefully, you'll usually find that a quoted line or two is torn out of context, and most of the time right-wing extremists don't even do that: Rather, they tell you what the founders said and meant in their own words, distorting the meanings as they do.

By contrast, here you will read the actual words of Thomas Paine, Benjamin Franklin, George Washington, Thomas Jefferson James Madison, Abraham Lincoln, and others. Some of these passages go on at some length, so that their messages are quite clear. As the founders speak to you **in their very own words**, you will more deeply understand the kind of nation they envisioned. This book of simple truths corrects many misconceptions. *For as long as it takes to read this book, I invite you to set aside the slogans and positions of whatever party or group of the right, left, or center you support and to reflect deeply and honestly on the thoughts that are our collective heritage.* I do not mean to give you a new party line to follow, but to provoke you to think more deeply and go beyond old truisms and clichés.

This work is not intended to be either "liberal" or "conservative." These words are in quotation marks because as commonly used today they are largely misleading or meaningless. They are like cerebral blood clots that slow our minds and dim our understanding. I know "conservatives" who advocate major changes, and "liberals" who want to keep most things largely as they are.

In fact, in many ways citizens of right, left, and center are pretty much alike. If so-called "progressive" and "conservative" parents are at the playground with their children, what matters to both is that their children enjoy themselves and don't fall off the swing. Such shared humanity has no national or cultural or class boundaries. I recall warming my hands one cold January morning over an oil drum fireplace in a vacant lot in Harlem along with men from the neighborhood. I remember squatting on earthen floors next to mud stoves in the kitchens of humble huts in places as diverse as Mexico and Chile, India and Indonesia. And I have attended grand catered events of multimillionaire friends, and hung out with them in their classy kitchens on days when they were just having a grilled cheese sandwich. Everywhere people gather around some kind of cooking fire. Everywhere people need food and shelter. Everywhere, most people are concerned about the well-being of their family and friends. The basic human needs and concerns are universal.

With a little help from "the better angels of our nature," as Lincoln put it, we can return to a path on which we will once again work together toward shared goals. Then perhaps the United States may even regain something of the respect from the rest of the world that it enjoyed back in the nineteen fifties and sixties, but since then has largely lost.

Let's put it plainly: Beginning in the 1970s, Radical Wrong extremists inside and outside right wing think tanks began *actively trying to hijack the intentions of the Constitution and the founding fathers*. Let's look at the dictionary:

> **hi-jack** (also **high-jack**)
> *verb [trans.]*
> Illegally seize (an aircraft, ship, or vehicle) in transit and force it to go to a different destination or use it for one's own purposes: three armed men hijacked a white van]
> [as n.] (**hijacking**) *an eight-hour hijacking.*
> . steal (goods) by seizing them in transit

. take over (something) and use it for a different purpose: *the organization had been hijacked by extremists.*

Reread that last sentence: "the organization had been hijacked by extremists." That's actually in the dictionary. In the U.S. today it is not just our political ideals that are being hijacked – it's the mantle of patriotism worn by the founders of our republic. To further their agenda, those who are bankrolling right-wing radicals have enlisted the most ethically challenged public relations hired guns that money can buy. Some are on political payrolls. Others are in right wing think tanks or top-tier ad agencies. And, yes, some are even editors and employees of the media themselves. Together they are taking us for a shrouded ride into a dark tunnel that is not in your interests, not in mine, and in many cases not even in their own.

"Not even in their own?" you might wonder. ""How can that be?"

It's simple. The plutocrats *(Dictionary: "plu-to-crat: a person whose power derives from their wealth")* who run the country in their own interest for their own profit have hoodwinked well-meaning, honest regular citizens who think of themselves as "conservative." In some cases they have bought them off with huge financial contributions to pseudo-messiahs who are the hard-hearted prophets of religious imperialism. In return, the ordinary middle class and working people hypnotized by these pseudo-messiahs have supported a plutocratic agenda that is opposed to their own real interests. Some of the other regular folks who have been taken in by the Radical Wrong's bombastic accusations and false promises are well-meaning old-timers (people who for the most part are a lot like me) who just want to keep things the way they used to be. Many are only now realizing that they're pawns in the extremists' games.

Many right wing extremists are interested only in pseudo-democracy that serves as a fig leaf to cover their own ambitions and greed.

Many Radical Wrongists are driven to dominate—such as in the "New World Order" agenda. They see themselves as the ruling class and our country as the ruling country and want to keep it all that way. Many of them don't care a whit about the well-being or freedom of your Aunt Sadie and Sister Sue and the millions of others like them. Meanwhile, they wrap themselves in the flag, play the national anthem loudly, and act as if they have a monopoly on those historic symbols. But as Bill Clinton remarked, "*You can put wings on a pig, but that doesn't make it an eagle.*"

Some right wing religious imperialists are even convinced that *their* church's doctrine should be written into law and imposed on everyone by the government (even though many other churches believe quite differently.) These authoritarian ideologues want the government to command you and me how to live our lives in matters that hae nothing to do with the rightful realm of governing, in direct violation of the First Amendment. Then they have the gall to proclaim, "That government is best that governs least." If we disobey, they are ready to have the government handcuff us, throw us in jail, and/or confiscate our property -- in direct violation of the Fifth Amendment. This tyrannical, punitive attitude is the opposite of a democratic one. The Republican Party of Dwight D. Eisenhower, which like the Democratic party of Franklin D. Roosevelt, was genuinely dedicated to realizing the egalitarian ideals of our founding fathers (". . . *we hold these truths to be self-evident: that all men are created equal.* . ."), has been lying on its deathbed in recent years, kept barely alive on life support by a few good men and women who are vilified day in and day out by blindly self-righteous ultra loudmouth politicians among the Radical Wrong's rigid true believers. For example, when a good Republican Senator who has dared to think for herself, Maine's Olympia

Snowe, recently chose not to run for re-election she said, "An atmosphere of polarization and 'my way or the highway' ideologies has become pervasive in campaigns and in our governing institutions. . . . I see a vital need for the political center in order for our democracy to flourish and to find solutions that unite rather than divide us. It is time. . . to return to an era of civility in government driven by a common purpose to fulfill the promise that is unique to America."

Don't "swallow whole" what anyone tells you – not me, not anyone else, nor "the authorities" of any group or party.

Today a widely accepted Big Lie is that either government or business is virtuous and the other is evil. This causes more confusion than clarity and hides more than it reveals. Perhaps you yourself realize that neither government nor business *per se* is the issue. You may have one next-door neighbor who is honest, decent, and kind, and another who lies, steals, and acts in almost every nasty way you can think of. Or you may have a neighbor who smiles and speaks in a soft, charming voice while he plots to bilk you out of everything you own – a textbook sociopath. Many people who met Soviet dictator and hatchet man Josef Stalin made such comments as, "I found him very likable" – even as he was having millions of people murdered. You will find these types in government, business, both major parties, and sometimes even in Churches. One will help you, while another will stab you in the back at every turn.

Trouble crops up in any social institution, whether government, commercial, political, or nonprofit, when greedy, insensitive, or power-driven people get into positions of influence—especially if they are unusually articulate, charming, or both.

Too often such people reshape goals, policies, procedures, and tactics of their legislative chamber, agency, or business to reflect their own twisted agendas. That means trouble for you and me. There are also many average Joes and Janes who respond to the incentives in their organization, then cover their backsides by denying responsibility when anything goes wrong. We could use more good men and women with President Harry Truman's attitude that "the buck stops here."

SIGN FROM HARRY TRUMAN'S DESK

But all this is so grave and serious. If we can't find something to laugh about in it all from time to time, we are in bad shape. So I have included comments by the great humorists and writers Mark Twain and Will Rogers, and also some contemporary figures.

My own reflections are labeled **Comment,** indented, or **SOLUTIONS,** indented with bullet points. These are what make sense to me now. They are not the agenda of any organized group or party. You will surely disagree with some of them. Good—as long as you're thinking and not just reacting automatically with a party-line knee-jerk response. I ask only that you truly think through the questions raised here *for yourself*, and *then* to act. To minimize injured feelings, I have tried to follow Thomas Paine's example in avoiding personal references to living individuals. But since I am no Thomas Paine, I have not *entirely* avoided them. I apologize for the lack of an index – the publisher tells me they are difficult to do with e-books because the pages change when you change the font size, but you can do a search of the text for whatever you want to find. Photographs give faces to the voices behind some of the messages. The quotations and pictures include a few people who were not political leaders at all, but who made comments that it pleased me to include, such as:

"For every complicated question, there is an answer that is short, simple, and wrong." *H.L. Mencken*

Now, on to what our nation's founders *actually said,* and how we can resurrect their vision. Whenever someone tries to convince you that *they* know about what our founding fathers' words mean and you are wrong, *be very skeptical.* Be careful not to "swallow whole" what anyone tells you—*not me, not anyone else, nor "the authorities" of any group or party.* When you chug-a-lug down the programs and platforms of others without thinking them through yourself, you are a sucker, a "mark" in the language of gambling casinos. *Ask yourself what the vested interests of the authorities or the party are—interests that might be measured in wealth, power, ideology—or even just people's wish to gain and keep the approval of others in their circle.* Instead of buying into sleazy slogans and malicious metaphors, consult your own direct experience. **Remember that every party's program is flawed. Yes, every** party. Some of the people quoted in these pages disagreed with each other. Some even disagreed with themselves when speaking to different audiences at different times. You always have the right to think for yourself about what makes sense, what seems true, and what does not.

There are major omissions here. I have skipped over the fact that Washington and Jefferson themselves owned slaves and benefited from their labor. Both accepted slavery as a part of their time and place, yet also spoke out against it, and Jefferson fought vigorously against its extension into newly-settled territories. I have also skipped over the systematic genocide carried out by the United States against American Indians. I have not included quotations from the continent's native peoples, or commentary about them, or done more than barely mention the role of the Iroquois Confederacy's model of government in the development of the American Constitution. To examine the history of our nation's relations with the Native American peoples would require another book as large as this one. Nor have I given extensive treatment to our relations with other nations. To keep a sharp focus, I have stayed close to events and people related to the American Revolution and the political history and traditions of the United States as viewed from the inside.

What's my attitude? When I'm fully present, it is empirical, pragmatic, and I like to think that I'm also at least somewhat visionary. I do my best to tune in to what is actually happening, including phenomena that it is more comfortable to avoid noticing. I try to assess what is best left as is, and what requires some kind of change. The essence of scientific training (of which I had quite a bit) is *a commitment to finding out what is actually so and what is not.* If we can't be certain about something, often we can at least assess how probable it is. I try to treat beliefs and opinions as hypotheses to be tested, and thereby proven, disproven, or revised. I try to solve problems by finding out what works. This means that when possible, great-sounding ideas for political or economic innovation can be tried on an experimental basis on a small scale, and the results assessed, before putting them into effect system-wide. Then they can be modified and improved, implemented widely, or discarded as not so hot.

In all this, remember that changes of almost every kind, whatever their direction and intent, are invariably called "reforms" by their advocates. (A prominent example is "tort reform," which is a code name for taking some of your rights away.) The name "reform" usually means *nothing but movement in a direction that fits somebody's agenda.* Tomorrow's "reform" can be in the very opposite direction from today's. The word means only doing something different than we're doing now. It's mostly meaningless.

Now as I sit writing, and take a moment to look out the window as shafts of sunlight filter through. I find myself pondering **the kind and quality of contact** that government, politicians, corporations, and you and I make with each other. Some forms of contact enrich us, while others impoverish us personally or spiritually—such as the enmity between people and groups that develops so easily and so often. *"What is the character of this contact?"* is a vital question. It is defined by behavior: Who does what to whom, how, under what circumstances? It is defined by emotion: What feelings does each of these people have as they act in ways that affect each other? What thoughts and beliefs does each have about the other, and about himself or herself in relation to the other? The kind and quality of our contacts with each other, and also with our natural world, is the essence of what is questioned here.

This work was written in a North American context, with reference to the history and central figures of the United States. Nonetheless, I hope that if you are from another country and culture, you may also find these pages useful. The cast of characters is local, but as Thomas Paine said, many of the circumstances to which it refers are universal, and "The cause of America is in great measure the cause of all mankind."

* * *

PART I:
DEMOCRACY IN CRISIS

These chapters offer insight into the great sweep of the founders' vision for a democratic republic, and the thinking that went into it. They address both ideas that were distilled into the Constitution, and related matters the founders viewed as important to the birth and success of the new nation. Even though some of their words and ideas recorded here did not manage to get the approval of the entire Constitutional Convention, they speak of the values that helped lay a strong foundation for a government that its citizens could trust.

Their words help us look at how their concerns are being honored and how they are being violated in our time. Close scrutiny of their statements lets us see how crucial elements of their intentions are getting trampled underfoot. It also provides a basis for asking, "Which values and ideals voiced by today's prominent political, economic, and media figures should we strive to uphold and develop, and which are unworthy of our respect?"

1. The Reasons for Government

From the early 1930s through 1980, our government was widely viewed as trying to improve the well-being of the people. That era's presidents –Franklin D. Roosevelt, Harry Truman, Dwight D. Eisenhower, and John F. Kennedy lived during that time and helped that outlook along. Beginning in 1980, the rhetoric from Washington shifted to exalting big business and demeaning government, bombarding the public day after day and year after year with messages that government was fundamentally bad and disreputable. People who had worked together and respected each other began taking the side of business or the side of government, poisoning the civic dialogue and leading to the antagonistic attitudes we hear today. Let's listen to what those who founded our government said about its role and character.

"We hold these truths to be self-evident: that all men are created equal, that they are endowed by their Creator with certain inalienable rights; that among these are life, liberty, and the pursuit of happiness; that to secure these rights, governments are instituted among men, deriving their just powers from the consent of the governed."
The Declaration of Independence

"Why has government been instituted at all? Because the passions of man will not conform to the dictates of reason and justice without constraint." **Alexander Hamilton**

"Government is instituted for the common good; for the protection, safety, prosperity, and happiness of the people; and not for profit, honor, or private interest of any one man, family, or class of men**." John Adams**

"Among the natural rights of the Colonists are these: First, a right to life; Secondly, to liberty; Thirdly, to property; together with the right to support and defend them in the best manner they can. . . . A commonwealth or state is a body politic, or civil society of men, united together to promote their mutual safety and prosperity by means of their union. . . . The first fundamental, positive law of all common wealths or states is the establishing the legislative power. . . Secondly, the Legislative has no right to absolute, arbitrary power over the lives and fortunes of the people. . . . There should be one rule of justice for rich and poor, for the favorite at court, and the countryman at the plough." **Samuel Adams**

Thomas Paine wrote, "Were the impulses of conscience clear, uniform and irresistibly obeyed," man would need no other lawgiver; but that not being the case, he finds it necessary to surrender up a part of his property to furnish means for the protection of the rest; and this he is induced to do by the same prudence which in every other case advises him, out of two evils to choose the least. . . . Security being the true design and end of government, it unanswerably follows that whatever form thereof appears most likely to ensure it to us, with the least expense and greatest benefit, is preferable to all others."

Paine also reflected on the origins of government. "Let us suppose a small number of persons settled in some sequestered part of the earth. . . Four or five united would be able to raise a tolerable dwelling in the midst of a wilderness, but one man might labour out the common period of life without accomplishing any thing. . . . in proportion as they surmount the first difficulties . . .which bound them together in a common cause, they will begin to relax in their duty and attachment to each other: and this remissness will point out the necessity of establishing some form of government to supply the defect of moral virtue. . . . In this first parliament every man by natural right will have a seat."

THOMAS PAINE

Paine commented on bad governments and good ones: "When, in countries that are called civilized, we see age going to the workhouse and youth to the gallows, something must be wrong in its system of government. . ."

"When we suffer, or are exposed to the same miseries BY A GOVERNMENT, which we might expect In a country WITHOUT GOVERNMENT, our calamity is heightened by reflecting that we furnish the means by which we suffer. . . "

"When it shall be said in any country in the world, 'My poor are happy; neither ignorance nor distress is to be found among them; my jails are empty of prisoners, my streets of beggars; the aged are not in want, the taxes are not oppressive . . . when these things can be said, then may that country boast of its constitution and its government."

Like Paine, **George Washington** saw both positive and negative aspects of government. In the first instance, he said, "The unity of government, which constitutes you one people, is . . . a main pillar in the edifice of your real independence; the support of your tranquility at home, your peace abroad; of your safety; of your prosperity; of that very liberty which you so highly prize. . . . It is of infinite moment that you should properly estimate the immense value of your national union to your collective and individual happiness; that you should cherish a cordial, habitual, and immovable attachment to it."

On the other side, he noted, "Government is not reason; it is not eloquent; it is force. Like fire, it is a dangerous servant and a fearful master."

Thomas Jefferson, principal author of the *Declaration of Independence* and the *Bill of Rights*, had much to say about the nature of government. "We acknowledge that our children are born free; that that freedom is a gift of nature, and not of him who begot them. . . . Every man, and every body of men on earth, possess the right of self government. They receive it with their being from the hand of nature. Individuals exercise it by their single will; collections of men by that of their majority. . . ."

"If we are made in some degree for others, yet, in a greater sense, are we made for ourselves. . . . Nothing could so completely divest us of that liberty as the establishment of the opinion, that the state has a perpetual right to the services of all its members. . . ."

THOMAS JEFFERSON

"A wise and frugal government," he declared, "which shall leave men free to regulate their own pursuits of industry and improvement, and shall not take from the mouth of labor the bread it has earned - this is the sum of good government. . . . "

He elaborated by saying, "Experience has proved it safer, for the mass of individuals composing the society, to reserve to themselves personally the exercise of all rightful powers to which they are competent, and to delegate those to which they are not competent to deputies named, and removable for unfaithful conduct, by themselves immediately."

Jefferson was careful to note that *"Where the people are well-informed,* (my italics) they can be trusted with their own government; whenever things get so far wrong as to attract their notice, they may be relied on to set them to rights."

He was no knee-jerk defender of the established order. "What country can preserve its liberties, if its rulers are not warned from time to time that this people preserve the spirit of resistance? . . . I hold it, that a little rebellion, now and then, is a good thing, and as necessary in the political world as storms in the physical. . . . An observation of this truth should render honest republican governors so mild in their punishment of rebellion, as not to discourage them too much. It is a medicine necessary for the good health of government."

In Jefferson's time there was active debate between those who wanted a stronger Federal government and those who wanted to see power more dispersed. Jefferson spoke for the latter group. "I see . . . with the deepest affliction, the rapid strides with which the federal branch of our government is advancing towards the usurpation of all the rights reserved to the states, and the consolidation in itself of all powers, foreign and domestic. . . . The three ruling branches [of the federal government] are in combination to strip their colleagues, the State authorities, of the powers reserved by them. . . . The states should be watchful to note every material usurpation of their rights."

Finally, he pointed out that, "The execution of the laws is more important than the making them."

"Where an excess of power prevails. . . no man is safe in his opinions, his person, his faculties, or his possessions." ***James Madison***

James Madison, who had the main responsibility for drafting the Constitution, wrote, "It will be of little avail to the people that the laws are made by men of their own choice if the laws be so voluminous that they cannot be read, or so incoherent that they cannot be understood. . . ." Madison continued, "The essence of Government is power; and power, lodged as it must be in human hands, will ever be liable to abuse. . . In framing a government which is to be administered by men over men you must first enable the government to control the governed; and in the next place oblige it to control itself."

John Adams, who edited the Declaration of Independence and succeeded Washington as President, wrote about representative government. "In a large society, inhabiting an extensive country, it is impossible that the whole should assemble to make laws. The first necessary step, then, is to depute power from the many to a few of the most wise and good."

Adams added, "Fear is the foundation of most governments; but it is so sordid and brutal a passion, and renders men in whose breasts it predominates so stupid and miserable, that Americans will not be likely to approve of any political institution which is founded on it."

Andrew Jackson, the seventh President, took office in 1829. He said, "As long as our government is administered for the good of the people, and is regulated by their will, as long as it secures to us the rights of persons and of property, liberty of conscience and of the press, it will be worth defending."

> **Comment:** I have seen no clearer evidence for Washington, Paine, and Madison's statements above than **Jesse Ventura's** remarkable book, *63 Documents The Government Doesn't Want You to Read.* The book's pages contain *photocopies of actual government documents* obtained through the Freedom of Information Act. These include the CIA assassination manual; a prescription for a faked terrorist attack to give the government an excuse to attack the alleged terrorists; and accounts of toppling democratic governments in other countries and replacing them with dictators. For years it has been whispered that these events took place. Now Ventura's book confirms it. Those documents, and Ventura's book, are ~~crystal~~ clear statements of what our government has no business doing. The sequel, *American Conspiracies* is equally hard-hitting. These books are not the work of some far-out radical. Ventura was a Navy SEAL and later served as Governor of Minnesota. He ran and was elected as an independent because he did not trust either of the major parties.

"Government can and must provide opportunity, not smother it; foster productivity, not stifle it," said **Abraham Lincoln.** In a few words, he addressed both sides of a question that faces us today: "Must a government, of necessity, be too strong for the liberties of our people, or too weak to maintain its own existence?"

"It is not my intention to do away with government. It is rather to make it work—work with us, not over us; stand by our side, not ride on our back." *Abraham Lincoln*

"A government for the people must depend for its success on the intelligence, the morality, the justice, and the interest of the people themselves. **Grover Cleveland.** The only president to serve a first term, be defeated for a second term, and then subsequently re-elected, Cleveland also said, "It is better to be defeated standing for a high principle than to run by committing subterfuge."

"Let us never forget that government is ourselves and not an alien power over us. The ultimate rulers of our democracy are not a President and senators and congressmen and government officials, but the voters of this country." **Franklin D. Roosevelt**

> **Comment:** Ensuring our security is a central task of government. Police and firefighters are a first line of defense. Having a source of livelihood that provides shelter, enough to eat, and

clothing is an aspect of security. Good health is part of security. Traffic lights are part of security. Many of the radical right's policies are aimed at securing security for only the privileged few.

Thomas Paine also referred to the mutual assistance in which people form a government to do for each what we cannot do alone. Governments build roads and bridges. They inspect restaurant kitchens. They require labels on our food that tell us what is in it. If we cut the funding for all that, who will fight fires, help people who call 911, and fill potholes in the roads? But there is more:

THEODORE ROOSEVELT

"Behind the ostensible government sits enthroned an invisible government owing no allegiance and acknowledging no responsibility to the people.
Theodore Roosevelt

"The government, which was designed for the people, has got into the hands of the bosses and their employers, the special interests. An invisible empire has been set up above the forms of democracy." **Woodrow Wilson**

"The President of the United States is the Executive Secretary of the ruling class." **Anonymous**

Comment: The "invisible empire" is stronger today than at any time since the 1920s. It is a nexus of oligarchic government by those who care more about increasing (not just preserving) their wealth and special privileges than about the well-being of the nation and its people. Occasionally the tip of the iceberg of this "invisible empire" becomes visible, as has recently happened with the notorious Koch Brothers and Koch Industries, who have been and are working ceaselessly to make America an unapologetic oligarchy and plutocracy.

(*Dictionary: "oligarchy: a small group of people having control of a country, organization, or institution; (2) government by such a group." "Plutocracy: (1) government by the wealthy; (2) an elite or ruling class of people whose power derives from their wealth.)*

Who are the oligarchs? CEOs and corporate board members who are committed to the idea that government exists to serve their companies' interests; figures in agencies like the CIA and the FBI who have the power to manipulate legislators and presidents by causing them to fear for their lives or those of their families; and the inner circle of strategists in think tanks and political parties—especially the very well funded think tanks of the far right. For more than half a century now there has been a well organized, carefully orchestrated, and skillfully executed collusion of the few to transform the United States in into a plutocratic right-wing oligarchy. Hidden behind a screen of pseudo-patriotic rhetoric, it has been remarkably successful. ("Pseudo-patriotic?" Use your x-ray vision to look carefully and you will find that the flags of many who are waving them are moth-eaten and full of holes. You need only mention closing any kind of corporate tax loophole, for example, and the response is immediate: "Well, we'll just move our company to another country.") Only when the people recognize and throw off the yoke of this invisible empire will full democracy have a chance to emerge in the United States. That is different from the agenda of most right-wing extremists. Many of them have accepted (or have been paid to accept) the oligarchy's ideology and to support the agendas of the corporate tycoons who are using their money and power to control vanishing resources.

Mark Twain wrote, "Reader, suppose you were an idiot. And suppose you were a member of Congress. But I repeat myself."

"There is no more independence in politics than there is in jail. . . The more you observe politics, the more you've got to admit that each party is worse than the other." **Will Rogers**

"About all I can say for the United States Senate is that it opens with a prayer and closes with an investigation." *Will Rogers*

"The business community is not much interested in good government and it wants the present Republican control to continue just so long as the stock market soars and the new combinations of capital are left undisturbed." **Franklin D. Roosevelt, 1929**

"It is perfectly true that that government is best which governs least. It is equally true that that government is best which provides most." *(When it can do both, that's pretty good.)* **Walter Lippmann**

"Many people consider the things government does for them to be social progress but they regard the things government does for others as socialism." Chief Justice of the Supreme Court **Earl Warren**

"The essential humanity of men can be protected and preserved only where government must answer-not just to the wealthy; not just to those of a particular religion, or a particular race; but to all its people." **Robert F. Kennedy**

"As nightfall does not come at once, neither does oppression. In both instances, there is a twilight when everything remains seemingly unchanged. And it is in such twilight that we all must be most aware of change in the air – however slight – lest we become unwitting victims of the darkness." Supreme Court Justice **William O. Douglas**

"I have seen in the Halls of Congress more idealism, more humanness, more compassion, more profiles of courage than in any other institution that I have ever known. Vice President **Hubert Humphrey**

"Too often I find that the volume of paper expands to fill the available briefcases." California Governor **Jerry Brown**

Jesse Ventura, former governor of Minnesota, suggests, "I'd like . . . every fourth year [to] become a year in no laws are made, but the old laws are reviewed, updated, or deleted as needed. That way we won't get endless, obsolete laws piling up on the books."

> **Comment:** Perhaps Mark Twain, Will Rogers, Robert F. Kennedy, and Hubert Humphrey are all correct. The less possible it is for congressmen and congresswomen to be bought off by corporate and other big money interests, the more likely they are to act in accord with Humphrey's observation.
>
> The Radical Wrong's agenda advocates shrinking government by cutting services to citizens. That overlooks the fact that **nothing** else requires more and bigger government than the war machine. Half of the entire world's military spending is made by the U.S. government. Instead of beggaring our educational programs and laying off police and firefighters, downsizing the expansive role of the military is the most obvious place to cut the budget.
>
> Another blatant Big Lie can be heard in the din from the right about Social Security. It is deceptive in the extreme. The biggest present problem with social security, which right-wing sources conveniently neglect to mention, is that the government has borrowed an enormous sum of money from the Social Security Trust Fund. It owes the Trust Fund more money than it owes China. Reliable sources claim that the Right's real motive for attacking Social Security is to privatize it so that more of every dollar that goes into it will go to investment and brokerage companies and less will go to recipients' benefit checks. The reality is that the expense ratio of Social Security—that is, the percentage of its receipts required to run the agency and its programs-- is significantly lower than that of any investment or brokerage company's retirement program. It is highly efficient, a case in which big government works well, and in all a model government program.
>
> Regarding states' rights, critics decry the federal government's takeover of powers that the Constitution does not delegate to it, and that might better be left to the states. In general I agree. Indeed, the same phenomenon often occurs between a state and its cities and counties. For example, in California, for decades under Republican and Democratic administrations alike the state periodically raided revenue sources that had belonged to localities. In a number of other nations, state governments have considerably more autonomy than in the U.S. *But here is the central problem:* Very often those who cry "state's rights" are defending a state's desire to enshrine prejudices against certain groups into law (most often women or a racial group) or to impose narrow agendas favored by specific groups such as the "religious right" on everyone. At that point the national government has to step in and do its best to ensure that states make no law and no policy that abridges the principles of equality, liberty, and justice for all. If factions in the states would stop trying to give one group more privileges than another, such as making it harder for some citizens to vote and easier for others, or such as giving taxpayers' money to sectarian schools, there would be no need for the federal government to step in. But when the state government abridges the rights of some of its people, or gives some special privileges not available to others, it is an open invitation to the federal government to intervene and ensure that the rights of *all* the people are protected.

SOLUTIONS

- **Every law should be written so clearly, concisely, and precisely that anyone can understand it and few will misunderstand it. Jefferson's words combine two** statements: "leaving men free to regulate their own pursuits of industry and improvement" applies especially to those in business, while "shall not take from the mouth of labor the bread it has earned" applies especially to working people. Both items are important.

- As long as legislators and administrations are dependent on the money and power of special interests, the "invisible empire" will continue. Ending that dependence is vital.

- Stop trashing government, and instead carry out regular evaluation and innovation, both internal and by the people it serves, to make it more efficient less expensive, lighter on its feet, and more responsive and responsible.

- To put Social Security back on a secure footing, make relatively small adjustments in benefits to account for the changing demographic structure, analogous to those made two decades ago. This will fix it. Leave the basic structure of the program alone. Require the government to gradually repay the money it has borrowed from the Social Security Trust Fund.

* * *

2. Power, Politics, and "The Goddamn People"

Politics is about how power and resources are exercised and distributed. Among dictionary definitions of politics are these: *(1) "activities associated with the governance of a country or other area, esp. the debate or conflict among individuals or parties having or hoping to achieve power; (2) "a particular set of political beliefs or principles."* People's inclinations inevitably differ. Such differences have political effects. For example, in the academic department where I worked for many years, the Department Chair who preceded me, and I myself when my turn came, both favored a "run a tight ship" approach. In contrast, the Chair who succeeded me favored an "undertake great bold initiatives" approach. A later Chair had a "decide everything possible herself" attitude (which led to substantial discontent in the faculty,) while her successor had a "make sure everyone has input into major decisions" attitude (which worked out well). Through all that, we found it important to have an agreed-upon decision-making and procedures policy. When that was forgotten, as it was for some years, we went through a troublesome period until we adopted a new policy. We needed "rules of the road" that everyone accepted.

Politics can be loving and compassionate, with its basis in trust and mutual respect. Or it can be mistrustful, hard-edged and antagonistic. At its worst it is prejudiced, rigid, narrow-minded, and punitive. In truly democratic politics everyone can have a voice. In authoritarian politics, some seize power (whether by force or by selling the people a dominant narrative that the latter accept), and then those in power command the rest.

"Just because you do not take an interest in politics doesn't mean politics won't take an interest in you." **Pericles**

"Politics would be a helluva good business if it weren't for the goddamn people." **Richard Nixon**

"Instead of gazing at each other with suspicious or doubtful curiosity, let each of us hold out to his neighbor the hearty hand of friendship, and unite in drawing a line, which, like an act of oblivion, shall bury in forgetfulness every former dissension. Let the names of Whig and Tory be extinct; and let none other be heard among us, than those of a good citizen, an open and resolute friend, and a virtuous supporter of the RIGHTS of MANKIND, and of the FREE AND INDEPENDENT STATES OF AMERICA." **Thomas Paine**

"The alternate domination of one faction over another, sharpened by the spirit of revenge, natural to party dissension, which in different ages and countries has perpetrated the most horrid enormities, is itself a frightful despotism." **George Washington**

Washington had a deep distrust of political parties, and refused to join one himself. He wrote, "However [political parties] may now and then answer popular ends, they are likely in the course of time and things, to become potent engines, by which cunning, ambitious, and unprincipled men will be enabled to subvert the power of the people and to usurp for themselves the reins of government . . . which have lifted them to unjust dominion. . . The common and continual mischiefs of the spirit of party are sufficient to make it the interest and duty of a wise people to discourage and restrain it. (My italics) It serves always to distract the public councils, and enfeeble the public administration. It agitates the community with ill founded jealousies and false alarms; kindles the animosity of one part against another; foments occasionally riot and insurrection and opens the odor to foreign influence and corruption, which find a facilitated access to the government through the channel of party passions."

Even with those comments, Washington was not quite finished. He added, "All obstructions to the execution of the laws . . . serve to organize factions, to give it an artificial and extraordinary force. [This puts] in place of the delegated will of the nation, the will of a party, often a small, but artful and enterprising minority of the community; and, according to the   of different parties, to make the public administration the mirror of the ill-concerted and incongruous projects of faction, rather than the organ of consistent and wholesome plans, digested by common counsels, and modified by mutual interests."

GEORGE WASHINGTON

Washington refused pleas to run for a third term, which he would have won easily. Poet **Robert Frost** wrote: "I often say of George Washington that he was one of the few in the whole history of the world who was not carried away by power."

Poet **Walt Whitman** advised, "Disengage yourself from parties. The have been useful, and to some extent remain so but the floating, uncommitted electors. . . watching aloof, inclining victory this side or that side—such are the ones most needed, present and future. . . These savage, wolfish parties alarm me. . . . It behooves you to convey yourself implicitly to no party, nor submit blindly to their dictators, but steadily hold yourself judge and master over all of them."

"The cherishment of the people then was our principle. . . . [We are with] those who identify themselves with the people, have confidence in them, cherish and consider them as the most honest & safe depository of the public interest." . . . . "I am not a federalist, because I never submitted the whole system of my opinions to the creed of any party of men whatever, in religion, in philosophy, in politics or in anything else, where I was capable of thinking for my self. Such an addiction is the last degradation of a free and moral agent. If I could not go to heaven but with a party, I would not go there at all." **Thomas Jefferson**

"Dissent is the highest form of patriotism."
Thomas Jefferson

"The latent causes of faction are . . . sown in every man, and we see them everywhere brought into different degrees of activity according to the different circumstances of civil society. A zeal for different opinions concerning religion, concerning government, and many other points . . . have in turn divided mankind into parties, inflamed them with mutual animosity, and rendered them much more disposed to vex and oppress each other than to co-operate for the common good."
James Madison

"I have no private purpose to accomplish, no party objectives to build up, no enemies to punish—nothing to serve but my country." **Zachary Taylor,** "Old Rough and Ready."

"Officeholders are the agents of the people, not their masters. Not only is their time and labor due to the government, but they should scrupulously avoid in their political action, as well as in the discharge of their official duty, offending by a display of obtrusive partisanship their neighbors who have relations with them as public officials." **Grover Cleveland**

"To announce that there must be no criticism of the president, or that we are to stand by the president, right or wrong, is not only unpatriotic and servile, but is morally treasonable to the American people." **Theodore Roosevelt**

"Foolish fanatics . . . the men who form the lunatic fringe in all reform movements." **Theodore Roosevelt**

"I remember when I first came to Washington. For the first six months you wonder how the hell you ever got here. For the next six months you wonder how the hell the rest of them ever got here." **Harry S. Truman**. Truman also remarked, "My choice early in life was either to be a piano-player in a whorehouse or a politician. And to tell the truth, there's hardly any difference."

"When fanatics are on top there is no limit to oppression." Journalist **H.L. Mencken**

"Let us not seek the Republican answer or the Democratic answer, but the right answer." **John F. Kennedy**

"Let us not seek the blame for the past. Let us accept our own responsibility for the future." *John F. Kennedy*

"It is not enough to allow dissent. We must demand it. . . We dissent from the monstrous absurdity of a world where . . .men must kill their fellow men. We dissent from the sight of most of mankind living in poverty, stricken by disease, threatened by hunger and doomed to an early death after a life of unremitting labor. . . We dissent from the willful, heedless destruction of natural pleasure and beauty. We dissent from all those structures-of technology and of society itself-which strip from the individual the dignity and warmth of sharing in the common tasks of his community and his country." **Robert F. Kennedy**

JOHN WAYNE

"I didn't vote for him, but he's my president, and I hope he does a good job." *John Wayne* on John F. Kennedy's election

"The concepts of love and power are usually contrasted as polar opposites. Love is identified with a resignation of power and power with a denial of love. What is needed is a realization that power without love is reckless and abusive and that love without power is sentimental and anemic. Power at its best is love implementing the demands of justice. Justice at its best is love correcting everything that stands against love." **Martin Luther King, Jr.**

"To err is human. To blame someone else is politics." **Hubert H. Humphrey**

"My esteem in this country has gone up substantially. It is very nice now when people wave at me; they use all their fingers." **Jimmy Carter**

"Power is the great aphrodisiac." **Henry Kissinger.** Kissinger also wrote, **"**The illegal we do immediately. The unconstitutional takes a little longer." In some cases, he wasn't kidding.

"The Democrats are the party that says government will make you smarter, taller, richer, and remove the crabgrass on your lawn. The Republicans are the party that says government doesn't work and then they get elected and prove it." **P.J. O'Rourke.**

"The most miserable, sterile clichés are to be found in party politics. . . Basically it is an illusion to follow party lines . . . for parties always base themselves on manifestos, systems and the like, i.e., on abstract notions." Austrian philosopher **Rudolf Steiner**

"To. . . the Democratic and Republican parties. . . I was dangerous because I was a threat to their good-old-boy network. . . . I began to realize how crooked party politics are. They're at each other's throats all the time, unless someone on the outside is threatening their turf. Then they join forces and tear the newcomer to pieces." **Jesse Ventura**

"Congress seems drugged and inert most of the time... its idea of meeting a problem is to hold hearings or, in extreme cases, to appoint a commission." First African-American congresswoman and female presidential candidate **Shirley Chisholm**

"In this world there happen to be huge concentrations of private power which are as close to tyranny and as close to totalitarian as anything humans have devised, and they have extraordinary power. They are unaccountable to the public. There's only one way of defending rights that have been attained or extending their scope in the face of these private powers, and that's to maintain the one form of illegitimate power that happens to be somewhat responsive to the public and which the public can indeed influence. So you end up supporting centralized state power even though you oppose it. People who think there is a contradiction in that just aren't thinking very clearly." Linguist, philosopher, and historian **Noam Chomsky**

"The real two-party system in America is the Meanies and the Weenies. The Meanies want to take away your benefits, and the Weenies want to compromise with them." Congressman **Alan Grayson**

"In looking for people to hire, you look for three qualities: integrity, intelligence, and energy. And if they don't have the first, the other two will kill you." Berkshire Hathaway CEO **Warren Buffett**

"I don't know a single legislator who doesn't anguish on a regular basis over the votes he or she has to take. . . Most of the time, legislation is a murky brew, the product of one hundred compromises large and small, a blend of legitimate policy aims, political grandstanding, jerry-rigged regulatory schemes, and old-fashioned pork barrels. In the Senate I was confronted with the fact that the principled thing was less clear than I had originally thought; that either an aye vote or a nay vote would leave me with some trace of remorse." **Barack Obama.**

Obama also said, "You don't need a poll to know that the vast majority of Americans—Republican, Democrat, and independent—are weary of the dead zone that politics has become, in which narrow interests vie for advantage and ideological minorities seek to impose their own version of absolute truth. . . We feel in our gut the lack of honesty, rigor, and common sense in our policy debates, and dislike what appears to be a continuous menu of false or cramped choices."

"Our politics are being hijacked by a comparatively small number of people who seek to dominate the debate by screaming the loudest. . . They attempt to impose strict litmus tests and insist on conformity. They demonize dissent and consider all political opponents their enemies. Fear is their favorite tactic as they try to divide and conquer. . . We should know the dangers of demagogues, politicized religion and ideological absolutists by now." **John Avlon**

> **Comment:** The way out, Steiner suggests, is to see those dogmas for what they are, to be interested in finding out what's actually real, and tune in to our inner spirit and those of the people around us. With greater awareness, we have greater potential to escape false certainties, fraudulent fabrications and dangerous dogmas. When yesterday's ideas and attitudes turn out to be mistaken or inadequate, we can frame new questions and seek new answers.
>
> In colonial days, the revolutionaries differed in some of their opinions, but tended to treat each other with respect and civility, and joined together in a pragmatic fashion when they could. Washington refused to join a political party and was explicit in saying that parties intensified antagonisms and made wise government more difficult. (The Constitution says nothing about political parties.) "What Washington and others after him, including Lincoln, feared was not the party system as such but "the spirit of party," writes philosopher Jacob Needleman. By this term he meant the attitude that one's own faction or part was more important than the whole, or what came to the same thing that one's own party's interests were the same as the interests of the whole. The "spirit of party" meant the commitment to fight for one's own interests and to overcome or even destroy, rather than learn from the opposition. This view, of course, is intimately related the adversarial structure of our legal system.
>
> One major political divide is between those commonly labeled "liberals" and conservatives." Barry Goldwater had a fairly clear vision of conservatism that has been largely lost. He defined it as "economic, social, and political practices based on the successes of the past." He wrote that the *conscience* of a conservative was "pricked by anyone who would debase the dignity of the individual human being." He later said he should have said, "pricked by anyone *or any action* that debases human dignity." When asked, "Doesn't poverty debase human dignity?" he replied, "Of course it does," and added that if family, friends, and private charity cannot handle the job, the government must."
>
> Finally, he said, "Politics is the art of achieving the maximum amount of freedom for individuals that is consistent with the maintenance of social order"—an almost perfect statement of an "individual libertarian." (That perspective is defined below.)
>
> "Liberals," as the word was typically used in the 20th century, trust reason and intellect to find new solutions to problems that old solutions have not dealt with well. They emphasize compassion, kindness, decency, equality of opportunity, political equality, and the welfare of ordinary working people. They are more inclined to support government

action to realize positive social goals than conservatives, with special emphasis on eliminating discrimination against people who are poor or different from the majority. They tend to be more suspicious of big corporations than of big government, and favor government regulation to protect people's health and well-being. (Oddly enough, in the 19th Century, "liberal" meant just the opposite—it meant those who favored big business dominance and government support for big business over working people.) "Progressives" have a lot in common with liberals, but are more likely to oppose foreign wars and to try to defend Earth's ecosystems against pollution and dissolution.

In recent decades those labels have become so misleading that I use them only with quotation marks. The quotation marks mean, "Don't believe almost anything you think this label means." My dictionary defines conservative as "holding to traditional attitudes and values and cautious about change or innovation." It defines liberal as "Open to new behavior or opinions and favoring maximum individual liberty in political and social reform." But these days all that often gets turned upside down. In my region, the "liberals" tend to want to keep the towns and countryside pretty much as they have been, while the "conservatives" bulldoze every living thing to bare earth and build huge new suburbs and business and shopping developments—in other words, they make *radical changes*. The "liberals" are more likely to be content with modest lifestyles, while the "conservatives" are more likely to build palatial homes and multiple very pricey vacation retreats and spend lavishly on upscale cars. It's just plain crazy to speak of those who are maiming ecosystems as "conservative," and those who are trying to stop that damage as "liberal" or "radical," because the very opposite is true: Those who are trying to protect the good health of an ecosystem are acting conservatively, and those wanting to change it quickly and in large-scale ways are acting radically. The explanation, of course, is that by "conservative," people often mean conserving their privileges, wealth, and status –or their knee jerk ideologies-- rather than conserving real things in the world.

The Keystone XL pipeline is an example. It would have carried oil 1,700 miles from Canadian tar sands (the most environmentally destructive, climate-hostile of all methods of oil extraction) from the facilities of multinational corporations that own the rights to extract it to a refinery in Port Arthur, Texas, which would have *exported* much of the diesel from tar sands crude – it wouldn't even help solve the U.S. energy problem. Who opposed the pipeline? Above all, farmers and ranchers in Nebraska and neighboring states who were afraid that pipeline leaks would pollute the precious Ogallala aquifer (vital for drinking water and agriculture) and did not want the U.S. government seizing their land and giving it to a Canadian oil consortium. To me that's pretty darned conservative. But Shell oil, Valero oil, Exxon-Mobil, Koch Industries, the French oil company Total, and the Saudi Arabian government tried to paint themselves as the "conservatives" in that contest, and paint the farmers and ranchers as the radicals. They spent about 37 times more supporting the pipeline than was spent by citizens who opposed it. It's an airtight case that the oil companies were really the wild screaming radicals in that contest. (Kudos to President Obama for vetoing XL and to the thousands of citizens who pressed him to do so, from withholding campaign contributions to demonstrating on the White House lawn, where hundreds were arrested.) Similarly, Valero and another Texas oil company, Tesoro, tried to hoodwink California voters into passing a 2010 ballot measure that would have scrapped that state's strongest law to prevent air pollution. There too, calculated misuse of the "C" word turns everything upside down.

"The enemy isn't conservatism. The enemy isn't liberalism. The enemy is bullshit." *Lars-Erik Nelson*

"Conservative" may mean conserving old beliefs, attitudes, and habits. It is less often applied to conserving practices that protect and enhance people's freedom, equality, and opportunity. Too bad.

With "liberal" we need to ask, "liberate what, or whom?" "Liberalize what restrictive rules, laws, or procedures? (That's often important to business, and is a first-rate idea when the restrictions are not really protecting anything or anybody.) With "progressive," the questions are "progress toward what? In what ways?" The term might be used for progressing in directions that neither you nor I would like at all. In that context it is as meaningless as "reform." For instance, we could "progress" toward a more lenient or a more restrictive immigration policy. Many "social liberals" favor the former, while many "liberal environmentalists" favor the latter. The generic labels don't tell us much. And there is the additional confusion that until the Twentieth Century, "liberal" meant allowing big business unlimited power, both domestically and in international affairs. In the latter case, that included access to the armed forces to further its agendas.

For the most part I find all these terms to be conceptual toxic waste that oftener than not leaves people confused and befuddled about the realities that underlie them. My view is to let them rest in peace, and be more specific and precise in our thinking, discussion, and action.

SOLUTIONS

- **Be very suspicious of these and other vague generalities and metaphors that can mean almost anything. Often such terms are meant to trigger conditioned emotional responses that short – circuit direct awareness and critical and creative thinking. Instead, we can speak more precisely, so that people respond to specific concrete events and policies instead of emotionally charged, knee-jerk, muddleheaded catchphrases that lump disparate items together.**

- **Develop a nose for bullshit, *even when it is consistent with your inclinations.* For starters, be on your toes for blatant contradictions. For instance, "'Senator Schmucko will lead the fight against big government spending and taxes, and he'll protect your security by voting to build twelve new aircraft carriers and thirty new nuclear submarines."**

- **Warren Buffett's remark about integrity applies to the politicians we hire to be our legislators and presidents as well as to businesspersons. Richard Nixon was an example of a brilliant man who lacked integrity. Had he developed that quality in himself, he could have been an excellent president. We need to put the element of character high on our list when we elect people to public office at all levels.**

* * *

3. The Constitution as a Ball of Wax: Its Timeless Vision and How It Has Been Realized, and Distorted

Some people think they know exactly what the Constitution really means, and furthermore, they think it means exactly what they want it to mean. Since some hold one view and some another, that leads to some major disagreements. For example, there is widespread reference to an alleged Supreme Court decision declaring a corporation to be a "person" *that never occurred,* as you will see below. Fortunately, there is one indisputable authority on the Constitution's overall intentions. It is that document's introduction, the Preamble. Here it is:

> *Preamble*
> *We the People of the United States,*
> *in Order to form a more perfect Union,*
> *establish Justice,*
> *insure domestic Tranquility,*
> *provide for the common defence,*
> *promote the general Welfare,*
> *and secure the Blessings of Liberty*
> *to ourselves and our Posterity,*
> *do ordain and establish this Constitution*
> *for the United States of America*

Comment: The Preamble states the central principles of the Constitution, which the body of the document spells out in detail. When it was written, "the People" meant property-owning white male citizens. As amended since, the "We the People" to whom the provisions of the Constitution apply now includes all women, all Native Americans, all African Americans, and all other citizens regardless of ethnicity or property ownership.

Given that reality, obviously the provisions of all lines that follow the word "Union" apply to **"We the People,"** that clearly means **All of We the People** – not just **Some of Us People.** In subsequent lines,

"establish justice" implies equal justice for all – not greater justice for those who can afford pricey lawyers or buy the favors of legislators or regulators.

"insure domestic Tranquility" can occur only if most people believe that the government has indeed established justice and furthers the general welfare. Promoting the welfare of the few at the expense the rest of us is sure to give rise to domestic anger, disturbance, and protest rather than tranquility.

"provide for the common defence" means protecting our own country – not conducting wars in which we invade other countries or endorse clandestine operations to replace democratic governments with tyrannies.

"promote the general welfare" gives clear approval to such programs as bank deposit insurance, Social Security, Medicare, building and maintaining highways, preventing disasters, providing disaster relief, etc.

"secure the Blessings of Liberty" suggests that the people must be free from oppression and exploitation both by government and by any other institution or organization, including corporations

"to ourselves and our Posterity" means carrying out the principles above in such a way as to avoid harming, and if possible to benefit, the interests and prospects of future generations.

"We have it in our power to begin the world over again."
Thomas Paine

As preparations to draft the Constitution were getting underway, **Thomas Paine** declared, "We have every opportunity and every encouragement before us, to form the noblest, purest constitution on the face of the earth. We have it in our power to begin the world over again. A situation, similar to the present, hath not happened since the days of Noah until now. The birthday of a new world is at hand."

"When you assemble a number of men, to have the advantage of their joint wisdom, you inevitably assemble with these men all their prejudices, their passions, their errors of opinion, their local interests, and their selfish views. From such an assembly can a perfect production be expected? It therefore astonishes me, Sir, to find this system approaching so near to perfection as it does." **Benjamin Franklin**

"The Constitution is not an instrument for the government to restrain the people, it is an instrument for the people to restrain the government - lest it come to dominate our lives and interests." **Patrick Henry**

"The basis of our political system is the right of the people to make and to alter their constitutions of government. . .The Constitution is the guide which I will never abandon. . . . This government, the offspring of your own choice, . . . containing within itself a provision for its own amendment, has a just claim to your confidence and your support. . . . The basis of our political systems is the right of the people to make and alter their constitutions of government. But the constitution which at any time exists, till changed by an explicit and authentic act of the whole people, is sacredly obligatory on all." **George Washington**

"Constitutions should consist only of general provisions; the reason is that they must necessarily be permanent, and that they cannot calculate for the possible change of things. . . . Do not separate text from historical background. If you do, you will have perverted and subverted the Constitution, which can only end in a distorted, bastardized form of illegitimate government." **James Madison,** principal writer of the Constitution.

"The Judges, both of the supreme and inferior Courts, shall hold their Offices during good Behavior." **Article III, The Judicial Branch,** *United States Constitution*

"Our lawyers and priests generally . . . suppose that preceding generations . . . had a right to impose laws on us, unalterable by ourselves, and that we, in like manner, can make laws and impose burthens on future generations, which they will have no right to alter; in fine, that the earth belongs to the dead and not the living. . . . Our creator made the earth for the use of the living and not of the dead. . . One generation of men cannot foreclose or burthen its use to another. . . A preceding generation cannot bind a succeeding one by its laws of contracts; these deriving their obligation from the will of the existing majority, and that majority being removed by death, another comes in its place with a will equally free to make its own laws and contracts. . . .

"Some men look at constitutions with sanctimonious reverence and deem them like the Ark of the Covenant, too sacred to be touched. They ascribe to the men of the preceding age a wisdom more than human, and suppose what they did to be beyond amendment. . . . I am certainly not an advocate for frequent and untried changes in laws and constitutions. . . . But I know also that laws and constitutions must go hand in hand with the progress of the human race. . . Institutions must advance also, and keep pace with the times. . . . Each generation. . . has a right to choose for itself the form of government it believes the most promotive of its own happiness." **Thomas Jefferson**

"The particular phraseology of the Constitution of the United States confirms .. . . that a law repugnant to the Constitution is void; and that courts, as well as other departments, are bound by that instrument. . . . Judicial review is in essence, taking both the contested law with the supreme law (i.e. the constitution) and deciding which is governing. All law that is statutes must conform to the constitution. . . .The people made the Constitution, and the people can unmake it. It is the creature of their will, and lives only by their will." Supreme Court Chief Justice **John Marshall**

"The Constitution has become a thing of wax to be molded as the Court sees fit. . . . **Thomas Jefferson,** criticizing the Supreme·Court's Marbury vs. Madison decision." Jefferson continued, "A Judiciary independent of a King or executive alone, is a good thing; but independence of the will of the nation is [not]. To consider the judges as the ultimate arbiters of all constitutional questions [is] a very dangerous doctrine indeed, and one which would place us under the despotism of an oligarchy. *Our judges are as honest as other men, and not more so. They have . . . with others, the same passions for party, for power, and the privilege of their corps. . . and their power is more dangerous as they are in office for life.* (my italics). . . Judiciary perversions of the Constitution will forever be protected under the pretext of errors of judgment, which by principle are exempt from punishment. . . . It is a misnomer to call a government republican, in which a branch of he supreme power is independent of the nation."

"All the rights secured to the citizens under the Constitution are worth nothing . . . except guaranteed to them by an independent and virtuous Judiciary." **Andrew Jackson**

"We the people are the rightful masters of both Congress and the courts, not to overthrow the Constitution but to overthrow the men who pervert the Constitution." **Abraham Lincoln**

> **Comment:** In the celebrated 1803 case of Marbury v. Madison, John Marshall, unilaterally declared that the Court had an ultimate and unchallengeable right of judicial review. This meant that it would have sole and unchecked power to determine what the Constitution meant. Jefferson was stunned. He was horrified to think that an unelected and uncontrollable branch of government, immune from the will of the citizens and from any check by the two elected branches of government, would henceforth have unchallenged power to decide what the Constitution meant. The Constitution itself does not appear to give such power to the Supreme Court. Marbury vs. Madison negated part of Lincoln's comment just above, making it impossible for the legislature, the executive branch, or the people in any form to overthrow Supreme Court Justices who pervert the Constitution except by removal from office for violation of Article III's "good behavior" clause (which has never yet been done.)

The **18ᵗʰ Century History** website's page, "John Marshall's Judicial Mind comments, "The power of contracts gives the government the ability to govern. The people are bound by the laws of the government and the constitution. The government is bound by the principles of the constitution, . . . the constitution being the **"supreme law of the land"**, where the states were subordinate to the central government and the central government subordinate to the constitution. . . . The government is not above the law, for if it were above the law, then it cannot be a government of laws, it would be a law unto itself."

It's a genuine dilemma. Nowhere does the Constitution give the Supreme Court an absolute power of Judicial Review, nor specify the terms for justices of that and lower courts, nor say almost anything at all about how many courts they shall be, how many justices they shall have, or how they shall be constitutes. All that is the result of various acts of Congress, and can be changed by Congress or by Constitutional amendment.

Marshall also made another major statement in the 1819 case of Dartmouth v. Woodward:

JOHN MARSHALL

"A corporation is an artificial being, invisible, intangible, and existing only in contemplation of law. . . Being the mere creature of law, it posses only those properties which the charter of creation confers upon it. . . It might reasonably be concluded that those properties, so beneficial in the economic sphere, pose special dangers in the political sphere. Furthermore, it might be argued that liberties of political expression are not at all necessary to effectuate the purposes for which states permit commercial corporations to exist. *So long as the Judicial Branches of the State and Federal Governments remain open to protect the corporation's interest in its property, it has no need, though it may have the desire, to petition the political branches for similar protection.* (My italics.) Indeed, the States might reasonably fear that the corporation would use its economic power to obtain further benefits beyond those already bestowed." **John Marshall**

> **Comment:** In 1978 when the First National Bank of Boston claimed that because it was a corporate "person" it had First Amendment rights to political speech and that money was the same as speech, the Court found for the bank on a 5-4 vote. But in a dissenting opinion, Chief Justice **William Rehnquist,** who was better known for militantly right-wing positions, quoted from Marshall's passage above.

In that same 1978 case, Supreme Court Justice **Byron White** added his own dissenting opinion: "The interest of Massachusetts and the many other States which have restricted corporate political activity . . . is . . . of preventing institutions which have been permitted to amass wealth as a result of special advantages extended by the law for certain economic purposes from using that wealth to acquire an unfair advantage in the political process."

"Money is the mother's milk of politics." Historian **Nathan Miller**

"The court made a serious mistake in finding that money is the equivalent of protected speech." Supreme Court Justice **John Paul Stevens,** in 2011, in response to the 'Citizens United' ruling,

"If they're going to pay tens of millions of dollars for an ad for a candidate, they ought to have to disclose whom this money is coming from. Stand by your ads. People have the right to know. I want them to disclose." **Nancy Pelosi,** first woman Speaker of the House of Representatives and current minority leader.

The assertion that so-called "conservatives" want "strict constructionists" on the Court is a classic Big Lie. [They] want justices who will rule in their favor. While hypocritically claiming to practice "judicial restraint," the present Court has actually been one of the most activist Supreme Courts in history.

Comment: "Strict constructionist" and "living document" approaches to interpreting and applying Constitutional meaning can each have shortcomings when applied to partisan agendas, or to phenomena that did not exist when the Constitution was written. Nevertheless, the Court is supposed to be nonpartisan and dedicated to impartial administration of justice. Current and recent Supreme Courts, composed of majorities appointed by Republican presidents and who vote their party line in almost every partisan dispute, are and have been among the most activist in the nation's history. Many such partisan decisions have been on 5-4 party-line votes that give giant corporate and other big money interests ever more influence over our politics. Recently two major decisions, most especially the "Citizens United" case (more accurately read "Plutocrats United Against the Citizens") also on 5-4 party line votes, have opened the floodgates for corporations and wealthy individuals to buy elections with enormous rivers of cash.

Whose interests do these ultra-activist judges who have no accountability to the people further? Almost always they serve the interests and welfare of the oligarchs. They increase their power over national policy and decision-making. Plutocratic Republican leaders openly applauded the "Citizens United" ruling, which defies and defiles the Constitution. Buy contrast, a year after the "Citizens United" case, a poll found that 87% of Democrats, 82% of independents, and 68% of Republicans favored a constitutional amendment to nullify the ruling and make it clear that corporations do not have the same rights as citizens. One letter to the New York Times asked, "If corporations are people, can I marry one? Is General Electric single?" Another quipped, "A corporation is not a person until Texas executes one."

The railroad's lawyers argued that corporations were "persons" with the same rights as a real human being. The Court did not rule on that issue. But the Court clerk. . . wrote the conclusion that a corporation "is a person" into the head-notes that summarized the case. . . . A headnote has no legal standing."

Where did all this start? Not in the Constitution. The word "corporation" does not appear anywhere in it. Absolutely nothing in the Constitution implies that any organization of any kind is a "person" with the rights that persons possess. And in John Marshall's **Dartmouth v. Woodward** decision Marshall's statement that a corporation is not a person is clear, unequivocal, and obviously correct in the eyes of any impartial observer. Political commentator Thom Hartmann finally tracked the origins of the "corporate personhood" myth down. In the year of 1886, during what is widely called the "Robber Baron" era of American history, a so-called "mistake" by a Supreme Court clerk did so much to swing the political balance of power toward giant corporations. In "Santa Clara County vs. Southern Pacific Railroad," the railroad's lawyers argued that corporations were "persons" with the same rights as a real human being. The Court did not rule on that issue, deciding the case on far narrower grounds. But the Court clerk, attorney C. Bancroft Davis *who was himself a former railroad company president,* wrote the statement that a corporation "is a person" into the head-notes that summarized the case. Chief Justice Morrison Waite, who was in poor health, apparently never noticed. The Court's discussion did not debate the Railroad's allegation of corporate "personhood," wrote no opinion mentioning it, and rendered no judgment on it. Rather, it decided the case on the basis of the county's desire to tax some of the railroad's fence posts, depending on their location. But ever since then, the backdoor reinterpretation of the Constitution found in the erroneous headnote written by Davis, which was not a Court ruling of any kind, has been assumed to be a legitimate court decision, even though a headnote has no legal standing. Attorney Jim Ritvo says, "Lawyers are trained to beware of headnotes because they're not written by judges or justices . . . They're just a comment by somebody who doesn't have the power to make or determine or decide law."

This silent coup against democracy was a factor in the present major confusion of "individual libertarian" and "big business libertarian" (in other words, "corporate dominance") ideologies. Anyone but a moron or a hopeless ideologue who is deaf and blind to reality can see that a corporation is not a person. It does not have a human body, can be in many places at once, under present laws is immortal, and in most cases has no heart—not even figurative. Sixty years after Davis wrote his headnote, Supreme Court Justice William O. Douglas said, "There was no history, logic, or reason given to support that view [offered in Davis' headnote]. See more about this confusion in the use of the term "libertarian" below.

The Fourteenth Amendment to the United States Constitution, passed in 1868, followed the Thirteenth Amendment, which abolished slavery. It was meant to end practices that tried to return slaves to something resembling their former condition by intimidating them with violence, restricting their movement, and preventing them from suing or testifying in court. Its central feature was to hold that all persons born in the United States are citizens with all rights pertaining to a citizen (with the exception of children of foreign diplomats--and, oh yes, Native Americans.) The Fourteenth Amendment had nothing to do with corporations, just as the original Constitution said nothing about them. But after the 1886 Headnote Mistake (or Intentionally Misleading Misreading), lawyers for corporations began arguing that since corporations were "citizens," they were entitled to the protections provided to former slaves by the Fourteenth Amendment and also to First Amendment protections of free speech. That's all just plain baloney. Let's get real.

To say that corporate money buying elections is "just free speech" is like saying that a candidate who appears on 500 TV stations and a candidate who has just a soapbox and a voice are equal in their exercise of free speech.

Also, in its "Citizens United" ruling the Supreme Court ignored the fact that many "U.S" companies are now foreign owned, and under this ruling have been handed the right to pour unlimited amounts of money into influencing our laws and elections. For instance, Australian Rupert Murdoch, whose British holdings have been unmasked for committing almost every crime in the book, owns the Fox News network, 22 U.S. television stations, and newspapers that include the Wall Street Journal. And day in and day out, ultra right-wing Murdoch, whose activities in England open him to the charge of having no ethics whatsoever, pours rivers of cash into promoting his brand of a poisonous Radical Wrong agenda throughout the United States. (More exciting details below.) Cash flows to influence U.S. politics can now come from North Korea, Russia, China, Iran, Syria, —or Satan himself, if you can find him.

No Supreme Court justice has ever been removed from office, even though the Constitution states that a Justice can be removed for lack of "good behavior." Legislating from the bench in a way that benefits a judge's supporters, as two current judges, Scalia and Thomas, have done on behalf of the notorious Koch Brothers, whose business, Koch Industries, received the 2012 Corporate Hall of Shame award as America's worst corporation, constitutes a clear conflict of interest. That is surely lack of good behavior. But acting on it requires a legislature willing to impeach them.

"Today's Constitution is a realistic document of freedom only because of several corrective amendments. Those amendments speak to a sense of decency and fairness that I and other Blacks cherish. . . . We must be careful, when focusing on the events which took place in Philadelphia two centuries ago, that we not overlook the momentous events which followed, and thereby lose our proper sense of perspective. . . If we seek, instead, a sensitive understanding of the Constitution's inherent defects, and its promising evolution through 200 years of history, the celebration of the "Miracle at Philadelphia" will, in my view, be a far more meaningful and humbling experience. . . . I plan to celebrate the bicentennial of the Constitution as a living document, including the Bill of Rights and the other amendments protecting individual freedoms and human rights." First African-American Supreme Court Justice **Thurgood Marshall**

THURGOOD MARSHALL

<<<<>>>>

SOLUTIONS

- We need a national commitment to basing our thinking and our laws on the *entire* preamble and the *entire* constitution, not just on the parts that some people like while ignoring other parts.

- Pass a Constitutional Amendment which specifies that never in law may a human being and a corporation be confused with one another. All decisions based on the premise that a corporation is a "person," with the same rights should be reversed, and replaced with a body of law uniquely appropriate to corporations. (see MoveToAmend.org online.)

- Require that every political advertisement disclose visibly and audibly who pays for it, naming the real people or companies (or showing their logos) and not some phony made-up name of a PAC that conceals their true identities.

- In choosing a President, we should be careful to choose one who is committed to appointing Justices who will do their best to serve Justice rather than a partisan agenda.

- Finding some appropriate check on the Supreme Court's power might be helpful. Jefferson suggested term limits, while an attorney who is a friend of mine points to the importance of protecting the Justices from prevailing political winds. Careful study of how such matters are handled in democracies around the world may be a good starting point.

* * *

4. Democracy: How Is It Broken?
How Can We Fix It?

Many of our noble fellow citizens on the far right maintain that they know what democracy is really about, while the rest of us poor louts wander around deluded. They are, however, willing to condescend to do us the favor of instructing us. In reality, even a cursory glance at recent history suggests that what the Radical Wrong really wants is to make the rules by which others must live – which is not what democracy is about at all. What *is* it about? Let's hear a word from Aristotle, and then jump through time to Samuel Adams.

"If liberty and equality, as is thought by some are chiefly to be found in democracy, they will best be attained when all persons alike share in government to the utmost." **Aristotle**

"Though the will of the majority is in all cases to prevail, that will to be rightful must be reasonable; . . . the minority possess their equal rights, which equal law must protect, and to violate would be oppression."
Thomas Jefferson

"An association of men who will not quarrel with one another is a thing which has never yet existed, from the greatest confederacy of nations down to a town meeting or a vestry," said **Thomas Jefferson.** But in such cases, he cautioned against the victors in a disagreement imposing their will on others:

"Experience hath shewn," **Jefferson** continued, "that even under the best forms of government those entrusted with power have, in time, and by slow operations, perverted it into tyranny. . . . Force is the vital principle and immediate parent of despotism. . . . Rogues . . . always contrive to nestle themselves into the places of power and profit. These rogues set out with stealing the people's good opinion, and then steal from them the right of withdrawing it, by contriving laws and associations against the power of the people themselves. . . . I am not among those who fear the people. They, and not the rich, are our dependence for continued freedom

"The issue today is the same as it has been throughout all history, whether man shall be allowed to govern himself or be ruled by a small elite."
Thomas Jefferson

"Every government degenerates when trusted to the rulers of the people alone. The people themselves are its only safe depositories." **Samuel Adams**

"A pure democracy is a society consisting of a small number of citizens, who assemble and administer the government in person." **James Madison. And also,** "We base all our experiments on the capacity of mankind for self-government."

"As the Colony encreases, the public concerns will encrease likewise, and the distance at which the members may be separated will render it too inconvenient for all of them to meet on every occasion as at first, when their number was small, their habitations near, and the public concerns few and trifling. This will point out the convenience of their consenting to leave the legislative part to be managed by a select number chosen from the whole body, who are supposed to have the same concerns at stake which those have who appointed them, *and who will act in the same manner as the whole body would act were they present.* (My italics) **Thomas Paine**

"Democracy shows not only its power in reforming governments, but in regenerating a race of men and this is the greatest blessing of free governments." **Andrew Jackson**

ABRAHAM LINCOLN

"As I would not be a slave, so I would not be a master. This expresses my idea of democracy."
Abraham Lincoln

"No man is good enough to govern another man without that other's consent." **Abraham Lincoln**

"The surface of American society is covered with a layer of democratic paint, but from time to time one can see the old aristocratic colors breaking through." **Alexis de Toqueville**

Of all dangers to a nation . . . there can be no greater one than having certain portions of the people set off from the rest by a line drawn – they not privileged as others, but degraded, humiliated, made of no account. . . . To become an enfranchised man [or woman], and now . . . to stand and start without humiliation, and equal with the rest, to commence . . . the grand experiment of development, whose end . . . may be the forming of a full-grown man or woman—that *is* something. . . . [Democracy] alone can bind, and ever seeks to bind, all nations, all men [and women], of however various and distant lands, into . . . a family. . . . Not that half only, individualism. . . . There is another half, which is adhesiveness or love, that fuses, ties and aggregates, making the races comrades, and fraternizing all." **Walt Whitman**

"Democracy is not so much a form of government as a set of principles."
Woodrow Wilson

"The defenders of every kind of regime claim that it is a democracy, and fear that they might have to stop using the word if it were tied down to any one meaning." Novelist **George Orwell**

"When public men indulge themselves in abuse, when they deny others a fair trial, when they resort to innuendo and insinuation, to libel, scandal, and suspicion, then our democratic society is

outraged, and democracy is baffled."
J. William Fulbright, Former Senate Foreign Relations Committee Chair

"You won the elections, but I won the count." Nicaraguan dictator **Anastasio Somoza**

"Man's capacity for justice makes democracy possible, but man's inclination to injustice makes democracy necessary." Philosopher **Reinhold Niebuhr**

"The flood of money that gushes into politics today is a pollution of democracy." Writer and journalist **Theodore H. White**

"People who have lost their hunger for justice are not ultimately powerful. They are like sick people who have lost their appetite for what is truly nourishing. Such sick people should not frighten or discourage us. They should be prayed for along with the sick people who are in the hospital." **Caesar Chavez**

"When the U.S. launched the second Iraq War, **David Letterman** remarked, "President [George W.] Bush has said that he does not need approval from the UN to wage war, and I'm thinking, well, hell, he didn't need the approval of the American voters to become president, either."

"You measure a democracy by the freedom it gives its dissidents, not the freedom it gives its assimilated conformists." Activist **Abbie Hoffman**

"We can have democracy in this country, or we can have great wealth concentrated in the hands of a few, but we can't have both." --Former Supreme Court Justice **Louis D. Brandeis**

"Why is it, when 638 people voted at a precinct in Franklin County, a voting machine awarded 4,258 extra votes to George Bush? Thankfully, they fixed it, but how many other votes did the computers get wrong? . . . This is my opening shot to be able to focus the light of truth on these terrible problems in the electoral system." Senator **Barbara Boxer**

"We are losing the democracy the democracy that we're trying to sell in the Mideast . . . right here in our own nation." **Humorist Rosie O'Donnell**

"You've got to vote for someone. It's a shame, but it's got to be done." Humorist **Whoopi Goldberg.**

"If there was one impulse shared by all the Founders, it was a rejection of all forms of absolute authority, whether the king, the theocrat, the general, the oligarch, the dictator, the majority, or anyone else who claims to make choices for us. George Washington declined Caesar's crown because of this impulse, and stepped down after two terms. . . . The procedural rules of our government help define the results—on everything from whether the government can regulate polluters to whether government can tap your phone—they define our democracy just as much as elections do." **Barack Obama**

"If you don't vote, you vote by default. A vote not used is implied consent. You're volunteering for taxation without representation. They can do whatever they want to you because you haven't challenged them." **Jesse Ventura**

JESSE VENTURA

Comment. Democracy means that all the people should have a voice in government, which exists to ensure their security and well-being. In "direct democracy" people participate directly in decisions; in "representative democracy" they elect representatives who presumably said and do the things they want said and done. Almost everyone likes to claim that they're for democracy, even if in reality, big money, big business, religious imperialists, or other interest groups call many of the shots. The best we usually get is semi-democracy, pseudo-democracy, or sometimes a blatant mockery of democracy—all almost always wrapped in the flag, perhaps with martial music playing in the background. But sometimes we're lucky enough to get the real McCoy.

Voting is no guarantee of democracy. Fascist dictatorships also hold elections, in which mysteriously the same despot or party is elected time after time. Who is allowed to vote, who is encouraged to vote and can vote easily, who counts the votes and observes the vote count, and who tallies the results—these are crucial elements of representative democracy.

In the U.S. today we have a semi-democracy. Most people don't want to believe that about our country, but unfortunately it's true. The most blatant recent example is when one party successfully carried out a tightly organized multistate conspiracy to keep hundreds of thousands of eligible voters from voting and apparently also rigged voting machines in Texas and Ohio. Then the Supreme Court, on a 5-4 party line vote, appointed George W. Bush to the presidency even though he had half a million votes fewer than his opponent. Vice President Al Gore would surely have gained a majority even in the anachronistic, anti-democratic Electoral College if the Court had not stopped the vote count. But the Court's Republican majority stopped the vote count before it was completed and said it was more important to have a president, any president, quickly than to have the candidate who actually won the election take office. *With that action, America lost its legitimacy as an example of democratic government.* I watched a smaller courtroom hearing on TV, in which before the votes were counted, two Republican operatives spent two weeks alone in a room containing absentee ballots from service personnel overseas. The Republican Party paid them half a million dollars for their two weeks in that room. What do you think they were doing there? What happened to them in the courtroom? Nothing. They walked free.

In the past, the river of shady cash flowing into state and national elections like effluent from a broken sewage system would have been considered extreme corruption, but now, since the 5-4 party line "Supreme Court Majority United Against the Citizens" case, the corruption has become legal. Unless "Citizens United" is repealed, the names of the justices who supported it may well be engraved on a tombstone of American democracy.

It is less widely known that a large body of data suggests that the 2004 presidential election was also stolen. (This is not something most Americans want to hear. We like to think that our elections are honest. For the most part, they used to be. Recently the situation has changed.)

In every previous U.S. election and every country around the world, exit polls have proven so reliable that they are widely used as a check on the honesty of elections. In 2004 in district after district and state after state –most notoriously Ohio— the exit polls showed John Kerry as the clear winner. In many districts the exit poll vote was not even close.

What happened? There was massive, systematic voting machine fraud, with no paper trail to detect it. Three of the four principal voting machine manufacturers were owned by strongly pro-Republican companies. The worst of them, Diebold, had been contributing to Republican candidates since 1998 and its CEO had even sent out a fund-raising e-mail that promised to make sure Bush would win in Ohio in 2004. Bob Fitrakis and Harvey Wasserman report that Kerry was far ahead at 12:20 A.M. and then information about the vote tally suddenly stopped. When the information flow resumed around 2 A.M, the totals had mysteriously shifted so dramatically that Bush was ahead by 118,000 votes. (The evidence for all this, and the facts in the paragraph below is reported in detail in Jesse Ventura's *American Conspiracies*; in Philips & Huff's *Censored 2010: The Top 25 Censored Stories of 2008-09;* and in Loo & Peter Phillips' *Impeach the President: The Case Against Bush and Cheney.*)

Major mistakes in tabulating occurred with the individual machines on which people voted, both with the computers that tallied local results, and with the nationwide tabulations. In almost all locations where there were discrepancies between exit polls and "official" vote totals, *the chips that contained the instructions that told the machines how to count mysteriously disappeared.* In some precincts voters reported with horror that they pushed the button for Kerry and then watched their vote show up as a vote for Bush. Before the vote, Republican officials who controlled the voting deleted thousands of eligible voters from the registration roles, supplied far too few voting machines to heavily Democratic areas, did not process cards from Democratic voter drives, and illegally stopped a recount in districts where there was a paper trail that could have given Kerry the election. Lou Harris of the famous Harris Polls declared, "Ohio was as dirty an election as America has ever seen."

Here are the details: Sophisticated computer hackers tracked the events that took place and found they could get into the vote reporting system through a "back door," remotely take control of it, and put in any result they wished. On election night, a registered Republican electronic security expert from Ohio who helped design computer systems for American Express, MasterCard, the State Department, and many other companies and agencies began noticing anomalies in various counties where Kerry started out ahead but then the totals swung radically over to Bush. He started thinking about a "kingpin attack" where hackers can change information at both ends of an information technology system. He traced the Ohio voting information superhighway to a company called SMARTtech in Chattanooga, Tennessee that just happened to do most of the GOP's web hosting.

As it turned out, Ohio Secretary of State J. Kenneth Blackwell, who was in charge of Ohio's vote-counting and was also co-chair of Bush's re-election committee (How could such a conflict of interest be permitted?) hired a company called GovTech Solutions to set up a *duplicate control center* for the 2004 election day. An Ohio state government contract unearthed through the Freedom of Information Act specified that GovTech was to create "a hardware VPN device [that would connect] the servers for database replication services as well as remote administration." *Remote administration?* That's another way of saying that hackers in the shadow control center could take over the vote counting and tabulation. The control center was the Tennessee SMARTtech headquarters. When Congressman John Conyers called for a recount of the Ohio results in Dec. 2004, the month after the election, it turned out that *the hard drive in the official Ohio computer that tabulated the results had been replaced since the election*, which made it impossible to examine the progression of the vote count and its numbers. GovTech was owned by Mike Connell. After a meeting between Connell and Conyers, a memo from Conyers to the House Judiciary Committee reported that "Well before the 2000 election, one of Connell's employees created a 'Trojan Horse' software application which, when installed on one computer, allows its remote control by another computer. Connell developed and ran important parts of the Blackwell's Ohio vote tabulation computer network for the 2004 and 2006 elections. Earlier, his employee Roy Cales ran all Florida's government computer systems during the 2000 election, with "unrestricted access" to all computers that were used by Florida's Secretary of State Kathleen Harris, notorious for numerous shady acts in that election. (See Ventura for more details and primary sources.)

In 2004 it was not just the presidency. Several state elections where there were huge last-minute reversals from polls to official final totals had one thing in common: Computerized voting machines with no paper trail.

Subsequent controlled experiments have shown that it is easy to program a voting machine to tally votes incorrectly. They have also shown that the best of touch-screen machines, working perfectly with no hanky-panky, have an unacceptably high error rate. All this is not happening in some small country in Africa or South America. It is happening in the United States of America, where we like to think of ourselves as being the home of representative democracy.

By my reading of their words, Paine, Franklin, Washington, Jefferson, Madison, and Lincoln would surely conclude that the monarchy has regained control of the country if they could see what has happened to our campaigns and elections in the last generation. Now, however, the alleged divine right of today's Kings and Queens and Lords and Nobles is bestowed by the great banks, investment houses, hedge funds, and other giant multinational corporations rather than by God.

Some right-wing extremists (and for that matter, some left-wing extremists too) have no interest in democracy at all. They just want the appearance of it. Their goal is to rule, by fair means or foul. True democracy seeks input from all and distributes power widely. It is opposed to imposing the wishes of some on others, and values freedom of thought and action, and equality of opportunity, as complementary sides of the same coin.

In the state of Maine, just 20 percent of candidates accept private campaign contributions. Rather, candidates who collect a specified number of $5 contributions from voters can finance their campaigns through the state Clean Election Fund. In Maine you don't have to be rich to run for office, you don't get bought or sold out by corporate special interests, and you can spend more of your time listening to voters instead of fundraising. *It costs less than $2 per taxpayer.* Connecticut, Arizona, and several other states have similar systems. A bill to institute such a system for the nation has been introduce in Congress several times, including one in 2007 co-sponsored by then-Senator Barack Obama, but has always been defeated by "our" Senators and Congresspersons.

What is the opposite of democracy? Authoritarianism. Authoritarians want control. They tend to belittle, harass, intimidate, or jail those who resist their agenda. Freedom is fine for them, but you and I had better shut up and do as we're told.

Authoritarian attitudes and actions are anti-libertarian and anti-democratic. Authoritarian views are widespread in the United States just as elsewhere. Often they are coupled with self-righteousness. Eternal vigilance is needed to keep those who hold such attitudes from crushing the fragile flower of democracy.

<<<<>>>>

SOLUTIONS

To make the United States a more genuine democracy we can move to:

- Address the matters of concern to most citizens—not just those that the major parties and candidates seize upon as "the issues."

- Clean up your state and local electoral policies and regulations to provide complete multi-partisan supervision of the electoral process, regardless of which party holds the governorship and legislature. Make sure that no party or interest controls the voting rolls and rules, that no eligible citizen is denied the right and opportunity to vote or faces undue difficulty doing so.

- Use a voting method that ensures that every vote is fairly counted in a way that has an indelible physical trail and leaves no possibility of fraud. For more than 40 years my county has without incident used optical scanning ballots marked with indelible ink that makes recounts easy. Old fashioned local hand-counting of foolproof ballots with observers from various parties is the most *conservative* (no quotation marks here) and reliable of all methods. Any voting method that precludes a recount should be strictly forbidden.

- Voting machines, when used, should be physically and electronically isolated from computers used to tally results. When voting machines or computer tallies are used, a foolproof method should be used to obtain and store all chips that were used to direct the vote counting, under nonpartisan supervision (such as state equivalents of the U.S. General Services Administration, or the latter itself if a state cannot guarantee the integrity of its voting and tallying process.) Just as with provisions for storing paper ballots for a specified time, any machine or computer used in voting should be protected against tampering by a partisan of any party until all counting and possibility of recounting is completed. (This may require computers dedicated to no other purpose.)

- Any tampering with voting or voting results should be a crime that results in: Prohibition against future use of the equipment of any company found to be involved; forfeiture of the election by the candidate connected with the party that engaged in the tampering; and consideration by legislatures of prohibitively effective criminal penalties for such tampering.

- A provision such as instant runoff voting (using methods described above) would make it attractive for citizens to vote for the candidate they really want to win rather than some mediocre hack from a major party who has the best chance to win because of the party's support. It would also break the iron grip of the two major parties on our political system. (Remember that the Constitution does not mention political parties.)

- Change the procedure for choosing Congressional committee chairs from automatically elevating the longest-serving member of the House or Senate majority party to secret-ballot election of the chair, regardless of party, by all members of the committee, at least every two years, without restriction on re-election. This would immediately raise the level of competence in congressional committee work.

- Remove the effects of bribery and corruption from our politics. Economist and former Secretary of Labor Robert Reich suggests an obvious second step: "Require that all political contributions go through 'blind trusts,' so that no candidate can ever know who contributed what." (The first step is to eliminate anonymous and unlimited slush fund spending such as that legitimized by the disgraceful "Citizens United" ruling.)

- Better yet, nationally or state by state, move to public funding of elections (such as in Maine) throughout the country so that our government again becomes more a servant of "We the People" and less one of "We the Corporations." One approach might be to begin lobbying reform with a constitutional amendment that applies only to the Federal government and not state governments, so that state legislators can support it without endangering their own cash taps. One that's in place and working well, individual states can move at their own pace toward similar reform.

- End government surveillance of citizens who are doing nothing more advocating positions different from those held by the government or major parties.

- Truly honor the Bill of Rights, and vigilantly striking down transgressions on our freedom like those in the misnamed and partly unconstitutional "Patriot Act."

- Enact term limits that encourage citizen-legislators rather than professional politicians. (But California passed a limit on Assembly members that is too short: Just three two-year terms, there are too few legislators with enough knowledge of long-term issues. These short terms transfer power to the executive branch. Ending the flow of corporate cash into lawmakers' pockets is crucial first step, because the money machine can buy votes of new and old legislators alike.)

- Provide, in states that allow citizens to vote directly on legislation through initiative or referendum ballot measures (such as in California), that signatures to qualify measures for the ballot may be gathered only by volunteers. This will end corporations putting measures that serve their own selfish interests on the ballot using paid signature gatherers. That use of direct citizen voting was never intended when that process was included in the state constitution.

- In states where citizens can vote on ballot measures, ensure impartial wording that tells what the measure is really about. Oregon law creates juries of randomly selected citizens to study the proposed legislation and separate fact from fiction, with their findings mailed to voters. California has an election booklet with "for" "against" and rebuttals for each ballot proposition, and an analysis by an impartial state legislative analyst. But the California system lets the measure's sponsor name it, even when the name is completely misleading. Either the legislative analyst or a citizen jury like Oregon's should be empowered to change misleading names to accurate ones.

- If you do nothing else, vote in every election, even small ones, even when it seems futile. Help make the corporate money machine backfire by consistently voting for candidates who have fewer and cheaper ads (due to less big money backing) unless you have clear reason to do otherwise. Beware of attack campaigns (other things equal, vote for the attacked rather than the attacker) and demand clear statements of people-oriented, small business and family farm oriented, and environment-oriented priorities. Use websites like Project Vote Smart to see where incumbents stand.

* * *

5. Liberty: Freedom to Do What Government, Corporate, and Religious Authorities Tell Us To?

There are those who claim to know better than the rest of us what the founders meant by freedom. Often enough this includes believing that anyone who disagrees with them is probably a socialist or Nazi who pals around with terrorists, so the government is justified in tapping all their communications and keeping close tabs on them. As it happens, some of the steps they advocate to "protect our freedom" are widely viewed by others as oppressive measures that reduce it, take power way from the people, and give it to the various kinds of secret police. And some in government have no qualms about defining anyone who opposes them or their program as a "suspected terrorist." For example, during the George W. Bush years the administration put 20 mostly elderly members of the "Peace Action Milwaukee" group opposed to the Iraq war, including a priest and a nun, on a "no fly list" that required airport authorities to stop them from boarding flights. That's a pretty flimsy excuse for "freedom"

PATRICK HENRY

"I know not what course others may take; but as for me, give me liberty or give me death!" **Patrick Henry**

"Where liberty is, there is my country." **Benjamin Franklin**

"It will be found an unjust and unwise jealousy to deprive a man of his natural liberty upon the supposition he may abuse it." **George Washington**

"The natural progress of things is for liberty to yield and governments to gain ground." **Thomas Jefferson**

"Necessity is the plea for every infringement of human freedom. It is the argument of tyrants. It is the creed of slaves." **William Pitt**

'Liberty may be endangered by the abuse of liberty, but also by the abuse of power." And, "I believe there are more instances of the abridgement of freedom of the people by gradual and silent encroachments by those in power than by violent and sudden usurpations." **James Madison**. He also wrote, "It is a universal truth that the loss of liberty at home is to be charged to the provisions against danger, real or pretended, from abroad. . . . If Tyranny and Oppression come to this land, it will be in the guise of fighting a foreign enemy."

A foreign visitor's view of the American scene: "In America the majority raises formidable barriers around the liberty of opinion; within these barriers an author may write what he pleases, but woe to him if he goes beyond them." **Alexis de Tocqueville**

"I deny the right to govern any other person, without that person's consent." **Abraham Lincoln**

"Prohibition goes beyond the bounds of reason in that it attempts to control a man's appetite by legislation and makes crimes out of things that are not crimes. A prohibition law strikes a blow at the very principles on which our government was founded." **Abraham Lincoln**

"Freedom makes a huge requirement of every human being. With freedom comes responsibility. For the person who is unwilling to grow up, the person who does not want to carry is own weight, this is a frightening prospect." **Eleanor Roosevelt**

"The only sure bulwark of continuing liberty is a government strong enough to protect the interests of the people, and a people strong enough and well enough informed to maintain its sovereign control over its government." **Franklin D. Roosevelt**

"History teaches that grave threats to liberty often come in times of urgency, when constitutional rights seem too extravagant to endure. . . . Big Brother in the form of an increasingly powerful government and in an increasingly powerful private sector will pile the records high with reasons why privacy should give way to national security, to law and order . . . and the like. . . . The liberties of none are safe unless the liberties of all are protected. . . . The Constitution places the right of silence beyond the reach of government. . . . The right to be let alone is indeed the beginning of all freedoms." Supreme Court Justice **William O. Douglas**

William O. Douglas also wrote, "We are rapidly entering the age of no privacy, where everyone is open to surveillance at all times; where there are no secrets from government. [There is] an alarming trend whereby the privacy and dignity of our citizens is being whittled away by sometimes imperceptible steps. Taken individually, each step may be of little consequence. But when viewed as a whole, there begins to emerge a society quite unlike any we have seen -- a society in which government may intrude into the secret regions of man's life at will."

ROSA PARKS, in the bus and the mug shot in jail

"Our mistreatment was just not right, and I was tired of it. . . . I would like to be remembered as a person who wanted to be free . . . so other people would also be free." **Rosa Parks** (She was sitting in the "colored" section of the bus when more white passengers got on and the driver came back and moved the "colored" sign farther back behind her. She refused to give up her seat, and was arrested for it.)

"We're losing our constitutional rights because of the so-called "war on terror". . . America is no longer what it has stood for since 1776. We've gone backwards. When you look at how religious fanatics and corporate America are teaming up, we today are on the brink of fascism." **Jesse Ventura**

And **Ventura** added, "What we do in our private lives is none of government's business. That position rules out the Republican Party for me."

"You wanna get rid of drug crime in this country? Fine, let's just get rid of all the drug laws." **Ron Paul**

"The 'national-security state' in all its aspects has continued to grow throughout the decades since the beginning of World War II. Defense budges, intelligence and surveillance networks, private military contractors [i.e. hired mercenaries] irregular forms of war: these and other executive-branch tools of international power work like a ratchet. Some presidents rapidly increase them in times of emergency, as George W. Bush did after the 9/11 attacks. No president scales them back." Historian **James Fallows**

"Now, tragically, folks, we are illuminating more and more of the Dark Side every day. Now that indefinite detention, enhanced interrogation, and domestic spying are acceptable, it is getting harder and harder to find those things that we as Americans theoretically cannot bring ourselves to do. . . . Every time the President comes up with a new secret tactic to take down Al Qaeda, the media blows its cover. Torture, monitoring our phone calls, monitoring our e-mails, secret prisons, all perfectly reasonable temporary concessions of freedom that will only be in effect as long as our never-ending war on terror." Humorist **Stephen Colbert**

> **Comment:** Colbert was talking about George W. Bush, but too many "enhanced" modes of surveillance remain in place. We all laud liberty; but we do not all mean the same thing. For some, the word means each person can do as he or she pleases with himself or herself and the product of his or her labor. For others, the same word means that some can do as they please *to* others, and with the product of others' labor. Some call that second meaning "liberty," while others call it "tyranny."
>
> Some people quite reasonably hold an "individual libertarian" view – that, as Jesse Ventura states, government has no place telling us what to do in our private lives. But some on the far right confuse things badly by mixing that up with a "big business libertarian" (i.e. corporate dominance) view. The two are entirely different.
>
> Individual libertarians hold that we should each be free to do as we wish as long as we do not harm others. This perspective follows from **Benjamin Franklin's** statement that "Every natural right not expressly given up, or, from the nature of a compact, necessarily ceded, remains. All positive and civil laws should conform, as far as possible, to the law of natural reason and equity." This applies to where you live, how you make your living, whether or not you wish to remain pregnant if you accidentally find yourself so, and for many libertarians, prostitution, drug use, and suicide. From a libertarian perspective, in no other way is a government as intrusive as when it presumes to tell us what we may or may not do with our own minds and bodies.
>
> We also want to remember, however, that some drugs are very bad news, and that on various occasions government security agencies have themselves distributed illegal drugs

to encourage people to zone out instead of protesting and demanding their due rights. Methamphetamines can blow out enough brain cells to make people unable to take care of themselves. Opiates can get people strung out forever. (Of former heroin addicts I have known, many ended up prematurely dead. Of meth addicts, some ended up completely crazy.)

Cocaine in its various forms wastes your nervous system. Even weed can cause people to chill out and forget about constructive social action. (During the desegregation actions in the 1960s, participants were forbidden to use drugs by the movement.) But use of drugs should not be a cause for putting people in jail. Do you want your tax dollars spent to keep someone in prison for smoking a joint? I don't. (Especially since weed is widely available in prisons and those imprisoned for possessing it will probably keep on smoking it there, with their room, board, guards, and barbed wire fences paid for out of your bank account and mine.) Widespread, effective, clinics and truthful information programs use a lot less of your tax money and mine than jailing people

"Individual libertarian" [and] "big business libertarian" views are entirely different. 'Individual libertarians' say, "*keep the state out of our private lives.*" "Big business libertarians" say, "*A corporation that may be more powerful than a small nation ought to be free to do as it pleases without any guidelines, oversight or social responsibility.*"

But many who hold "big business libertarian/corporate dominance" views also lobby constantly for government contracts, subsidies, tax incentives, land grants, anti-labor and anti-union laws—even subsidies for herbicide and pesticide farming that poisons farmers and consumers. The corporate dominance outlook holds that Wall Street, the big banks, other great corporations, and "the invisible hand of the market" will look out for ordinary people's interests and put people to work. A true fairy tale! Yet many in this camp also seek government regulations that will give them a competitive advantage or wedge of entry into some market. That's a long way from "free markets." On the other hand, even small mom and pop businesses are often hobbled by an excess of rules and regulations and forms to fill out that don't help anybody anywhere.

(The confusion of the individual libertarian and corporate dominance perspectives owes much to Ayn Rand, an unbending elitist whose antidemocratic philosophy rightly lauded the individualism of the perceptive and able few, but forgot that the people as a whole can be educated toward a tolerant individualism and an evolving higher consciousness. Rand's books have a strong cult following of those who believe themselves superior to others and therefore feel entitled to everything they can get regardless of the effects on anybody else. Interestingly enough, research shows that those who are "superior" in amassing wealth (Rand's central cadre of supporters) are almost all people who are good at organizing and finance, and include almost no one who is creative in the sciences or arts, and not a single Nobel Prize winner. In other words, in real life many of the would-be creative heroes whom Rand lauds are shut out of the utopian conditions for the few that she advocates.

To be truthful about today's realities, Ralph Nader has suggested changing the pledge of allegiance to
"*. . . with Liberty and Justice for Some.*"

Forms of freedom include **freedom from** intimidation by others or government or businesses as well as **freedom to** do as you please. Your **freedom to** is subject to limits that keep you from harming others.

Recently, provisions of the so-called "Patriot Act" have further limited our freedoms, such as by allowing the government to spy on us without a warrant. Such abuses occur even at the local level. And now there is the 2012 National Defense Authorization Act (NDAA) that permits "indefinite detention" in military jails without a charge or a trial. Although President Obama said that his administration would not authorize such detention of American citizens, future administrations may act differently.

<<<<>>>>

SOLUTIONS

- Eliminate laws against mere possession of a drug in amounts appropriate for individual use, and shift anti-marijuana funding into shutting down brain-cell-killing methamphetamine production and distribution.

- Guarantee every woman's right to end a problem pregnancy if she wishes and declare that any law abridging this right is an unconstitutional intrusions on her right to be let alone.

- Enforce the 9th and 10th Amendments by ending prohibitions against behavior not injurious to others and non-warranted spying on citizens by government agencies.

- Declare that laws governing individuals and those governing corporations exist in distinct and separate spheres, that laws written to protect individual rights were never intended to apply to corporations, and that corporations are and should be subject to separate laws.

- By legislative action or constitutional amendment, provide greater protection for us all against "emergency" government security agency roundups of citizens the government considers "suspicious" but has no real evidence against.

* * *

6. True Education, and How to Tell It and Fake Education Apart

Our nation's founders shared a belief that the success of democracy and of our nation depends on an educated citizenry. This principle has been put into practice by building and staffing schools everywhere. But today access to quality education is shrinking fast rather than growing, even though it is increasingly needed to get good jobs. Now we are making larger incomes for the wealthy and larger profits for corporations a higher priority. And many people do not yet comprehend that indoctrination with their pet beliefs is fake education. True education requires teaching our children to question, to examine critically, to think creatively, and to develop the ability to go beyond what their teachers think and know. The story unfolds below.

"The best means of forming a . . . virtuous and happy people will be found in the right education of youth. Without this foundation, every other means, in my opinion, must fail. . . . Promote then as an object of primary importance, institutions for the general diffusion of knowledge. In proportion as the structure of a government gives force to public opinion, it is essential that public opinion should be enlightened." **George Washington**

"Educate and inform the whole mass of the people. . . They are the only sure reliance for the preservation of our liberty. **Thomas Jefferson**

JOHN ADAMS

"It should be your care, therefore, and mine, to elevate the minds of our children and . . . excite in them an habitual contempt of meanness, abhorrence of injustice and inhumanity, and an ambition to excel in every capacity, faculty, and virtue. If we suffer their minds to grovel and creep in infancy, they will grovel all their lives." **John Adams**

"A well-instructed people alone can be permanently a free people. . . . What spectacle can be more edifying or more seasonable, than that of Liberty and Learning, each leaning on the other for their mutual and surest support? . . . A popular government without popular information or the means of acquiring it, is but a prologue to a farce, or a tragedy, or perhaps both. . . . Learned Institutions ought to be favorite objects with every free people. They throw that light over the public mind which is the best security against crafty and dangerous encroachments on the public liberty." **James Madison**

In addition, **Madison** wrote, "Whenever a youth is ascertained to possess talents meriting an education which his parents cannot afford, he should be carried forward at the public expense."

"Upon the subject of education, not presuming to dictate any plan or system respecting it, I can only say that I view it as the most important subject which we as a people can be engaged in." **Abraham Lincoln**

MARK TWAIN

And there is this sage observation, "Don't let schooling interfere with your education." Also, "Education consists mainly of what we have unlearned." **Mark Twain**

"Democracy cannot succeed unless those who express their choice are prepared to choose wisely. The real safeguard of democracy, therefore, is education. . . We cannot always build the future for our youth, but we can build our youth for the future." **Franklin D. Roosevelt**

"Education is a kind of continuing dialogue, and a dialogue assumes different points of view." Yale Law School Dean **Robert M. Hutchins**

"Liberty without learning is always in peril; learning without liberty is always in vain." And also, "Let us think of education as the means for developing our greatest abilities, because in each of us there is a private hope and dream which, fulfilled, can be translated into benefit for everyone and greater strength for our nation. . . Our progress as a nation can be no swifter than our progress in education. The human mind is our fundamental resource." **John F. Kennedy**

"Enlighten the people generally, and tyranny and oppressions of body and mind will vanish like evil spirits at the dawn of day."
Thomas Jefferson

"No one has yet realized the wealth of sympathy, the kindness, and generosity hidden in the soul of a child. The effort of every true education should be to unlock that treasure." **Emma Goldman**

"Years of misguided teaching have resulted in the destruction of the best in our society, in our cultures and in the environment. . . . "The end of all knowledge should surely be service to others [and] the building up of character." **Caesar Chavez**

"Do not worry about your difficulties in mathematics. I assure you that mine are greater." **Albert Einstein**

"Education. . . is not only to discipline and instruct, but above all to free the mind. . .from the darkness, the narrowness, the groundless fears and self-defeating passions of ignorance. . . A free mind insists on seeking out reality. . . . It is not easy, in the middle of one's life or political career, to say that the old horizons are too limited—that our education must begin again. But neither are the challenges ahead easy. The best responses will not be easily found, nor once found, will they command unanimous agreement. But the possibilities of greatness are equal to the difficulty of the challenge." **Robert F. Kennedy**

"'No Child Left Behind' is the most ironically named piece of legislation since the 1942 Japanese Family Leave Act." Senator **Al Franken.**

"Cutting the deficit by gutting our investments in innovation and education is like lightening an overloaded airplane by removing its engine. It may make you feel like you're flying high at first, but it won't take long before you feel the impact." **Barack Obama**

"The Koch brothers . . . grant agreements with universities come with very significant strings attached. . . . They are setting up a pattern where Universities are expected to give up their values in exchange for money. The programs that they start tend to be one point of view only. At over 150 universities they have spent tens of millions of dollars to get their point of view instilled. . .

[When it accepts a Koch Brothers grant] . . . "The University signs a contract that says they will hire someone who says they share the [extreme right-wing] point of view held by the Koch Brothers. They have an immense amount of influence over who those professors are and what they teach and what they publish and what research they do and what they say in the classroom. This is a major threat to the country, not just to the educational system or the students or the faculty. This is a major threat to our way of life." **Cary Nelson, President of the American Association of University Professors**

> **Comment:** In the economic downturn at the beginning of the twenty-first century, education suffered severely. In many states class sizes have ballooned, even though a teacher's first-hand knowledge of what is going on with a specific student is often one of the most important elements in education. This year in Texas, for example, many high school teachers find themselves with 10 more kids in every class than they had last year. It takes a toll on them, and on the quality of their students' education. I know one teacher who loved her work last year and is almost in despair about it this year. With some kinds of learning, one-to-one interaction is needed. In elementary school, middle school, and high school, above about a 1 to 17 student-teacher ratio, the quality of education goes downhill.
>
> But as Mark Twain points out, training is not enough. The wrong kind of schooling teaches people **not** to think. We learn by stories. Everyone has some kind of story about how the world is, and how they would like it to be. Such stories often include the mental pictures we call metaphors, and also "mind movie" action clip. These stories, mental pictures, and mind movies may be about the past, the present, or future possibilities that we fear or hope for. You may have borrowed some parts of your own stories from listening to others tell their stories, without even knowing you were doing so. It's all right to question perceptions and feelings associated with them. Are you sure they're accurate? Do they truly reflect your values?

The wrong kind of schooling can train people NOT to think. In a "monologue" or "one-sided narrative," the authorities constantly

broadcast their story about the way things are, while everyone else listens mutely.

A story can include the implicit or explicit statement: "I am the authority. Do not question this." Or by contrast, it can include the statement, "Please ask questions and say how you feel about this. Any story can be wrong, or partial, or mistaken, including this one." It's especially important to pay attention to which stories are being told to children regarding matters they've never heard about.

PAOLO FREIRE

Stories are also called narratives. Somebody describes what's happening like a TV narrator's voice–over. Such narrations may closely describe real events and be fairly accurate (like an unbiased, competent sports announcer) or may wildly distort what's occurring. Brazilian educator Paolo Freire, who worked among peasants who had been serfs on haciendas, spoke of a **"monologue" or "one-sided narrative"** in which the rulers continually repeat their story about the way things are. He called this the **"dominant narrative."** Everyone else is "submerged in a **"culture of silence"** in which they listen mutely. In a classroom, for example, when the educational system or the school emphasizes unquestioning consumption of the dominant narrative, students are treated like piggy banks with little slots in their heads. The teacher moves up and down the rows, depositing coins of knowledge that embody their "knowledge" (whether it is correct or not) into the slots. Freire calls this the "banking model of education." When you can regurgitate the dominant narrative to others, you are considered educated. Fantasy? After the so-called "No child left behind" program went into effect, teachers complained that its intense emphasis on standardized tests was turning them and the students into robots devoted to memorization. It decreased genuine thinking and creativity. (Teachers I know referred to it as "No child left standing.") In a monologue, freedom dies.

In today's politics, monologues are pervasive. Each candidate has "talking points" that are repeated *ad nauseum.* In education that liberates, everyone is both teacher and student—forever. They learn from each other, challenge each other, and engage in true dialogue, constructively rethinking the dominant narrative or even rejecting it, in contrast to a monologue's relationship of dominance and submission.

Often it is accurate to call a widely shared narrative an ideology. An ideology is a collection of stories shared by a number of people. Many serve to justify our own actions and attitudes. Many explain complex phenomena with simpleminded or misleading ideas.

It is fashionable for both "liberals" and "conservatives" to say, "Other people have ideologies, but not me." Self-deception rears its self-congratulatory head. As I use the word "ideology," everybody has one—even if their ideology is a pragmatic orientation toward finding practical solutions to problems.

In some states, not only are the schools in deep trouble but the universities are in shambles due to years (or in some states, like California, decades) of budget cuts coming one after another like an invasion force of ugly monsters popping out of a sewer pipe. Some right-wing extremists applaud this as "smaller government," since most of our schools are public schools run by states or cities or public school districts. I doubt that the founding fathers would be pleased.

Finally, Robert F. Kennedy points to a promising phenomenon that has become more common in recent years: adults returning to school for re-education or simply opening up their minds wider. Beyond that, we all need to re-educate ourselves, by giving up old dogmas and obsolete knowledge, and open ourselves to discovering anew.

SOLUTIONS

- **In schools, money talks. It can buy smaller class sizes. More money can come from trimming bloated administrations (this varies from one college and school district to another), and from shifting money over to education that is saved by not incarcerating drug offenders.**

- **Businesses can contribute in a variety of ways to education in their communities.**

- **Junior Colleges could establish vocational training programs analogous to those in Germany, with great attention to making sure they are training students for emerging needs rather than yesterday's needs.**

- **Schools at all levels need to give more attention to fostering creative and critical thinking and to science education (U.S. colleges are filling up with physics and math teachers from other countries because we do not educate enough of them ourselves. Incentives might be offered to students who go into advanced training in such areas.)**

- **The Armed Forces, already outstanding in some areas of training and education, could make training that transfers to peacetime pursuits a larger part of their mission. They should also do as good a job of training those who are leaving the service to function well in civilian society as they do of training recruits to kill.**

- **Communities can self-organize local education and training programs, with people who have diverse abilities, including retired people, volunteering to teach them to others.**

*   *   *

7. Freedom of Speech and the Media:
The Great Manipulators

The First Amendment is straightforward in its ban on Congressional interference with the people's right of free speech. Things get more complicated when we get into the realm of government secrecy categories, libel, copyrights, radio and TV, and the internet. Throughout our history, some people, agencies, and companies have nibbled away at that right, others have cursed it, others have defended it, and still others have reflected thoughtfully about it. Details follow.

"Whoever would overthrow the liberty of a nation must begin by subduing the freedom of speech." **Benjamin Franklin.** Franklin also wrote, "If all printers were determined not to print anything till they were sure it would offend nobody, there would be very little printed."

"If the freedom of speech is taken away then dumb and silent we may be led, like sheep to the slaughter." **George Washington**

"If a nation expects to be both ignorant and free, it expects what never was and never will be." *Thomas Jefferson*

"If [a book] be false in its facts, disprove them; if false in its reasoning, refute it. But, for God's sake, let us freely hear both sides. . . . Our liberty depends on freedom of the press, and that cannot be limited without being lost. " **Thomas Jefferson**

On another occasion and in a different context, Jefferson also wrote, "Nothing can now be believed which is seen in a newspaper. Truth itself becomes suspicious by being put into that polluted vehicle. . . . Nonetheless, he reflected, "Indeed the abuses of the freedom of the press here have been carried to a length never before known or borne by any civilized nation., But it is so difficult to draw a clear line of separation between the abuse and the wholesome use of the press, that as yet we have found it better to trust the public judgment, rather than the magistrate, with the discrimination between truth and falsehood." **Thomas Jefferson**

There was also early support for advertising in newspapers: "It is the advertiser who provides the paper for the subscriber. It is not to be disputed, that the publisher of a newspaper in this country, without a very exhaustive advertising support, would receive less reward for his labor than the humblest mechanic." **Alexander Hamilton.** (Hamilton did not mention, and may not have foreseen, that one day advertisers would influence editorial policy.)

"To the press alone, chequered as it is with abuses, the world is indebted for all the triumphs which have been gained by reason and humanity over error and oppression," wrote **James Madison.** "Nothing could be more irrational than to give the people power, and to withhold from them information without which power is abused. A people who mean to be their own governors must arm themselves with power which knowledge gives. A popular government without popular information or the means of acquiring it is but a prologue to a farce or a tragedy, or perhaps both."

JAMES MADISON

Abraham Lincoln could have been speaking of many of today's hatemongering talk show and TV hosts and spin-doctors when he said, "He can compress the most words into the smallest ideas of any man I ever met."

Another "log cabin president" who attacked political corruption said, "Publicity is the strong bond which unites the people and their government. Authority should do no act that will not bear the light." **James A. Garfield**

"If the fires of freedom and civil liberties burn low in other lands, they must be made brighter in our own. If in other lands the press and books and literature of all kinds are censored, we must redouble our efforts here to keep them free. If in other lands the eternal truths of the past are threatened by intolerance, we must provide a safe place for their perpetuation." **Franklin D. Roosevelt**

"When even one American - who has done nothing wrong - is forced by fear to shut his mind and close his mouth - then all Americans are in peril." **Harry S. Truman**

"The First Amendment does not speak equivocally. It prohibits any law 'abridging freedom of speech or of the press.'" Supreme Court Justice **Hugo L. Black**

"To misstate or suppress the news is a breach of trust." Former Supreme Court Justice **Louis D. Brandeis,** who also said, "Sunlight is the best disinfectant" for all kinds of mischief.

Former Supreme Court Justice **Felix Frankfurter** pointed to another dimension: "Without a lively sense of responsibility a free press may readily become a powerful instrument of injustice."

"If this nation is to be wise as well as strong. . . .then we. . . . must know all the facts and hear all the alternatives and listen to all the criticisms." *John F. Kennedy*

"We are not afraid to entrust the American people with unpleasant facts, foreign ideas, alien philosophies, and competitive values. For a nation that is afraid to let its people judge the truth and falsehood in an open market is afraid of its people. . . . Let us welcome controversial books and controversial authors. For the Bill of rights is the guardian of our security as well as our liberty." **John F. Kennedy**

JOHN F. KENNEDY

JFK also remarked, "It is never pleasant to read things that are not agreeable news, but I would say that it is . . . invaluable to check really on what is going on in the administration. . . . There is a terrific disadvantage not to have the abrasive quality of the press applied to you daily, to an administration, even though we never like it, and even though we wish they didn't write it, and even though we disapprove, there isn't any doubt that we could not do the job at all in a free society without a very, very active press."

"The job of the newspaper is to comfort the afflicted and afflict the comfortable."
Humorist **F.P. Dunne.**

"A democracy ceases to be a democracy if its citizens do not participate in its governance. To participate intelligently, they must know what their government has done, is doing, and plans to do in their name. Whenever any hindrance, no matter what its name, is placed in the way of this information, a democracy is weakened, and its future endangered." Newsman **Walter Cronkite**

Definition: "Editor: a person employed by the newspaper, whose business it is to separate the wheat from the chaff, and to see that the chaff is printed." **Elbert Hubbard**

"If you want a watchdog to warn you of intruders, you must put up with a certain amount of mistaken barking. . . . But if you muzzle him . . . and teach him decorum, you will find that he doesn't do the job for which you got him in the first place. Some extraneous barking is the price you must pay for his service as a watchdog. A free press is the watchdog of a free society. Columnist **Alan Barth**

We can put television in its proper light by supposing that Gutenberg's great invention had been directed at printing only comic books." **Robert M. Hutchins**

"Nothing can be more notorious than the calumnies and invectives with which the wisest measures and most virtuous characters of The United States have been pursued and traduced [by American newspapers]." **Thurgood Marshall**

"If the First Amendment means anything, it means that a state has no business telling a man, sitting alone in his house, what books he may read or what films he may watch." **Thurgood Marshall**

HUBERT H. HUMPHREY

"In real life, unlike in Shakespeare, the sweetness of the rose depends upon the name it bears. Things are not only what they are. They are, in very important respects, what they seem to be." Vice President **Hubert H. Humphrey.** Also, "The right to be heard does not automatically include the right to be taken seriously."

"A cynical, mercenary, demagogic, corrupt press will produce in time a people as base as itself." Newspaper owner and editor **Joseph Pulitzer**

The **code of ethics of the Society of Professional Journalists** states: "Members of the Society of Professional Journalists believe that public enlightenment is the forerunner of justice and the foundation of democracy. The duty of the journalist is to further those ends by seeking truth and providing a fair and comprehensive account of events and issues. Conscientious journalists from all media and specialties strive to serve the public with thoroughness and honesty."

"The choice of what we say and how we say it, what we report, do have an impact, and we need to care what that impact is. Journalists need to be more committed to objectivity and thoroughness and accuracy and fairness. We need to respect other people's privacy, whether those people are public figures or private figures. . . If we don't, people are going to reject the very rights that are essential to their own freedoms." *Rocky Mountain News* editor **Jean Otto**

Supreme Court Justice **William O. Douglas** wrote, "The framers of the constitution knew human nature as well as we do. They . . . knew the suffocating influence of orthodoxy and standardized thought. They weighed the compulsions for restrained speech and thought against the abuses of liberty. They chose liberty. . . . Free speech is not to be regulated like diseased cattle and impure butter. The audience that hissed yesterday may applaud today, even for the same performance. . . When a legislature undertakes to proscribe the exercise of a citizen's constitutional right to free speech, it acts lawlessly; and the citizen can take matters in his own hands and proceed on the basis that such a law is no law at all. . . . No matter what the legislature may say, a man has the right to make his speech, print his handbill, compose his newspaper, and deliver his sermon without asking anyone's permission. The contrary suggestion is abhorrent to our traditions. . . . The struggle is always between the individual and his sacred right to express himself and the power structure that seeks conformity, suppression, and obedience

> **Comment:** Today we see clearly that the U.S. power structure mentioned by Douglas includes both bureaucrats and corpocrats. (In the interest of evenhanded use of loaded language, if we're going to call public servants who work in government bureaus or agencies "bureaucrats," we can call those who work in big business "corpocrats.")

WILLIAM O. DOUGLAS

"You work your butt off and somebody says you can't have your record played because it offends them. Tyrants are made of such stuff." Humorist **Richard Pryor**

"What might be most remarkable about this remarkable document [the First Amendment] is not what it says but what it does not say. There are no restrictions, contingencies, or other provisions dealing with heresy, blasphemy, pornography, obscenity, defamation, national security, sedition, public morals, racism, sexism, libel, slander, political correctness, or a host of other social concerns that have threatened to dilute the strength of the First Amendment for more than 200 years." *Project Censored* founder **Carl Jensen**.

"If only the corporate and even progressive media in America would catch on to the meaning of a free press. This is not about agreeing with particular conclusions on controversial topics, it's about agreeing to have an open, transparently factual, public dialogue about the most crucial issues our society faces. . . . It is our duty to fight censorship in any form, even or especially, when it comes from those we respect the most." **Peter Phillips and Mickey Huff,** past and present directors of *Project Censored.*

Phillips and Huff also state, "*Managed news* includes both the release of specific stories intended to build public support as well as the deliberate non-coverage of news stories that may undermine U.S. goals. . . . Managed news creates a *Truth Emergency* for the public inside the US/NATO Military Industrial Media Empire. Deliberate news management undermines the freedom of information on the doings of the powerful military/corporate entities through overt censorship, mass distractions, and artificial news—including stories timed for release to influence public opinion (i.e. propaganda). . . .

"A Truth Emergency is . . . the state in which people, despite potentially being awash in a sea of information, lack the power of discernment, resulting in a knowinglessness about what is going on. . . . We are living in a time where people do not know whom to trust for accurate information."

"It's like watching a Disney movie about the news." Humorist **Stephen Colbert,** about Fox News.

"The Faux News Network." Online comment by **Artful**

"I think that Madison's view on government is still unequalled. That people determined to be in a democracy, to be their own governments, must have the power that knowledge will bring. . . . You can either be informed and your own rulers, or you can be ignorant and have someone else, who is not ignorant, rule over you. The question is, where has the United States betrayed Madison and

Jefferson, betrayed these basic values on how you keep a democracy? I think that the U.S. military-industrial complex and the majority of politicians in congress have betrayed those values." **Julian Assange** founder of *Wikileaks*, which publishes information from whistleblowers. **Assange** also comments, "I have a lot of sympathy for journalists who are trying to protect their sources. It's very hard now. Unless you're an electronic-surveillance expert or you have frequent contact with one, you must stay off the Net and mobile phones. You really have to use just the old techniques, paper and whispering in people's ears. Leave your mobile phones behind. Don't turn them off, but tell your source to leave electronic devices in their offices. We are now in a situation where countries are recording billions of hours of conversations, and proudly proclaiming that you don't have to select which telephone call you're intercepting, because you intercept every telephone call."

In 2011 **Assange** was arrested in England for alleged sexual misconduct in Sweden (At this writing no charges have been filed but he nonetheless remains under indefinite detention, while the U.S. government tries to have him extradited to the U.S. for trial for disclosing government secrets). In an interview with *Rolling Stone*, he says,

The U.S. government is trying to redefine what have been long-accepted journalistic methods. If the Pentagon is to have its way, it will be the end of national-security journalism in the United States. They're trying to interpret the Espionage Act to say that any two-way communication with a source is a collaboration with a source, and is therefore a conspiracy to commit espionage where classified information is involved. . . They're trying to create a new legal precedent that includes a journalist simply asking a source to communicate information. A few years ago, for example, the CIA destroyed its waterboarding interrogation videos. In the Manning hearing, prosecutors described how we had a most-wanted list, which included those interrogation videos if they still existed. This list was not put together by us. We asked for nominations from human rights activists and journalists from around the world of the information they most wanted, and we put that on a list."

Rolling Stone: "From a journalist's perspective, a list like that would be the equivalent of a normal editorial meeting where you list the crown jewels of stories you'd love to get."

Assange: "Exactly."

Rolling Stone: "So if you're going to jail, then Bob Woodward's going to jail."

Assange: "Individuals like . . . Bob Woodward constantly say to their sources, "Hey, what about this, have you heard anything about it? . . . Do you have any more details, and can you prove them with paper?" And all those would be defined as conspiracy to commit espionage under the Pentagon's interpretation."

At this writing U.S. Army Private Bradley Manning, from Crescent City, Oklahoma, is in U.S. prison for sending *Wikileaks* a U.S. Government video of, in the words of the *New York Times* "The so-called 'Granai massacre, ' when American aircraft dropped 500lb and 1000lb bombs on a suspected militant compound." *Wikipedia* refers "to the killing of a large number of Afghan civilians. . . on May 4, 2009, in the village of Granai in Farah Province, south of Heart, Afghanistan. The U.S. military have admitted [that] 'the inability to discern the presence of civilians and avoid and/or minimize accompanying collateral damage resulted in the unintended consequence of civilian casualties.' The . . . Afghan government has said that around 140 civilians were killed, of which 93 were children and only 22 were adult males." For releasing the video, along with diplomatic cables and footage of a 2007 Baghdad airstrike, Manning is now awaiting a court martial that may result in life in prison. Freedom of speech?

When asked whether he thought Wikileaks should post that video online, **Daniel Ellsberg,** who released the *Pentagon Papers* that blew open government lies about the Vietnam war, said, "First of all, I'd call for President Obama to post that videotape online. Let's see whether it confirms what his officials and the Bush officials said about it earlier, or what the truth is. Has he seen it himself? He certainly should. He has access to it. And if he does, what excuse would he have for not revealing it?"

Ellsberg adds, "I agree that there are things that should be kept secret. . . . The fact is that when it comes to judgment as to what should be kept secret and what should not be secret, Julian Asssange's judgment has been pretty good so far." Of his own release of the Vietnam Pentagon Papers, Ellsberg comments, "We were young, we were foolish, we were arrogant, but we were right. . . . There should be at least one leak like the Pentagon Papers every year."

Comment: There are other disturbing incidents, especially since the start of Iraq War II in 2000 until the present. In early 2010 Lieutenant Colonel Anthony J. Schaffer published a book titled, **Operation Dark Heart: Spycraft and Special Ops on the Frontlines of Afghanistan—and the Path to Victory**. When I opened it, almost every page had several words or even several sentences blacked out with marker ink. A note from the publisher that begins the book explains:

"Just as St. Martin's Press was readying its initial shipments of this book . . . the Department of Defense contacted us to express its concern that [its] publication could cause damage to U.S. national security. This was unexpected, since . . . the author had worked closely with the Department of the Army, and had made a number of changes to the text, after which it passed the Army's operational security review. However, the . . . Defense Intelligence Agency in particular insisted that the Army's review was insufficient. . ." Col. Schaffer is a security professional himself, with some twenty-five years experience as a special operations agent with the CIA, the Marines, and the Army. He knows how to stay undercover, how to keep a secret, and how to avoid revealing sensitive information. Based on the discussions our author had with the government, he requested that we incorporate some of *the government's changes* (my italics) into a revised edition of his book while redacting other text he was told was classified, though he disagreed with that assessment."

Instead of eliminating the censored passages, St. Martins blacked them out so readers could see how much was cut. St. Martin's had already sold a few of the original uncensored copies. The Department of Defense bought the remainder of the first printing run of ten thousand copies, then allowed the printing and sale of the censored version. Hello--where are we now? Nazi Germany? Stalinist Russia?

The DOD's handling of Operation Dark Heart was clumsy. The George W. Bush administration was much slicker. A favorite tactic was alluded to by Robert Louis Stevenson—just don't mention what you're doing—such as the thoroughgoing gutting of the government's securities regulations and environmental regulations. "The cruelest lies," wrote Stevenson, "are often told in silence."

As for Assange, whom the U.S. government is pulling out all stops to try to bring to trial for revealing government secrets, I have a friend who has taken an informal, unscientific poll of acquaintances, asking: "Julian Assange: Hero or villain?" The majority answer "Hero."

Moving now to the mainstream media, they inevitably have split personalities. They:

1. Report "the news" that they consider important. This includes many trivial items while ignoring other crucial ones. The conventional wisdom is that they focus on what is catchy, sensational, and commercial. In reality, many catchy, sensational, and commercial stories are buried because they call the dominant narrative into question.

2. Need to keep the attention of viewers and readers, so the showy and sensational often makes the news while vital but less showy items languish. (If the news is not entertaining, "click" goes the channel changer.

3. Routinely misquote and take things out of context to make a non-story into a story, and specifically the story they want to tell.

4. Are filled with advertising designed to sell products and make money. No problem with that. But even though some advertisements are shameless lies, since money talks, the TV or radio station or magazine or paper runs them anyway. And since they depend on advertising revenue to operate, their editorial policy is often tailored to trying to please their advertisers.

5. Reinforce the dominant cultural narratives and political preferences favored by their owners, by their choice of what to report and how to report it both in "news stories" and in ads.

You can seldom get accurate sense of what's going on from just one news source. It's wise to check out multiple sources with diverse viewpoints, especially in the online world where some sites are so biased that they're totally silent about any facts that don't fit their preconceptions.

Who owns most newspapers, stations, and TV stations? Giant corporations and the very rich. What outlooks do they broadcast to the people? For the most part, those of their owners. Reporters and editors know whose hand feeds them.

Some people are for a "free press" as long as it says what they want it to and doesn't disagree with what they think are the facts. So-called "conservatives" often claim that they are discriminated against by the so-called "liberal media" when a news item contradicts their preconceptions. Think about it. How many left-wing talk shows are there in comparison to right-wing talk shows? The recent scandals involving ultra right wing media mogul Rupert Murdoch (who now owns the Wall Street Journal, Fox TV, and numerous other U.S. media outlets, are instructive about what many media owners want.

The arms of the octopus of Murdoch's empire are longer and more numerous than almost anybody knows. One afternoon last year I got a phone call from Fox News.

Me? Fox News? Strange.

Then a recorded message came on and said that Fox News was getting together a focus group of people who oppose President Obama and who would like to help defeat him in 2012 to discuss him and his policies, and that Fox would like me to participate. After about two minutes of trashing Obama, the tape ended and a real live person came on. He said almost exactly ("almost" because I wrote this down from memory just afterward),

"I'd like you to help us with a little survey --blah blah blah."

After I agreed to take the survey, he continued,

"We'd like your opinion of how President Obama is doing. On a five-point scale in which 1 is terrible and 5 is excellent, how would you rate his present performance?"

"About a 3.5."

"Thank you. Good afternoon." [CLICK]

Ah so. They wrote me off as not a hot candidate for a hate group about Obama. No news there.

But just one minute. *What is a supposedly NEWS program --especially one that constantly calls itself "fair and balanced" doing taking such a blatantly partisan stance and explicitly engaging in partisan political activity?*

Then I remembered my wife telling me that recently she was visiting someone who had the Fox political "news" on and it was a parade of one person after another trashing Obama.

A little light went off in my head: If I had given Obama a rating of "1" they might well have seen me as a promising gutter rat not just for the focus group but also to talk trash on one of their ultra rightist wingnut shows.

Fox News President and the Chairman of Fox Television Stations, Roger Ailes, was a media consultant for Republican presidents Richard Nixon, Ronald Reagan, George H.W. Bush, and George W. Bush. Can he really be "Fair and Balanced?"

I mentioned the telephone incident to my wife, puzzled because I have never had any contact with Fox News. Where did they get my name?

She looked at me silently for a minute, then said, "Who did you call on the phone last night?"

"Well," I replied, "I voted for two of the singers on American Idol."

American Idol. Fox TV. Nice clean entertainment. Millions of people's phone numbers straight into the Fox News political database?

"All they have to do is click your number on their electronic calling list and hit "return," said my wife. "They don't even have to look at your name." Or maybe they got my number off some mailing list—or by hacking my e-mail, Rupert Murdoch's London antics style.

But that incident was just a glimpse of the tip of the iceberg. Here's another endearing story. Not so long ago Fox News hired two reporters and told them to go out and do some real investigative reporting. Great! Or so it seemed.

One of their first stories was about the widespread presence of rBST (bioengineered growth hormone) in Florida milk. The hormone makes cows produce more milk. The manufacturer, Monsanto, was running a TV commercial in dairy farming areas that boldly announced, "Prosilac is the single most tested new product in history, and is now available for you specifically so you can increase your profit potential." Actually thousands of other products have been tested more, and tests on Prosilac have produced such conflicting results that Canada, Australia, New Zealand, Europe, and many other countries totally ban it. The U.S. Food and Drug Administration (which is infested like a termite-ridden house with former Monsanto executives in top positions) pronounced it safe, but Canadian tests found that it could be absorbed by the body and had implications for human health. A Canadian scientist said, "I personally am concerned that there are very serious problems of secrecy [and] conspiracy." Monsanto has been busy leaning on state legislatures throughout the U.S. to make it illegal for milk producers and distributers who do not use rBST on their milk to say so. (Talk about Big Brother and freedom of speech!)

Friday night before the investigative reporters' TV show was to run, Fox received a letter from a Monsanto lawyer threatening a lawsuit and loss of advertising revenue if the program aired. The general manager at Fox pulled the reporters upstairs and said, "What would you do if I killed this story?"

They replied, "We're not going to lie for you."

In response, Fox said basically, "Okay, we will redo the story so that Monsanto doesn't object to it. The result? **Eighty three** subsequent drafts, and in every one of them the Monsanto lawyers asked for more changes, such as changing the word "cancer" to "negative health implications" throughout the script. Fox told the reporters, "We just paid three billion dollars for these television stations. *We'll tell you what the news is. The news is what you say it is.*" (my italics)

When the reporters refused to present the story as Monsanto and Fox wanted it, they were fired for insubordination. In court they claimed whistleblower status for exposing Fox's lies and won. An appellate court dismissed the case on the grounds that it is not illegal for TV stations to lie.

Of course! We knew that, didn't we? Nor newspapers – just look at the lying trash in tabloids at your supermarket check-out stand! And Fox's owner Rupert Murdoch is one of the world's tabloid kings. So remember that the First Amendment, which has many virtues, protects free speech but not truth. Let the buyer beware: Any radio or TV station, magazine, newspaper, website, or other media source can legally lie shamelessly and claim that they're telling the gospel truth. A corporation or government agency can lie and tell you it's the truth. And do you really believe the official government or corporate reports about certain major irregularities in recent U.S. history, which the government calls "conspiracy theories" but Phillips and Huff (see above) call "managed news" and "truth emergencies"? Your only protections are a source's reputation for integrity, and your own critical and thoughtful mind.

In these days of multiple corporate Big Brothers, it seems only sane to be a little paranoid. If Fox news is "Fair and Balanced," I wonder what bias looks like. But let's be serious. Rupert Murdoch owns Fox. His personal reputation tells all. He might as well just say straight out, "We are an ultra right wing extremist network." (In fairness, I like the local anchors of the Fox station in my area.) If you want a real in-depth look at the "liberal media" myth and how it compares to reality, however, read Minnesota Senator Al Franken's *Lies and the Lying Liars Who Tell Them.*

During Iraq War II another mega-corporation, Clear Channel, told the 1,200 radio stations it owns not to play the music of a popular group, the Dixie Chicks, who let it be publicly known that they opposed the war. In response, millions of country music fans dutifully shifted their attitudes from liking to disliking the Dixie Chicks. This is a good example of the frightful power that has resulted from the immense concentration of media ownership that took place under the Reagan and Clinton administrations. Before the Telecommunications Act of 1996, one owner could have only 40 stations. When I was a kid, the limit was 5.

When the 1980's began there were more than 50 large media companies. Now there are ten. If not monopoly, it is certainly oligopoly, and in something as essential to our culture as telecommunications, oligopoly threatens democracy. It's as simple as that.

In 2011, coverage of "Occupy Wall Street" was minimal in mainstream media until it became too big to ignore. And almost nonexistent in the news were the dramatic and powerful photos of 700 United and Continental Airlines pilots marching in disciplined formation in front of the New York Stock Exchange. I ran across them on a British website. (I wanted to include one of the photos here but the asking price to use it was too rich for this book's production budget. You can view the picture at Getty images.com--image 127273467.)

It is not just Fox and Clear Channel. Today a large share of what you hear and read in mainstream corporate media – radio, TV, and newspapers – is *managed news.* Deliberately misleading

Management of the news is often used to cover up what the government-corporate axis wants covered up and give you garbage in its place. We live in a multimedia theater of flickering lights and shadows where much of what we see and think is the work of the masters of illusion who control the information, metaphors, and myths that we see and hear, and who keep us from seeing and hearing others. They tell us what is allegedly real and what is not, what is supposedly important and what is not. Often enough they lie, and that's perfectly legal. And we, like suckers and marks in a gambling casino, believe them. When something the power structure wants is unlawful, they pass a law to make it legal, helped along by a chorus of approval from the media. That's the way the dominant narrative is devised and disseminated.

There are a few mostly honest newspapers: The Christian Science Monitor is one; the St. Petersburg Times in Florida is another. And there may be an honest small time local newspaper in your local community that doesn't owe its soul to the company store. Online, there are many websites now that are outside the mainstream. Some are completely dedicated to creating a full menu of canned ideologies for you to consume. Others focus on unearthing and presenting facts and ideas that bureaucratic, corpocratic, and sometimes even theocratic Big Brother does not want you to hear.

Here's a little exercise for you. It works especially well with talk radio, where there are words and sounds but no pictures. Turn on any broadcaster and, first, do not listen at all to the content of what he or she is saying, but listen only to the voice qualities – to the tone, the cadences, the loudness or softness. Without reference to the content, does this person sound reasonable, and respectful of listeners (and guests or callers if there are any)? Is the tone pleasant and inviting, concerned, or bullying or judgmental in a nasty way? What features do you find your own face forming itself into as you listen? Regardless of content, what attitudes do the speaker's words evoke? Sometimes hearing just one sentence is enough to answer all these questions.

Next, continue to ignore the content, but change from listening to the sound to listening to the language the broadcaster is using. Notice the choice of words and phrases. Do they encourage thoughtfulness or are they designed to manipulate you into adopting the same attitude as the speaker? Pay special attention to *adjectives,* whether positive or negative. What *comparisons and metaphors* does the speaker use? They're probably all meant to make you think about the subject as if it really were the mental picture the comparisons and metaphors bring up.

Then, listen to content in terms of whether it directly addresses a point being made or goes of on a tangent that somehow avoids it—especially in dialogues, where the broadcaster and guests or callers respond to each other. Practice attending to these items and you'll get better at noticing when others' comments are manipulative.

Lieutenant Colonel Daniel L. Davis served two tours of duty in Iraq and two in Afghanistan, logging more than 9,000 miles during the latter. In his report *Dereliction of Duty,* he presents compelling evidence that the American Forces Press Service is only minimally a news organization, and is primarily a propaganda arm of the armed forces. Moreover, the working circumstances of mainstream media reporters "embedded" with the armed forces tend to turn them into propaganda mouthpieces for the military and dull the critical faculties of the reporters. They basically see and hear everything with the same eyes and ears as the units in which they are embedded, making objectivity almost impossible.

Today "Informations Operations (IO) " designed to "protect" the support of the American people for U.S. war missions are an integral part of military strategy. Military strategists and tacticians in every country have always tried deceive the enemy--no news there. But a 2006 Information Operations article recommends trying to bring about changes in the 1985 Smith-Mundt act that was passed specifically to prohibit US government organizations from using information "to influence public opinion in the United States [in order] to protect a key friendly center of gravity, to wit US national will." The 2011 July-August edition of the *Military Review* states: states that "IO should be incorporated into "every facet of a unit's daily framework. . . . For years, commercial advertisers have based their advertisement strategies on the premise that there is a positive correlation between the number of times a consumer is exposed to product advertisement and that consumer's inclination to sample the new product. The very same principle applies to how we influence our target audiences. . . . I cannot overemphasize the importance of such 'message saturation.' Such repetition and constancy is a critical prerequisite to influencing a target audience." In other words, marketing strategies for selling combat operations are the '"very same" as those for selling fast food hamburgers.

In 2011 the Pentagon's Inspector General investigated a charge that the Bush Administration's Department of Defense inappropriately used former generals to shape public opinion with "expert commentary" in the news. The investigation asked, "Was the outreach campaign an earnest effort to inform the public, or improper media manipulation?" On December 25, 2011 the *New York Times* reported on the Inspector General's findings (reprinted in Colonel Davis' report):

"Secretary of Defense Rumsfeld's staff often provided military analysts with 'talking points' for their media appearances. A military analyst described the talking points as 'bullet points given for a political purpose." Another military analyst said that the outreach program's intent "was to move everyone's mouth on TV as a sock puppet." Four military analysts said they were fired from the program "because they were critical" of the Pentagon. When a top NBC analyst, retired Four Star General Barry McCaffrey, "started challenging" Defense Secretary Rumsfeld on the air, he was immediately removed for not being a "team player." And another CNN commentator, retired Four Star General Wesley Clark (his class valedictorian at West Point, who commanded NATO forces during the Kosovo war without losing a single U.S. soldier's life) "was told that the White House had asked CNN to release him from his contract as a commentator." That's no way to inform citizens in a democracy.

On 9/11 while still on CNN, Clark got a call from the White House asking him to say the attack was connected to Saddam Hussein. Clark reports, "I said, "I'm willing to say it, but what's your evidence? And I never got any."

The FCC and the Media. Washington, Jefferson, Adams, Madison, and Lincoln all spoke eloquently of the need for an educated, well-informed public in order for democracy to function. Indeed, Lincoln declared that, "I view [education] as *the most important subject that we as a people can be engaged in*."(my italics) In the present multimedia era, people are educated (or not, or rendered stupid) not only through the schools but through a spectrum of information sources. In the Radio Act of 1927, Congress declared that the Radio Commission, which later became the Federal Communications Commission (FCC) should only issue broadcast licenses when it serves the public interest. After all, the airwaves belong to the people, and a limited number of broadcast frequencies are available.

In the media environment of 1949, during the Truman era, lawmakers became concerned that the three major television networks could misuse their broadcast licenses to shape public opinion as they wished. In response, the FCC drafted a "Fairness Doctrine" that had two basic elements: It required broadcast license holders to devote some of their airtime to controversial matters of public interests, and required them to provide contrasting viewpoints on those matters, whether through news segments, public affairs shows, or editorials. It prohibited stations from broadcasting a single perspective, day after day, without presenting alternative views. The basic idea was that viewers should have access to multiple perspectives. No one should be able to monopolize the airwaves with their own narrative, their version of the way things are, whether the monopolizer is the left, the right, the government, or the multinational corporate establishment. The doctrine arises from the principle that broadcasters have special trustee obligations, which they voluntarily accept in exchange for exclusive use of scarce public airwaves.

In 1969 the Fairness doctrine was challenged in *Red Lion Broadcasting Co. vs. the FCC*. In a unanimous vote the U.S. Supreme Court upheld the FCC's right to enforce the Fairness Doctrine. Supreme Court Justice Byron White wrote,

"A license permits broadcasting, but the licensee has no constitutional right to be the one who holds the license or to monopolize a radio frequency to the exclusion of his fellow citizens. There is nothing in the First Amendment which prevents the Government from requiring a licensee to share his frequency with others.... It is the right of the viewers and listeners, not the right of the broadcasters, which is paramount.

In the 1970s the FCC called the doctrine "the single most important requirement of operation in the public interest—the *sine qua non* for grant of a renewal of a license."

But in 1980 Ronald Reagan became President. Opponents of the Fairness Doctrine (especially owners of radio and TV stations) argued that the requirement of fairness abridged free speech, and hey ought to be able to say anything they wanted, without allowing others to differ on their stations. By 1985 the FCC was composed entirely of Reagan appointees. All was ready. The FCC set out to kill the various parts of the Fairness Doctrine one after another, with the rationale (or cover story, as you prefer) that because of the many media voices in the market place, listeners could go from one station or channel to another to get their news.

Supporters of the Fairness Doctrine replied, "The Doctrine doesn't restrict your speech at all. It just requires that you offer others who disagree with you on important public matters that same right of free speech. Since you're broadcasting on a bandwidth that belongs to all the people, that's quite reasonable." Congress agreed, and in 1987 both the House and the Senate voted put the Doctrine into law, so that the FCC would have to enforce it whether it wanted to or not. But Reagan vetoed the bill, and there were not enough votes in Congress to override the veto. During the George H.W. Bush administration Congress tried again, and Bush vetoed the legislation again.

In 2000, the Fairness Doctrine's last restriction, the personal attack rule, was removed. That freed up media to attack anyone they wanted with no chance for rebuttal. These days a sociopathic maniac can get away with saying almost anything on radio or TV (and some do—and some stations encourage it). Public interest lawyer Robert F. Kennedy Jr. says that today, "The FCC's pro-industry, anti-regulatory philosophy has effectively ended the right of access to broadcast television by any but the moneyed interests." And after a study of two Eugene, Oregon radio stations' programming, attorney Edward Monks concluded that *"Political opinions expressed on talk radio are approaching the level of uniformity that would normally be achieved only in a totalitarian society."* A much larger survey by the Center for American Progress and Free Press found that, "In the spring of 2007, of the 257 news/talk stations owned by the top five commercial station owners, 91 percent of the total weekday talk radio programming was conservative, and only 9 percent was progressive."

At Johns Hopkins University, Mark Crispin Miller has tracked the increasing concentration of media ownership. Miller's charts trace the holdings of four major conglomerates: Time Warner, Disney/Cap Cities, General Electric, and Westinghouse. Each owns a news network: CNN, ABC, NBC, and CBS, respectively. They also own radio stations, magazines, cable TV, motion pictures, music, and newspapers. And this doesn't even include Fox, which is owned by a foreigner, the notorious tabloid king Rupert Murdoch, who owns a large chunk of what the other four don't own, including the *Wall Street Journal* and Twentieth Century Fox studios. As for the other four, can they be fair in covering news that involves the corporations that own them, which are involved in everything from nuclear reactors to the weapons manufacturing? Miller argues that this concentrated ownership wipes out Reagan's rationale for killing the Fairness Doctrine, and that it is needed more than ever now that a few owners control most of what most people see and hear on radio and TV.

Is it presumptuous to ask, "Who is the country for, the people or big business? The millions of viewers and listeners or the handful of station owners?" On one hand an owner of many TV and radio stations asserts the right to broadcast whatever he damn well pleases, while on the other hand there is the public's right to be well-informed enough to be able to participate as an active citizen in a democratic society. (In any case the station holds most of the cards, since it can just not cover what it doesn't want to public to know about, and then there is no viewpoint explicitly presented and no responsibility for airing other viewpoints.)

For now, however, in U.S. broadcast media, fairness and balance are largely dead. Can they be reborn? If not, then the defense of the people's right to know what's really going on, if such a defense occurs, will take place only elsewhere in the world. Would that please you?

SOLUTIONS

- Extend the First Amendment protection of free expression, "Congress shall make no law. . . abridging the freedom of speech." The extension might read something like, "Likewise, *no other arm or agency of government,* shall make such a law or regulation or adopt such a policy or procedure, officially or unofficially. (A carefully worded, narrowly written exception could be made in cases of national security.)

- Before the Reagan and Clinton presidencies, one owner could have no more than forty radio stations. Now media corporations are lobbying to scrap the present limit of 1/3 of the total market. A limit of *one* station per owner makes sense to me, with provision that a specified share of those that would have to be sold off by media conglomerates be made available to community citizens' associations. Big media companies could still offer content to many stations, provided that stations were free to accept or not accept particular programs.

- Pass a constitutional amendment that explicitly states that the people's right to be fully informed about political and economic decisions and events that affect our lives is as important as the right of free speech.

- Create forums for widespread public input on how to manage our media to encourage the most widespread access and coverage, including more community- and citizen-based radio and TV stations, with input from experts on media freedom.

- It makes no sense to resurrect the old Fairness Doctrine just as it was in 1949. But it makes excellent sense to rewrite in a way that fits today's realities, in accord with the founding fathers' (and Lincoln's) great vision of a truly informed people.

- When you turn on mainstream media, listen critically and make your own call about them, based on what they cover and don't cover, and how they present stories.

- Make a habit of doing internet searches on news you're interested in, and look especially at sources that you seldom read (such as those in other countries), to broaden your perspective. Vigorously fight government and private initiatives to censor the internet. With newspapers dying like flies, the internet is our last best chance at a "free press."

- If our country goes to war again, or war by any other name, ensure access for independent media that are not "embedded" with U.S. forces and therefore subject to de-facto censorship of what they can and cannot cover.

- Donate what you can afford to at least one public radio or TV station. (My personal favorite is Link TV, which shows how people live in countries very different from our own.)

- Bradley Manning has already endured great punishment that few people would be willing to risk. I think he has been punished enough. Do taxpayers want to pay to keep this guy in prison for life? Not me. Give him a discharge and turn him out on the street to support himself. Julian Assange is brilliant and could be invaluable to U.S. e-intelligence where others fail. How about playing, "Let's make a deal." Instead of trying to crucify him, ask him to help the government in one or more crucial cases where it would not violate his sense of ethics and integrity by doing so.
(For instance, put him in charge of supervising prevention of dirty tricks in the national vote counting in U.S. elections.)

* * *

8. Pathways to Equality, and Efforts to Destroy Them

The Declaration of Independence begins, *"We hold these truths to be self-evident: that all men are created equal. . ."* In drafting the Declaration (which was edited by John Adams and Benjamin Franklin on the way to its final form), Jefferson made the statement that "all men are created equal" the **first** of its "self-evident truths." He put equality first, even before freedom and independence. It took more than half a century and a terrible war to establish that "all men" truly meant all, rather than just white men of European ancestry, and it took decades more to establish that "men" really meant "human beings, male and female alike" rather than just males. It has been a long road and we are not yet at the end of it, since racial and gender prejudice are still widespread. Those who hold such prejudices keep trying to find ways to embody them in law, so they can continue to think of themselves as "better than" and justify keeping nonwhites and women down. It is long past time to let go of all that.

Thomas Paine said simply, **"**I believe in the equality of man.**"**

ABIGAIL ADAMS

"If particular care and attention is not paid to the ladies, we are determined to foment a rebellion, and will not hold ourselves bound by any laws in which we have no voice, or representation. . . If we mean to have heroes, statesmen and philosophers, we should have learned women." First Lady *Abigail Adams*

"Patriotism in the femals sex is the most disinterested of all virtues. Excluded from honours and from offices, we caannot attach ourselves to the State or government from having held a place of eminence. . . Yet all history and every age exhibit instances of patriotic virtue in the female sex; which considering our situation equals the most heroic of yours." **Abigail Adams,** wife of President John Adams

Abraham Lincoln was articulate about equality. Of slavery, he remarked, "Our progress in degeneracy appears to me to be pretty rapid. As a nation, we began by declaring that *'all men are created equal.'* We now practically read it 'all men are created equal, *except negroes.'* When the Know-Nothings get control, it will read 'all men are created equal, except negroes, *and foreigners, and Catholics.'* When it comes to this I should prefer emigrating to some country where they make no pretence of loving liberty. . . . The master not only governs the slave without his consent, but he governs him by a set of rules altogether different from those which he prescribes for himself."

"Whenever I hear anyone arguing for slavery I feel a strong impulse to see it tried on him personally."
Abraham Lincoln

Lincoln's comments about equality were not limited to slavery. "[The Declaration of Independence] gave promise that in due time the weights would be lifted from the shoulders of all. . . and that all should have an equal chance. . . . Let us discard all this quibbling about this man and the other man, this race and that race and the other race being inferior and therefore they must be placed in an inferior position. Let us discard all these things, and unite as one people throughout this land, until we shall once more stand up declaring that all men are created equal."

Lincoln added, "I think the authors of . . . the Declaration of Independence. . . intended to include all men, but they did not intend to declare all men equal in all respects. They did not mean to say all were equal in color, size, intellect, moral developments, or social capacity. They defined with tolerable distinctness, in what respects they did consider all men created equal-equal in "certain inalienable rights, among which are life, liberty, and the pursuit of happiness." This they said, and this meant. They did not mean to assert the obvious untruth, that all were then actually enjoying that equality, nor yet, that they were about to confer it immediately upon them. In fact they had no power to confer such a boon. They meant simply to declare the right, so that the enforcement of it might follow as fast as circumstances should permit. They meant to set up a standard maxim for free society, which should be familiar to all, and revered by all; constantly looked to, constantly labored for, and even though never perfectly attained, constantly approximated, and thereby constantly spreading and deepening its influence, and augmenting the happiness and value of life to all people of all colors everywhere. The assertion that "all men are created equal" was of no practical use in effecting our separation from Great Britain; and it was placed in the Declaration, nor for that, but for future use. Its authors . . . knew the proneness of prosperity to breed tyrants, and they meant when such should re-appear in this fair land and commence their vocation they should find left for them at least one hard nut to crack." Finally, **Lincoln** linked equality to democracy:

"Allow all the equal voice in the government and that, and that only, is self-government." *Abraham Lincoln*

"If a woman earned a dollar by scrubbing, her husband had a right to take the dollar and go and get drunk with it and beat her afterwards. It was his dollar." **Lucy Stone,** early abolitionist and women's rights advocate

"I grew up like a neglected weed – ignorant of liberty, having no experience of it. . . I freed a thousand slaves. I could have freed a thousand more if only they knew they were slaves." **Harriet Tubman**, central figure in the Underground Railroad for escaped slaves.

HARRIET TUBMAN

Comment: Lincoln's incisive comments show that freedom and equality are opposed only when one person wants the freedom to deny another person's equality. In other cases freedom and equality are both the opposite of slavery and subservience. I am not equal in possessions to a multimillionaire, nor in hardships to someone who lives under a bridge, but we are equal in our common humanity. I feel better when I show respect for each of them, regardless of their circumstance or position in life. And "We the People" do better as a nation when we do our best to provide equality of opportunity for each other, and demonstrate an equality of respect for other peoples and other nations.

"We would have every arbitrary barrier thrown down. We would have every path laid open to women as freely as to men. If you ask me what offices they may fill, I reply—any. . . Let them be sea captains, if you will." **Margaret Fuller,** author of America's first major feminist book. She also wrote, "Two persons love in one another the future good which they aid one another to unfold. . . What woman needs is . . . as a nature to grow, as an intellect to discern, as a soul to live freely and unimpeded to unfold such powers as were given her when we left our common home."

"The history of mankind is a history of repeated injuries and usurpations on the part of man toward woman, having in direct object the establishment of an absolute tyranny over her. . . He has compelled her to submit to laws, in the formation of which she had no voice. He has withheld from her rights which are given to the most ignorant and degraded men – both natives and foreigners. . . . In the covenant of marriage, she is compelled to promise obedience to her husband, he becoming, to all intents and purposes, her master—the law giving him power to deprive her of her liberty, and to administer chastisement. . . He has [given] to the world a different code of morals for men and women, by which moral delinquencies which exclude women from society, are not only tolerated but deemed of little account in man. . . He has endeavored. . . to destroy her confidence in her own powers, to lessen her self-respect, and to make her willing to lead a dependent and abject life." **Elizabeth Cady Stanton, 1848**, abolitionist and women's rights advocate.

ELIZABETH CADY STANTON & SUSAN B. ANTHONY

"It was we, the people, not we, the white male citizens. . . but we, the whole people, who formed the union."
Susan B. Anthony

"No man is good enough to govern any woman without her consent. . . I think the girl who is able to earn her own living and pay her own way should be as happy as anybody on earth. The sense of independence and security is very sweet." **Susan B. Anthony**, a leader in the campaign for women's right to vote.

> **Comment:** Among some peoples inequality is especially pronounced in regard to gender. In the U.S., gains, such as voting rights have been hard fought, and bans on workplace discrimination have come only slowly. In some traditionally male occupations, discrimination and harassment are still widespread. Violence against women by men is still a regular item in the news. The Equal Rights Amendment to the Constitution, "Equality of rights under the law shall not be denied or abridged by the United States or by any state on account of sex," first introduced in the Senate in 1923, has been introduced again and again, but never passed in a majority of (male dominated) state legislatures. At this writing twenty-one states have some version of it in their state constitutions.

"I think there can be no question that women should have equal rights with men.". . . . "Women should have free access to every field of labor which they care to enter, and when their work is as valuable as that of a man it should be paid as highly. . . .Especially as regards the laws relating to marriage there should be the most absolute equality between the two sexes. I do not think the woman should assume the man's name." **Theodore Roosevelt**

Where Theodore Roosevelt saw the ideals, his cousin –in-law **Eleanor Roosevelt** saw the limits: "Too often the great decisions are originated and given form in bodies made up wholly of men, or so completely dominated by them that whatever of special value women have to offer is shunted aside without expression."

SIMONE DE BEAUVOIR

"The ideal of the average Western man is a woman who freely accepts his domination, who does not accept his ideas without discussion, but who yields to his arguments, who resists him intelligently, and ends by being convinced. . . . Children's books, mythology, stories, tales, all reflect the myths born of the pride and the desires of men; thus it is that through the eyes of men the little girl discovers the world and reads therein her destiny." **Simone de Beauvoir,** French writer and philosopher (and partner of Jean-Paul Sartre) who provided the mid-20th Century's seminal critique of patriarchal oppression and the feminine situation.

"It is easier to live through someone else than to become complete yourself. . . A girl should not expect special privileges because of her sex but neither should she adjust to prejudice and discrimination. . . . Men are not the enemy, but the fellow victims." **Betty Friedan**, writer who extended de Beauvoir's analysis to the United States.

"I have sacrificed everything in my life that I consider precious in order to advance the political career of my husband." **Patricia Nixon**

"If any class or race can be permanently set apart from, or pushed down below the rest in political and civil rights, so may any other class or race when it shall incur the displeasure of its more powerful associates, and we may say farewell to the principles on which we count our safety. . . . Negroes have been preyed upon by all types of exploiters, from the installment salesman of clothing, pianos, and furniture to the vendors of vice. The majority of our Negro people find but cold comfort in shanties and tenements. Surely, as freemen, they are entitled to something better than this." **Harry S. Truman, 1940**

"If one man's rights are denied, the rights of all are in danger--that if one man is denied equal protection of the law, we cannot be sure that we will enjoy freedom of speech or any other of our fundamental rights. . . We must recognize the full human equality of all our people—before God, before the law, and in the councils of government . . for the single and fundamental reason that it is the right thing to do." **Robert F. Kennedy**

"If you can convince the lowest white man that he's better than the best colored man, he won't notice you're picking his pocket. Hell, give him someone to look down on and he'll empty his pockets for you." **Lyndon B. Johnson**. Johnson also said, "It is not enough to open the gates of opportunity. All of our citizens must have the ability to walk through those gates."

"A people who extend civil liberties only to preferred groups start down the path either to dictatorship of the right or the left." **William O. Douglas**

JACQUELINE KENNEDY

"What is sad for women of my generation is that they weren't supposed to work if they had families. What were they going to do when the children are grown - watch the raindrops coming down the window pane?" **Jacqueline Kennedy**

"I figured, okay, I'll move to the White House, do the best I can, and if they don't like it, they can kick me out. But they can't make me someone I'm not. . . . The search for human freedom can never be complete without freedom for women." **Betty Ford**

"No one knows what leadership has gone undiscovered in women of all races, and in black and other minority men." **Gloria Steinem**, founder of **Ms.** magazine and central spokesperson for women's rights in the late 20th Century and today. Steinem also remarked, "If women are supposed to be less rational and more emotional at the beginning of our menstrual cycle when the female hormone is at its lowest level, then why isn't it logical to say that, in those few days, women behave the most like the way men behave all month long?"

GLORIA STEINEM

"A child born to a Black mother in a state like Mississippi... has exactly the same rights as a white baby born to the wealthiest person in the United States. It's not true, but I challenge anyone to say it is not a goal worth working for. . . . I wish I could say that racism and prejudice were only distant memories. We must dissent from the indifference. We must dissent from the apathy. We must dissent from the fear, the hatred and the mistrust.... We must dissent because America can do better, because America has no choice but to do better. **Thurgood Marshall**

"My God, what do we want? What does any human being want? Take away an accident of pigmentation of a thin layer of our outer skin and there is no difference between me and anyone else. All we want is for that trivial difference to make no difference. . . Racism is so universal in this country, so widespread and deep-seated, that it is invisible because it is so normal. . . I am not anti-white, because I understand that white people, like black ones, are victims of a racist society. They are products of their time and place." First black Congresswoman and first black female Presidential candidate **Shirley Chisholm.**

"I never believed in Santa Claus because I knew no white dude would come into my neighborhood after dark." African-American humorist **Dick Gregory.** He also said, "If it wasn't for Abe Lincoln, I'd still be on the open market."

DICK GREGORY

"There's a lot more hypocrisy than before. Racism has gone back underground." African-American actor and humorist **Richard Pryor**

"I'd rather have the illusion that [politicians] had ideas and high inspirations and principles, that they foster something in people that makes them want to be part of it instead of all this exclusion stuff, which is really horrible." Actress and humorist **Lily Tomlin**

"The American experiment was achieved by a complex synthesis of both Iroquois and European contributions. But there was one Iroquois contribution that was so advanced it may have shocked and alarmed the founding fathers. . . . The Iroquois judiciary was made up entirely of women. Clan mothers and women's councils reviewed the behavior of men they nominated to office. If any of those men erred and failed to heed three successive warnings, the women members of the judiciary swiftly and surely impeached them. Iroquois womanhood enjoyed freedoms hundreds of years ago that have still not been given to modern American women." Broadcaster **Hugh Downs**

"Some in our party miss no opportunity to roundly and loudly condemn affirmative action that helped a few thousand black kids get an education, but hardly a whimper is heard from them over affirmative action for lobbyists who load our federal tax codes with preferences for special interests." First African-American Secretary of State **Colin Powell**

COLIN POWELL

"WOMEN OF AMERICA, UNITE! Any law, rule, or custom that limits women's rights or freedoms more than men's is exploitive, unacceptable gender discrimination. We will not vote for, and will actively work against any candidate who supports such a law, rule, or custom. We will withhold all financial support from any political party or religious organization that supports such discrimination. We will consider permanently leaving any such party or other organization to join with sisters and brothers who actively oppose such restrictions. In whatever ways we find appropriate (which may go so far as to include days of fasting and prayer during which no work may be performed and no items will be bought) we actively commit to achieving full freedom for all women to live their lives and control their bodies as they choose, without gender-related discrimination, domination, or oppression of any kind. We invite all men who support women's self-determination to join us." **The American Women's Freedom Movement Declaration**

> **Comment:** Jungian psychiatrist Jean Shinoda Bolen suggests that our culture is obsessed with the power to dominate at the cost of our ability to truly love. We equate power with the "hard front" and a façade of total self-sufficiency. That is, I define **your needs** in terms of **my wishes,** and if I am more powerful, then "Keep your mouth shut and do as I say." Men who have trouble expressing love settle for control over others and lock women into complementary roles of being subservient and nurturing. As a result, men and women both end up emotionally crippled like hunchbacks, missing out on much of what we potentially could be. (The craving for power is often an attempt to compensate for abuse, humiliation powerlessness, and invalidation experienced from someone somewhere during our childhoods.)
>
> Now, as the women's movement moves beyond insisting that women and men are no different, many are realizing that on the average, with full regard for the man exceptions, some gender differences have implications for how we set up our culture. Today and in the future we will need every source of logic, insight, and intuition we can find, including the best of traditionally "male" and traditionally "female' energies, aptitudes, and attitudes. It is time for men and women to cooperate as equal partners in choosing the community's, the nation's and the world's future directions.
>
> Many nations now have or have had female presidents or prime ministers. Costa Rica currently requires that 40 % of its congress must be female, and in two years the male - female ratio will be 50-50. I suspect that we would soon see more money spent on education and cleaning up the air and water and less spent on bombs and wars if the U.S. followed Costa Rica's example.

GERALD R. FORD

"In this Land of the Free, it is right, and by nature it ought to be, that all men and all women are equal before the law." *Gerald R. Ford*

<<<<>>>>

SOLUTIONS

- Personally, we each can be alert to noticing whenever our thoughts and feelings that some people are better than others are triggered, and do our best to release them and avoid letting them affect our actions.

- Pass the Equal Rights Amendment—finally. Identify all legislators of either gender who oppose it and who support any form of discrimination against women, publicize their positions, and vote them out of office.

- We can be sensitive to gender imbalance it city councils, the legislatures, and judiciaries, and if all else is equal in terms of competence and values, support candidates of the underrepresented gender.

- Pay attention to *your own* hidden racism and ethnic bias.
  Almost everybody has some, so don't get on your case about it. Just remember to keep it in its place, avoid acting on it, and give every person from every race, national or ethnic group, or gender the equality of respect that everyone deserves.

* * *

9. Justice for Whom?
Down the River of No Return?

A quick search of the web shows that the term "justice" has many meanings and covers an immense territory. Much of what is found throughout this book has something to do with some kind of justice. This section is restricted to matters clearly related to those parts of the Constitution reproduced just below. Its emphasis is on what is or is not to be considered a "crime," and on how local, state, and federal institutions of the United States deal with such matters.

"The Judges, both of the supreme and inferior courts, shall hold their Offices during good Behavior." **Article III, Section 1, United States Constitution**

"The right of the people to be secure in their persons, houses, papers, and effects, against unreasonable searches and seizures, shall not be violated, and no Warrants shall issue, but upon probably cause, supported by Oath of affirmation, and particularly describing the place to be searched, and the persons or things to be seized." **Amendment 4, United States Constitution**

"No person shall be held to answer for a capital, or otherwise infamous crime, unless on a presentment or indictment of a Grand Jury, except in cases arising in the land or naval forces, or in the Militia, when in actual service in time of War or public danger, nor shall any person be subject for the same offense to be twice put in jeopardy of life or limb; nor shall be compelled in any criminal case to be a witness against himself, nor be deprived of life, liberty, or property, without due process of law; nor shall private property be taken for public use, without just compensation." **Amendment 5, United States Constitution**

"In all criminal prosecutions, the accused shall enjoy the right to a speedy and public trial, by an impartial jury of the State and district wherein the crime shall have been committed . . . and to be informed of the nature and cause of the accusation; to be confronted with the witnesses against him; to have compulsory process for obtaining witness in his favor, and to have the Assistance of Counsel for his defence." **Amendment 6, United States Constitution**

"Excessive bail shall not be required, nor excessive fines imposed, nor cruel and unusual punishments inflicted." **Amendment 8, United States Constitution**

". . . nor shall any State deprive any person of life, liberty, or property, without due process of law; nor deny to any person within its jurisdiction the equal protection of the laws." **Amendment 14, United States Constitution**

"The right of citizens of the United States to vote shall not be denied or abridged by the United States or by any State on account of race, color, or previous condition of servitude." **Amendment 15, United States Constitution**

"Justice in the life and conduct of the State is possible only as it first resides in the hearts and souls of the citizens." **Plato**

"The sentiment of justice is so natural, and so universally acquired by all mankind, that it seems to be independent of all law, all party, all religion." French philosopher **Voltaire**

"Justice is the insurance which we have on our lives and property. Obedience is the premium which we pay for it." **William Penn**

"The natural liberty of man, by entering into society, is abridged or restrained, so far only as is necessary for the . . . best good of the whole. . . . By entering into society he agrees to an arbiter or indifferent judge between him and his neighbors; but he [does not renounce] his original right. . . He must pay the referees for time and trouble. He should also be willing to pay his just quota for the support of government, the law, and the constitution; the end of which is to furnish indifferent and impartial judges in all cases that may happen." **Samuel Adams.** In addition, Samuel Adams asked, "What liberty can there be where property is taken away without consent?"

"The strictest law sometimes becomes the severest injustice." **Benjamin Franklin**

"The most sacred of the duties of a government [is] to do equal and impartial justice to all citizens," declared **Thomas Jefferson.** He added, "Taste cannot be controlled by law." Even though a Southern slave-owner himself, he wrote, **"**There must doubtless be an unhappy influence on the manners of our people produced by the existence of slavery among us. The whole commerce between master and slave is a perpetual exercise of the most boisterous passions, the most unremitting despotism on the one part, and degrading submissions on the other. Our children see this, and learn to imitate it; for man is an imitative animal. This quality is the germ of all education in him." Finally, he spoke a line with which people of every political outlook will surely agree: "Justice require eternal vigilance."

"Justice is the means by which established injustices are sanctioned." French poet, journalist, & novelist **Anatole France.**

"Law in origin was merely a codification of the power of dominant groups, and did not aim at anything that to a modern man would appear to be justice." British philosopher **Bertrand Russell**

"When there are too many policemen, there is no liberty. Where there are too many soldiers, there is no peace. Where there are too many lawyers, there is no justice." Chinese writer **Lin Yutang**

"Judging from the main portions of the history of the world so far, justice is always in jeopardy." **Walt Whitman**

"A government had better go to the extreme of toleration, than to do aught that could be construed into an interference with, or to jeopardize in any degree, the common rights of its citizens." **Abraham Lincoln**

"I have always found that mercy bears richer fruits than strict justice." **Abraham Lincoln**

"Too much mercy . . . often resulted in further crimes which were fatal to innocent victims who need not have been victims if justice had been put first and mercy second." **Agatha Christie,** English novelist and playwright

"Unjust laws exist: shall we be content to obey them, or shall we endeavor to amend them, and obey them until we have succeeded, or shall we transgress them at once? . . . Why is [the government] not more apt to anticipate and provide for reform? Why does it not cherish its wise minority? Why does it . . . not encourage its citizens to put out its faults, and do better? . . . What I have to do is to see, at any rate, that I do not lend myself to the wrong which I condemn." **Henry David Thoreau**

HENRY DAVID THOREAU

Thoreau also wrote, "Law never made men a whit more just; and by means of their respect for it, even the well-disposed are daily made the agents of injustice. . . The mass of men serve the state. . . not as men mainly, but as machines, with their bodies. . . A very few—as heroes, patriots, martyrs, reformers in the great sense. . . serve the state with their consciences also, and so necessarily resist it for the most part; and they are commonly treated as enemies by it. . . [Nonviolent] Disobedience is the true foundation of liberty. The obedient must be slaves."

"Every actual State is corrupt. Good men must not obey laws too well. **Ralph Waldo Emerson**

"[It] is revolting to have no better reason for a rule of law than that it was laid down in the time of Henry IV. It is still more revolting if the grounds upon which it was laid down have vanished long since, and the rule simply persists through blind imitation of the past. **Oliver Wendell Holmes, Sr.**

"When the [Supreme] Court moved to Washington in 1800, it was provided with no books, which probably accounts for the high quality of early opinions." **Robert H. Jackson**

"A jury consists of twelve persons chosen to decide who has the better lawyer." Poet **Robert Frost**

"This is a court of law, young man, not a court of justice." Supreme Court Justice **Oliver Wendell Holmes, Jr..** Holmes also wrote, "The young man knows the rules, but the old man knows the exceptions."

OLIVER WENDELL HOLMES, JR.

"Justice cannot be for one side alone, but must be for both." **Eleanor Roosevelt**

"Peace and justice are two sides of the same coin." **Dwight D. Eisenhower**

"You sit up there, and you see the whole gamut of human nature. Even if the case being argued involves only a little fellow and $50, it involves justice. That's what is important." Supreme Court Chief Justice **Earl Warren**

Warren also wrote, ""It is the spirit and not the form of law that keeps justice alive. . . . Police must obey the law while enforcing the law. . . Life and liberty can be as much endangered from illegal methods used to convict those thought to be criminals as from the actual criminals themselves." **Earl Warren**

"Surely the fact that a uniformed police officer is wearing his hair below his collar will make him no less identifiable as a policeman." **Thurgood Marshall**

"Justice must be blind to the hardness or softness of a man's hands, as well as to the leanness of fatness of his pocketbook." **B.C. Forbes**, editor of Forbes magazine

"Every society gets the kind of criminal it deserves. What is equally true is that every community gets the kind of law enforcement it insists on." **Robert F. Kennedy**

"Guilt or innocence becomes irrelevant in the criminal trials as we flounder in a morass of artificial rules poorly conceived and often impossible to apply." Supreme Court Chief Justice **Warren Burger**

"The mugger who is arrested s back on the street before the police officer, but the person mugged may not be back on the street for a long time, if ever." New York Governor **Mario Cuomo**

Evangelical leader **Pat Robertson** says, "This war on drugs just hasn't succeeded. . . . I believe in working with the hearts of people, and not locking them up." This country, he continues, "has gone overboard on this concept of being tough on crime. . . . It's completely out of control. Prisons are being overcrowded with juvenile offenders having to do with drugs. And the penalties . . . some of them could get 10 years for possession of a joint of marijuana. It makes no sense at all. . . . If people can go into a liquor store and buy a bottle of alcohol and drink it at home legally, then why do we say that the use of this other substance is somehow criminal? . . . We here in America make up 5% of the world's population, but we make up 25% of the [world's] jailed prisoners. . . . I think on this one, I'm on the right side." (Other sources put the U.S. total at half the world's prisoners. In either case, it's too many.)

"Mass incarceration on a scale almost unexampled in human history is a fundamental fact of our country today. Over all, there are now more people under 'correctional supervision' in America – more than 6 million – than there were in the Gulag Archipelago under Stalin at its height." Adam Gopnik in the New Yorker

"The U.S. has 760 prisoners per 100,000 citizens. . . . Japan has 63 per 100,000, Germany has 90, France has 96, South Korea has 97, and Britain – with a rate among the highest, has 153. . . . This wide gap between the U.S. and the rest of the world is relatively recent. In 1980 the U.S.'s prison population was about 150 per 100,000 adults. . . . More than half of America's federal inmates today are in prison on drug convictions, . . . more than were arrested on assault or larceny charges. And 4 of 5 of those arrests were simply for possession. . . . Americans are creating a vast prisoner underclass in the country at huge expense, increasingly unable to function in normal society, all in the name of a war they have already lost." **Fakreed Zakaria** in Time magazine.

"ATLANTA – The nation's largest private prison company made an enticing offer to 48 states that went something like this: We will buy your prison now if you agree to keep it mostly full and promise to pay us for running it over the next two decades. . . . Corrections Corporation of America sent letters to the prison leaders in January [of 2012], saying it had a pot of $240 million to buy facilities as part of an investment." **Greg Bluestein,** Associated Press

"In our criminal justice system, once a person has been convicted, no matter how shaky the conviction, the presumption of innocence disappears. The defendant is assumed to have had a fair trial. New evidence, even enough to sow a field of doubt, does not necessarily entitle a defendant, even one on death row, to a new trial." New York Times and New Yorker writer **Raymond Bonner**

> **Comment:** In our daily lives, the justice most of us are most concerned about involves being secure against attack or robbery by others. Capable law enforcement and penalties for wrongdoing are a major part of this. Unfortunately, the biggest crimes, like the heists pulled off by crooked banks and brokerage houses in the 2008 economic crash, are often least visible and hardest to combat and prosecute.
>
> But all too often, the justice system gets perverted to other ends than protecting people's well-being. Your neighbors or mine may decide to make behavior they like legal and behavior they dislike illegal, despite Jefferson's astute remark that "taste cannot be controlled by law," or his comment that "It does me no injury for my neighbor to say there are twenty gods, or no God. It neither picks my pocket nor breaks my leg." And so we have a multiplication of local, state, and federal laws and statutes that prescribe what you and I can and cannot legally do, even when failing to obey them would hurt no one and damage no property, no other living being, and no ecosystem.
>
> And the government! There is a general principle in most times and places that almost any organization that endures for a considerable time has a tendency to gradually create more and more laws and regulations and other forms of red tape that make perfectly reasonable behavior difficult and inconvenient. Corporations often do this just as government does, but in the latter case the police can come and handcuff you and throw

you in jail and the judge can fine you or send you to prison if you did something someone somewhere didn't like, even though it picks no one's pocket and breaks no one's leg. By contrast, corporations can only bankrupt you in extended lawsuits or hire goons to harass you or work you over.

To my knowledge, not one of our founding fathers said that any action that does no harm to another person or to public or private property should be unlawful. Not one of our founding fathers condoned city ordinances that decree what a person may or may not plant in their yards, except in cases of resource allocation, such as plants requiring excessive water use in areas where supplies are scarce. *Not one of our founding fathers ever imagined that a prison might be privately owned and run for profit, with the inevitable conflicts of interest and possibilities of abuse that such a practice involves, as lobbyists for the private prison industry push legislation that will fill their cells and beds.* Not one of our founding fathers ever suggested that a fertilized ovum, in its various stages of development, should be legally designated a "person," with the rights and responsibilities thereto appertaining, and the consequent stripping away of rights and responsibilities from a woman who, by her will or not, finds herself pregnant. And not one of our founding fathers suggested that . . . (the list goes on and on). Anything somebody somewhere can think of to make illegal can be made illegal, and then your pocket and mine can be picked for tax dollars to arrest, try, and imprison whoever violates that law. This is the very essence of an anti-libertarian view. And it is the very essence of what the founding fathers said our government has no business doing.

Perhaps the worst abuse of freedom in the U.S. today is widespread imprisonment of people who have done nothing that harms another.

When the United States was founded, a widespread abuse in Europe was imprisonment of debtors. America's founders prohibited such imprisonment in the United States. Today's imprisonment of those convicted of simple possession of drugs looks to me like a direct parallel to Europe's old debtors' prisons. This all began after 1980. At first it was orchestrated by the Reagan administration, which dramatically ratcheted up imprisonment of African American males. (White males with identical drug possession "offenses" were typically able to hire lawyers who got them released from their criminal charges, or at least placed on probation instead of thrown into prison.) Later the "war on drugs" escalated, as Republicans and Democrats alike vied to sound tougher on crime. And after release, the former prisoners they are marked for life as second-class citizens due to their jail record, making it hard to get a job or renting a house. Some states even strip them of their right to vote. (When you have "paid your debt to society," especially for an act that in Jefferson's words "neither picks my pocket nor breaks my leg," why does it still follow you for the rest of your life? Is that not "cruel and unusual punishment?"

Today the prison-industrial complex makes huge profits off the portion of these unfortunate prisoners in private jails. That whole situation is corrupt and un-American. You and I spend enormous sums of tax money to keep these people behind bars. It is a hopeful sign that very few states showed any interest in Corrections Corporation of America's 2012 offer to buy their prisons. Although most people don't realize it, in many cases *it costs as much to keep someone in prison for four years as it would cost to give them a college education at an Ivy League university*. Sometimes that's just for getting picked up with a a joint in your pocket. Think about it, Mr. and Ms. Taxpayer: Do you want the government picking your pocket for that kind of money for that purpose? Zakaria provides these figures: "In 2011, California spent $9.6 billion on prisons vs. $5.7 billion on the UC system and state colleges. Since 1980, California has built one college campus and 21 prisons. A college student costs the state $8,667 per year (far below pricey Ivy League schools); a prisoner costs it $45,006 a year" [comparable to student costs in Ivy League universities]. Prospective students are getting turned away in droves in California because the colleges are so severely underfunded.

I suspect that most ordinary citizens have had one or another run-in with the police or the bureaucracy in which they were treated less than well. Last year I woke up at 3 A.M. in Philadelphia to catch a 6 A.M. flight across the country. After a layover and change of planes change I got to the West Coast around 10 P.M. I had a couple of cups of coffee for the drive home. A few minutes north of San Francisco I was pulled over by a Highway Patrol car because I was allegedly "weaving" as I changed lanes and the two officers in the car thought I might be a DUI. The older officer was professional in his conduct. The younger one had an obsessive craving to find me guilty. He was hostile, intimidating, threatening, obnoxious, and apparently a former playground bully who had never grown up. The older officer largely ignored his young colleague, ran his tests in which I visually tracked his flashlight beam and answered all his questions in a clear and articulate manner, and correctly concluded that I was just tired. I was certainly glad he was there, and not just his emotionally defective sidekick.

It could have been worse. Based on recent events in the local news, I imagine that if I had been Black or Latino instead of an old white man with a gray beard, the obnoxious young punk cop might have pulled me from the car, slammed my head against the hood, and handcuffed my hands behind my back before proceeding with his questions. (Yes, that's a stereotype on my part, although one based in day in, day out news reports.) In sum, while I have found most police to be respectful, courteous, and helpful—and some have even gone out of their way to be so-- others are out of hand and off the wall and ought not to be on the force, just like DA's who care more about getting a conviction than seeing justice done.

Excessive police actions costs big money. About twenty-five years ago, using federal dollars from an anti-marijuana program, my county's sheriff's department dispatched a helicopter to hover over my house every day for a week. Then one day five trucks and cars roared up my driveway and screeched to a stop. Three of them contained men in fatigue combat gear with machine guns (How exciting – just like in *Rambo*), one had a team of dogs, and one had a policewoman to take our children away. To their credit they were at least moderately polite, but I have never seen anyone's jaw drop as fast and far as theirs when I escorted them to our house's interior patio and they discovered that what they thought was a small crop of marijuana plants, about three feet square, were new growth shoots on a redwood tree-trunk that had been felled a couple of years before. They were not pleased to find a law-abiding citizen instead of a lawbreaker. My best guess is that in all, the helicopter time and the raid must have cost at least fifty thousand dollars, paid for by the Federal "CAMP" program, which would be several times that much in today's dollars. Your tax dollars.

One of the most glaring problems with our legal system is that, as Oliver Wendell Holmes pointed out, often there is not even a pretense of trying to see that justice is done. A crime is committed. Then the District Attorney and his or her staff, eager to please citizens screaming for revenge, often are convinced in advance of the guilt of whatever suspect they might turn up. Too often finding out whether a suspect is really guilty is not even on the agenda. Our system does not reward the D.A. for finding out the truth, but for getting convictions. The more skins of the accused a D.A. can nail to the wall, the greater is his or her reputation—and chances for re-election or promotion.

Likewise, the defense attorney is rewarded for getting the charges dismissed, even when he or she knows the client is completely guilty.

You've probably read that recently in Texas, large numbers of prisoners with life sentences who had been locked up for many years were found innocent by DNA evidence.

We can applaud the present efforts to retroactively objectively determine guilt or innocence. We can likewise condemn the original inquiries in which so many were falsely found guilty (almost all of them black). In capital cases, the simple principle is that the principle of "guilt beyond reasonable doubt" should be amended to "absolute certainty" that a person committed the crime of which he or she is accused.

In plea bargains, your constitutional guarantees go right out the window. But many who are accused yet innocent accept them, in matters both large and small, because they can't afford the costs and time of a trial, or because the prosecutor obviously has no interest in finding out whether they are innocent. In addition, in some states citizens have now imposed mandatory sentencing on themselves. California's "Three strikes and you're out" law, passed in understandable widespread horror in the wake of a particularly brutal and gruesome kidnapping and rape of a young child, eliminates judicial discretion. Anyone who commits three felonies, even if they are lightweight "crimes" that harm no one or nothing, faces automatic life imprisonment, and a judge has no power to judge whether that is appropriate or not. Why bother with a judge who has no power to judge? A robot could fill out the forms and pass the sentence. Besides the detail of possibly destroying the person's life, when someone who is innocent get sent to jail, you and I pay the taxes to feed, shelter, and guard him for life. I do not think Franklin, Washington, Jefferson, Madison, Paine, and Lincoln would approve.

At various times in our nation's history the law has conscripted young men and sent them off kill or be killed, whether they had any wish to go or not. I believe this was clearly justified only once during my lifetime, in World War II. (Korea—I don't know. Never since then.)

Hundreds of thousand of Americans, or perhaps even millions --maybe including you-- have been harassed and charged with "crimes" that should never have been called crimes by local police, the FBI, the CIA, the Drug Enforcement Administration, and now the sprawling invisible octopus of the Department of Homeland Security which has tentacles that reach everywhere. I have been informed by a source I think is reliable that the CIA, established to operate strictly outside the United States, now has an office and operatives in every major U.S. city. If so, that's your tax money and mine, shaken from our pockets by the same fear-mongering used to pass the Patriot Act's vast expansion of government powers of surveillance that is now used to spy on you and me and our neighbors. Be warned: Today almost nothing you do or say online is confidential. Both big government and big business track your every move.

In Thoreau's "Essay on Civil Disobedience," quoted in part above, his central objection was to being taxed to pay for the Mexican War. I resented being taxed to pay for the Vietnam and Iraq wars, and numerous smaller and less well known military and clandestine operations, but I lacked the integrity of Thoreau's willingness to go to jail for refusal to pay war taxes.

Also, the immense number of lawsuits by businesses against each other, and by stockholders against businesses, for the most part is of no benefit to you and me but is another drain on our tax moneys and a full employment program for attorneys.

One last important point: The Internal Revenue Service is now in an ungodly alliance with other agencies—especially the Drug Enforcement Administration and state and local law enforcement bodies that work with it. Today a police or sheriff's department can arrest a person for a crime –even for allegedly growing a plant the government has chosen to make illegal— and then the IRS can and often does seize and impound the arrested person's house, land, car, and all their personal property, EVEN THOUGH THE PERSON HAS NOT BEEN CONVICTED AND MAY LATER BE FOUND INNOCENT. Often the items are not returned, or just some are returned, and no compensation whatsoever is made. **The U.S. Constitution's Fifth Amendment reads explicitly, "No person shall. . . be deprived of**

life, liberty, or property, without due process of law; nor shall private property be taken for public use, without just compensation." (Nowhere does it say that although the police are not allowed to do that, the IRS is.) The Fourteenth amendment reinforces the point in the passage just quoted. In how many places are we as a people willing to close our eyes and ears to actions that treat our Constitution as if it did not exist?

An attorney who read a draft of this section offers this perspective: "I think Walt Whitman was right. Justice is always in danger. What is legal and what is illegal is generally a legislative function that almost by definition is what one group wants over what another group wants. Yes the IRS will overreach, yes the Homeland Security folks will violate rights, and yes money will always have power."

SOLUTIONS

- **Most of our legal system has grown up to supplement the Constitution, which is concise and spare in its outline for the judiciary. I suspect that its framers would be appalled to see what our legal system has become. The legal system needs a thorough overhaul, the specialized details of which are beyond my limited knowledge to think through and prescribe. The general principles, however, are fairly simple:**

- **Follow the articles of the Constitution at the beginning of this section to the letter. This includes the Fifth Amendment's prohibition against the "taking" of private property before a person is convicted of a crime, with the sole exception of property that is clear potential evidence of a crime. It also includes the "taking" of any property not used in committing a crime without just compensation, with the exception of items that it is illegal to possess.**

- **The present administration should immediately end, and Congress should explicitly outlaw, the patently unconstitutional IRS seizures of property when someone has been accused but not convicted. They are patently unconstitutional.**

- **Do away with all laws that basically consist of one group (or groups) of citizens attempting to impose their preferences or agendas in matters in which no discernible injury is done to anyone or anything.**

- **Wipe victimless crimes off the books, unless it can be shown that some identifiable harm to others would be done by keeping them. If documented harm is done only to oneself, the proper response seems to me to be some kind of treatment rather than jail. (A friend who is an attorney says, "We have to be thoughtful and careful in defining 'victimless' crimes. It's about as subjective as defining 'reasonable.'")**

- **Eliminate all for-profit privately run prisons, with a five- or ten-year phase-out period, due to their inherent conflict of interest (which results in lobbying to criminalize enough activities to keep their beds full and their profits gushing.)**

- **Require all allocations to the FBI, the CIA, military espionage and police divisions, and all other branches of the Department of Homeland security or any agency that replaces it to be on the books, visible, and embodied in** funding bills that contain no other items.

- Prohibit the Transportation Security Administration from paying bounties to airline and other personnel for turning in supposedly suspicious characters. (That practice creates an inherent conflict of interest and invites abuse.)

- Require that the principle of habeas corpus apply in military as well as civil justice, and make special provision for speedy and fully impartial (i.e. by someone with no interest in padding his resumé with a successful prosecution) examination of anyone turned in by an informer for a bounty, which too often leads to highly questionable accusations.

- Develop and carry out a procedure to systematically review and revision federal, state, county, and city criminal justice procedures with the goal of making them actually serve justice and focus on protecting people against genuine crimes that do them harm. Require lawsuits involving corporations to be fully paid for by the parties to the suits rather than by taxpayers.

- Provide that any President and other members of an administration that in any manner orders, justifies, or condones torture be immediately subjected to impeachment procedures or fired as soon as the facts of the torture (even if labeled by euphemisms) become known

* * *

PART II:

DIMENSIONS OF OUR CONCERNS

Here we address vital concerns of our time. These include many people's inability to find jobs and the rapidly increasing gap between rich and poor. They include militant religious imperialism that directly violates the Constitution's First and Fifth Amendments by making sectarian beliefs into state or national law, and then commanding the police to throw anyone who disobeys them into jail. There is also widespread concern about the size and scope of the worldwide U.S. military machine and what it has done in recent decades in response to presidential orders. And many people are concerned about the multitude of ways in which civilization is damaging the natural environment, not only in the United States but also around the world. In most of these matters the founding fathers' views were crystal clear, yet they are being widely violated now.

10. The Strangely Named "Tea Party"

SAMUEL ADAMS

"We have the truth, we know how everything ought to be, and we're going to cram it down your throat whether you like it or not" seems to be the so-called "Tea Party" motto, if I can judge by what I hear and read. When I check out its website, of course that message is heavily cloaked in patriotic rhetoric and the colors red, white and blue. But patriotism, those colors, and our founding fathers belong equally to all Americans. In fact, the "Tea Party's" very name is based on a distortion that turns the meaning of the original Boston tea party inside out and upside down.

"How strangely will the Tools of a Tyrant pervert the plain Meaning of Words!" **Samuel Adams**

"All tyranny needs is for people of good conscience to remain silent." **Thomas Jefferson**

"I want to just take a moment to thank the Teabaggers. Thank you so much for helping us pass health care. . . I know they're saying, 'Why are you thanking me? I was so against it, I marched on Washington with tea bags hanging off my Founding Fathers costume, with a gun on my hip and a picture of Obama dressed as Hitler, screaming about his birth certificate.' And America saw that and said, 'I think I'll go with the calm black man.'" Humorist **Bill Maher**

> **Comment:** Samuel Adams and other participants in the real 1773 tea party were protesting not against the British government itself, but against that government's alliance with the era's largest corporation, the East India Tea Company, and the monopoly Parliament granted to it for importing tea to the colonies, enforced by the ships and guns of the Royal Navy. All other merchants who owned ships, and even the shopkeepers who bought and sold their tea, were labeled "smugglers," subject to attack by the British Navy or British agents on shore. In late November the East India Tea Company ship *Dartmouth* arrived in Boston Harbor, and soon was joined by two more tea ships, the *Eleanor* and the *Beaver*. On December 16, about 7,000 people gathered around the Old south Meeting House to protest the tea monopoly and a tax that Parliament had passed on tea. That evening a group variously estimated at between 30 and 130 men, some disguised as Mohawk Indians, boarded the three vessels and dumped 342 chests of tea into the water. The sailors on three British Man-O-Wars that were anchored in Boston Harbor lounged around and looked on nonchalantly as the tea party members chopped open and threw overboard the crates of

tea on the East India Company ships. In days that followed, Samuel Adams defended the action. He argued that it was not the act of a lawless mob, but was instead a principled protest and a defense of the people's rights.

In sum, the 1773 tea party was a protest against corporate lobbying and influence on government policy that was jacking up prices and putting hundreds of small enterprises (independent ship-owners and mom and pop tea importers) out of business. Its action in the harbor was *against the company whose payoffs were buying the government's backing, and against the British government's support of the company's monopoly,* which worked just about the same way as todays' corporate political donations to Congress.

If the present "Tea Party" succeeds in its declared goal of "shrinking government" (except that it shows no interest at all in shrinking the most gigantic element of big government, the Department of Defense, which until the mid-Twentieth Century was more accurately named the Department of War), then even greater corporate influence in Washington than exists today is the likely result. The "Occupy Wall Street" demonstrators who are protesting corporate influence on government appear to be the truer heirs of the spirit of the 1773 tea party. As a reminder that t today's "Tea Party" has turned the ideals and intentions of the Boston tea party upside down and is making illegitimate use of its name, I have put the name of the recent "Tea Party" in quotation marks throughout this book.

Many of today's "Tea Party" members have been taken in by the stories and symbols produced by lavishly funded right-wing think tanks and a few media-savvy elitist leaders. These leaders include such figures as Dick Armey, who was previously a lobbyist for the People's Mojahedin Organization of Iran. Armey tried to push through legislation that would provide U.S. taxpayer support for that organization --"MEK"—which was branded a terrorist group by the State Department. (Great role modeling for your members, Dick!) The tragedy is that ordinary citizens who make up the cadres of "Tea Party" members, who for the most part have been duped by Big Money and Big Business oligarchs, are acting against their own interests as well as those of the nation. Be careful about whom you follow, and what their interests are.

The original 1774 tea party patriots would probably soil their undergarments if they could see how their name is being used today.

The "Tea Party" has claimed to be populist, standing up for ordinary people against big government. I call that baloney—real populists don't look down on working people or poor people. Historically, populists are for the people and against abuse, tyranny, lying and cheating from any source, whether government, business, political parties, or anyone else. But most of the "Tea Party" congresspersons who swept into office in 2010 raced faster than hungry pigs to the big business cash troughs to rake in corporate donations, violating every principle the original Boston tea party stood for. In response to the antidemocratic 2010 "Citizens United" ruling (i.e. "Corporate Moneybags United vs. We the People), the "Tea Party's" utter silence was utterly deafening. Whoever chose the "Tea Party" name was either incompetent at reading and understanding history, or a very clever manipulator who liked the name and intentionally spread a grotesquely distorted version of the original tea party's motives.

Perhaps you have been disgusted by some of the ultra-rightist positions and rhetoric, and dislike their policies that seem to ignore the ordinary citizen. Perhaps you have a hard time accepting the fact that a former Speaker of the House of Representatives made a list of every filthy name in the book and instructed Republicans in Congress to use an epithet or adjective from the list every time they talked about any Democrat or Democratic program.

Perhaps politicians' actions paved the way for the biggest company in your community to fire some of your relatives and close friends along with thousands of others. And perhaps now, reading this, you find yourself perplexed. Can you forgive and forget? Is that the best way? What actions can you take now? Well, at the very least, you can work to keep the wrong people out of positions of power--especially those who appear to be morally and ethically challenged. And be well aware that in order to promote their hyper-partisan program they are well organized and focused on specific goals, and to defeat them you will have to do likewise, and be more creative too.

There is an interesting true story about how ordinary people can turn politics around when they act with compassion and integrity. Kathryn Watterson tells of a Jewish couple that received repeated threats from the Grand Dragon of Nebraska's Ku Klux Klan, Larry Trapp. They contacted him on a human level in a way that no one else had done, suspecting that he was "a destructive but vulnerable, messed-up person who needed a new perspective on the world." They listened to his life story, shared theirs and how he was affecting them, and stayed with him emotionally as he left the Klan and the American Nazi Party. Larry went on to apologize to people and groups he had hurt or harassed. At one point he said, "They're confused people, the Klan and the Nazi Party. They really hate themselves is what their problem is. They don't want to punish themselves, so they want to try to punish someone else."[1] Ultimately the couple, Michael and Julie Weisser, took care of the wheelchair-bound Trapp for the last year of his life.

If Michael and Julie could find a way to make their peace with a Ku Klux Klansman who had threatened them personally, then just about anyone ought to be able to find some kind an opening to discover common ground with those whom they have seen as their opponents. And vice versa. Kindness, combined with true listening to what is deepest in others' hearts, are good starting points to offset intolerance. (Handling someone else's tendency to turn another person or group into an "enemy" is more challenging. We might call defusing unscrupulous behavior an advanced practice in handling injustice.)

By contrast if you have been committed to an extreme right-wing view, you face a different question. Is it really possible to let go of an ideology that you've been advocating and take a step toward something that incorporates its best ideas and lets go of its worst ones? You can ask yourself that from time to time as you continue to examine the truth, or lack of it, underlying any action being taken.

Ironically, recently the "Tea Party" vowed to do its best to run out of office all elected representatives who did not vote exactly as it told them to. That stance directly opposes the liberty of letting their members follows their own consciences and best judgment, by backing only candidates who kowtow to what the "Tea Party" leadership tells them to do (in direct violation of Article 10 of their own platform.) There is no individualism there. It is The Political Organization making itself into Big Brother: "Act as we tell you to. Think our thoughts, not your own." When you listen with awareness to right-wing radio and TV talk show programs, you will notice that many are filled with intolerance and hate. Those who disagree with the hosts are interrupted, cut off, and ridiculed. Is that the national attitude you to which you want to contribute?

SOLUTIONS

- **First, be aware that few mental maneuvers are more dangerous than self-deception. (More about this later)**

- Always ask *who is benefiting* from the political choice being made? For example, many in the current Tea Party actually think they are acting to further freedom when actually their actions contribute directly to suppressing it. They advocate budget deficits worse through enormous military spending that is completely contrary to the spirit of the nation's founders (see below). They try to force the government to make some people live as others want them to.

- Second, be alert to the Tea Party's vigorous efforts to set up a well-strategized, well-organized political machine designed to defeat everyone who disagrees with their rigid ideology. Lend a hand to those who are taking vigorous, well-organized steps to counter such measures, or take such steps yourself.

- Third, do your best to help throw out of office every last one of the Tea Party legislators who are taking corporate bribes (often labeled "campaign contributions") for backing their policies and who are more committed to ideology than to their country. That includes just about all who were elected in 2010. Throw them overboard like crates of East India Company tea.

- Support those who have been working and voting to make the government serve all its people, middle class and working class, small businesspersons and independent farmers and ranchers, and to protect the environment, rather than kneeling at the feet of big money interests. Check on what your legislators are saying and how they are voting, and if they're not for the good health of our people and land and waters, lend your voice to making changes that can help heal their misperceptions.

* * *

11. How Jefferson's Premonition Came True

The American revolutionaries knew the oppression of governments well, from the examples of Europe's monarchies. To find one that was not greedy, corrupt, and heavy-handed was a difficult, perhaps even impossible, task. At that time, oppressive corporations were less common. At first only the British East India Company was a major player in England's American colonies. (Elsewhere, the Dutch East India Company played a similar role.) Long before the events that provoked the American Revolution, the East India Company operated as a band of lawless pirates that attacked and plundered India's commercial ships, including the notorious attack on the Ganj-i-Sawaii, in which East India Company Captain Henry Every and his crew stole 500,000 gold and silver pieces in the richest pirate haul in history. In England the company established a lobby in Parliament. A competing company arose, but the British East India Company soon absorbed it to maintain a monopoly. The Seven Years War with France led to French defeat, to British imperial hegemony in India (with the East India Company playing a leading role), and to the Company's capture of Manila. Government alliances with crooked companies are nothing new.

As ambassador to France, Thomas Jefferson must have known this history well. Meanwhile in the colonies, other corporations were formed and began to be influential. As described below, Jefferson and Madison tried to include an eleventh Amendment in the Bill of Rights to limit corporate power, but were rebuffed by certain other participants in the Constitutional Convention. Nonetheless, Jefferson was worried about the growing influence of corporations from the time the Constitution was written until his death. Throughout the rest of his life he was uneasy about the potential for unelected private entities to accumulate great wealth and power and affect the course of the nation's affairs. He favored defined and limited government power and also defined and limited corporate power, as his words below show.

"I hope we shall take warning from the example [of England] and crush in its birth the aristocracy of our monied corporations which dare already to challenge our government to a trial of strength and bid defiance to the laws of our country. . . . [The corporation] penetrating every part of the Union acting by command and in phalanx, may in a critical moment upset the government. I deem no government safe which is under the vassalage of any self-constituted authorities."
Thomas Jefferson

Jefferson also remarked, "I sincerely believe, with you, that banking establishments are more dangerous than standing armies."

"All men having power ought to be mistrusted to a certain degree," said **James Madison.** He also remarked, "What prudent merchant will hazard his fortunes in any new branch of commerce when he knows not that his plans may be rendered unlawful before they can be executed?"

> **Comment:** Madison did not say "all in government who have power" or "all in business who have power." His statement was inclusive. Essential questions are, "Does government exist for the people or for business? Does business exist for people, or do people exist for business?
> Many big corporations and other companies are doing a good and conscientious job of producing needed goods and services. Most of the corporations I deal with serve me efficiently and well. The same is true of most government agencies and civil servants with whom I interact. The point is that b0th government and business alike –and nonprofits too-- can act in either helpful or harmful ways.
> In Madison's day, "Merchants" and "commerce" referred almost entirely to local mom

and pop concerns. By the late 18th Century that had changed dramatically, as huge corporations (especially railroads) almost ran the country. Jefferson foresaw and feared that change. Madison and Jefferson together tried hard but unsuccessfully to include an 11th Amendment in the Bill of Rights that would have prohibited "monopolies in commerce." It would have made it illegal for corporations to own other corporations or give money to politicians or try to influence elections. Imagine how different our nation might be if they had succeeded!

When the Constitution was written and for several decades afterward, a corporation had to be chartered by a state. To get a charter, most states required the company to provide that it would serve a valued social or public purpose, like building a canal or offering education. A corporate charter could be revoked if this were not done—a far cry from present practice, in which many corporations make no pretense of trying to benefit anyone except their stockholders and executives. Contemporary practice was intensified by influential economist Milton Friedman's misrepresentations of the philosophy of Adam Smith, who agreed with early American views that business should serve the needs of the people as well as the pockets of stockholders and executives. Corporate charters also had term limits, for which the corporations had to seek renewal after 15 or 20 years. "Profit for profit's sake" is the mantra these days. (See the section "Sleight of hand with Adam Smith's ideas" below).

Jefferson mistrusted not just big banks, but big corporations of any kind. He and Madison tried their best to include an Eleventh Amendment in the Bill of Rights that would have prohibited "monopolies in commerce." The amendment would have required corporations to treat farmers, small businesses, and suppliers fairly, and would have made it illegal for one corporation to own others, to give money to politicians, or to try to influence elections in other ways. Jefferson and Madison also wanted the Constitution to require owners and executives of corporations to be responsible for their actions, instead of being protected by the "limited liability" ploy that was pioneered by British companies in which crooked owners could pocket their ill-gotten gains and be free of any prosecution (like numerous big banks and investment houses too well known to need mention here in the 2008 meltdown). They failed to get their Amendment included because a majority in congress thought that existing state laws would suffice to constrain corporate power, not realizing that state congresspersons would turn out to be even more easily bought than national legislators.

Not so long afterward, the effects of corporate money on politicians was already having a corrosive effect on American democracy, as we see here:

"I weep for the liberty of my country when I see . . . that corruption has been imputed to many members of the House of Representatives, and that the rights of the people have been bartered for promises of office."
Andrew Jackson

ANDREW JACKSON

"The strongest bond of human sympathy, outside of the family relation, should be one uniting all working people, of all nations, and tongues, and kindreds." **Abraham Lincoln**

Lincoln also wrote, **"These capitalists generally act harmoniously and in concert to fleece the people, and now that they have got into a quarrel with themselves, we are called upon to appropriate the people's money to settle the quarrel."** *(Sound familiar?)* Later in his career, he was appalled by war profiteers like J.P. Morgan, who knowingly sold a Union general 5,000 defective rifles that exploded in soldiers' hands." As a result of such observations, he uttered these words that confirmed Jefferson's worries about unchecked corporate power: "I see in the near future a crisis approaching that . . . causes me to tremble for the safety of my country. As a result of the war, corporations have been enthroned and an era of corruption in high places will follow, and the money power of the country will endeavor to prolong its reign by working upon the prejudices of the people until all wealth is aggregated in a few hands and the Republic is destroyed."

"If any man tells you he loves America, yet hates labor, he is a liar. If any man tells you he trusts America, yet fears labor, he is a fool." *Abraham Lincoln*

As if in fulfillment of Lincoln's prophecy, the late nineteenth century was an era dominated by the "robber barons" who built the country's railroads, and were incredibly enriched by the government's gifts to them of millions of acres of land along the railroad routes. The spirit of the time is summed up in **Cornelius Vanderbilt's comment**, "What do I care about the law—Haint' I got the power?" That era also saw the beginning of institutionalized segregation as a replacement for slavery.

> **Comment**: Theodore Roosevelt did his best to break up monopolies that practiced all sorts of shady and crooked tactics, most especially Standard Oil of New Jersey, which was eventually reincarnated as ExxonMobil (In Europe, Esso). Presidents Taft, Harding, Coolidge, and Hoover basically let big business run the country, until Judgment Day in October, 1929. Then things changed. But since 1980 the situation has gradually become eerily similar to that of the Coolidge and Hoover days.

"Multinational corporations do control. They control the politicians. They control the media. They control the pattern of consumption, entertainment, thinking. They're destroying the planet and laying the foundation for violent outbursts and racial division." California Governor **Jerry Brown**

Comment: Something has gone terribly wrong. Today the deck is stacked against the American worker, the middle class, and most American families. Many people now see that politicians who are supposedly looking out for our common good are greedy, ignorant of what really needs to be done, or both. At this point almost everybody knows that Washington and the statehouses are filled with lobbyists for big-money interests that throw enormous sums of money at legislators to buy votes. In many state capitals the situation is even worse than in Washington, because it usually takes less money to buy a state legislator or election than a federal one. In California, a legislator told me, "The lobbyists are like a plague of locusts. There is almost nothing the big companies are not trying to buy. And many of the legislators are very cooperative."

It is now well known that much of today's political game is not government versus business but government and business allied against the people. The radical right would have us believe otherwise-- that business is always good and government always bad. The radical left leans toward the opposite position. Don't be fooled. Either government or business, at any level from the local to the international, can be honest, decent and act with integrity—or none of the above.

"Bigness is indeed often a problem, in government and business alike. Its lesson should by now have been burned into our memory . . . The 'Curse of Bigness' shows how size can become a menace – both industrial and social. It can be an industrial menace because it creates gross inequalities against existing or putative competitors. It can be a social menace – because of its control of prices. . . . All power tends to develop into a government in itself. . . . Industrial power should be decentralized. It should be scattered into many hands so that the fortunes of the people will not be dependent on the whim or caprice, the political prejudices, the emotional stability of a few self-appointed men." **William O. Douglas**

In regard to jobs and employment, **Thomas Paine** wrote, "Our present numbers are so happily proportioned to our wants, that no man need be idle."

Comment: Paine's words were most accurate in regard to the American Indian peoples. Among the colonists from Europe, there was a labor shortage, so a need for jobs was not an issue. Recruiters talked people in Europe into coming across the Atlantic to work, or even to come on indentured servant contracts. But even that was not enough to meet the appetite for labor, so the violent capture of Africans to serve as slaves began. Since unemployment was not a big problem, it was not much discussed by the founders of the republic.

"It is assumed that labor is available only in connection with capital; that nobody labors unless somebody else, owning capital, somehow by the use of it, induces him to labor. This assumed, it is next considered whether it is best that capital shall hire laborers, and thus induce them to work by their consent. Having proceeded so far, it is naturally concluded that all laborers are either hired laborers or what we call slaves. Now, there is no such relation between capital and labor as here assumed. . . Labor is prior to, and independent of, capital. Capital is only the fruit of labor, and could never have existed if labor had not first existed. Labor is the superior of capital, and deserves much the higher consideration. Capital has its rights, which are as worthy of protection as any other rights." **Abraham Lincoln**

"Ability to work constitutes the capital and the wage of labor the income of a vast number of our population, and this interest should be jealously protected."
Grover Cleveland

"The laboring classes constitute the main part of our population. They should be protected in their efforts peaceably to assert their rights when endangered by aggregated capital, and all statutes on this subject should recognize the care of the State for honest toil, and be framed with a view of improving the condition of the workingman." **Grover Cleveland**

GROVER CLEVELAND

"A truly American sentiment recognizes the dignity of labor and the fact that honor lies in honest toil. Contented labor is an element of national prosperity. . . . Our workingmen are not asking unreasonable indulgence, but as intelligent and manly citizens they seek the same consideration which those demand who have other interests at stake. They should receive their full share of the care and attention of those who make and execute the laws, to the end that the wants and needs of the employers and the employed shall alike be subserved and the prosperity of the country, the common heritage of both, be advanced." **Grover Cleveland**

Comment: Larger questions are seldom asked, such as "How do we cope with the immense transfer of assets from labor to capital that has taken place over the past five decades? Sometimes this has occurred through self-centered or malicious intent on the part of owners and executives—by mechanizing and robotizing, they themselves come to own more of their companies' labor power and their workers own less, because there are fewer workers. But often there is no malicious intent. All those telephone operators whose jobs are gone, all those factory workers who have been replaced by robots, even people in the little shops and concession stands who have been replaced by vending machines—all that is technology gobbling up jobs—at the same time that our population keeps expanding. Fewer jobs for more people means that structural joblessness increases. Poverty rises. The underclass grows. No one ever seems to ask, "After most of the jobs are gone, where will people get money to buy the goods the robots produce?"

"The law does not pretend to punish everything that is dishonest. That would seriously interfere with business." Attorney *Clarence Darrow*

Comment: Meanwhile, the big corporations and wealthy individuals who own equipment and machinery get even richer. For the most part many in the Radical Wrong camp actually do not care very much about unemployment, except as a side issue to corporate profits, bond yields and stock prices, and as a campaign issue. Most of the policies they advocate channel even more capital to the very rich and leave even fewer jobs for middle- and working class people who are already losing them. (Job loss is frequently labeled "increased productivity" and "enhanced profit margins."

Another cause of unemployment among American workers is the huge number of immigrants, illegal and illegal alike, we admit each year. That makes some kinds of jobs harder to find for native-born citizens. *The United States takes in as many immigrants every year as the rest of the world combined.* We do not have work for them all. No wonder our unemployment rate stays high. Population growth is pushed up by both legal and illegal immigration. We need a complete rethinking of our approach to population that takes the needs of workers, employers, and everybody else into account.

It would be helpful for right wing extremists to stop spreading such lies as, "Governments don't create jobs—businesses do." Does a commercial pilot have a job? You bet. Does an Air Force pilot have a job? You bet.

Does a janitor who works for a corporation have a job? Of course. Does a janitor who works for the General Services Administration have a job? Of course. And who employs terachers, police, and firefighters? And what are all those positions held by people who fix bridges, pave roads, and fill potholes, if not jobs? The assertion that business creates jobs, and government does not, is a very tall tale indeed.

In sum, the time has come to deeply rethink both local and global economic structures and processes, to cope with not only today's challenges, but the far greater ones that are starting to be visible on the far horizon.

WILL ROGERS

Will Rogers said, "A holding company [i.e. conglomerate] is a thing where you hand an accomplice the goods while the policeman searches you."

In 1913, **Theodore Roosevelt** wrote, "We demand that big business give the people a square deal; in return we must insist that when anyone engaged in big business honestly endeavors to do right he shall himself be given a square deal." And then Teddy Roosevelt added, "This country has nothing to fear from the crooked man who fails. We put him in jail. It is the crooked man who succeeds who is a threat to this country."

No less an authority on business and investment than **Malcolm Forbes,** in response to the widespread right-wing slogan that "We ought to run government just like a business," observed that, "Few businessmen are capable of being in politics, they don't understand the democratic process, they have neither the tolerance or the depth it takes. Democracy isn't a business."

Comment: A widespread right-wing statement is that government does terrible things while corporations do not. It is absolutely true that government does terrible things. But don't be fooled: As Corporate Accountability International's "Corporate Hall of Shame Awards" (given on the basis of website visitors' votes) shows, corporations also do terrible things.

THE CORPORATE ACCOUTABILITY HALL OF SHAME'S RECENT "WINNERS" AND RUNNER-UPS FOR THE AWARD OF "AMERICA'S WORST CORPORATION" ARE:

2011 Worst Company in America: Koch Industries. For spending hundreds of millions of dollars to try to replace what remains of our democracy with corpocracy and plutocracy.

2010 Worst Company in America: Monsanto, the world's largest monopoly, for "mass producing cancer causing chemicals, aggressively running small farms out of business, . . . "reckless promotion of genetically modified organisms," and for its "40 year long history of producing dangerous pesticides, herbicides, and cancer causing chemicals" dating back to Agent Orange" It has sent Pinkerton Guards to intimidate farmers into using its products, and dragged farmers to court for patent violations when its own GMO varieties cross-pollinated the neighboring farmers' crops through no fault of theirs. No small farmer has the money for a court battle against a huge company with unlimited funds.

Monsanto is still aggressively pressuring the U.S. government to intimidate countries that ban the growing and importation of GMO crops into accepting them, and to get other countries to agree to a worldwide ban against labeling foods made with GMOs as such. Monsanto executives have said that in their ideal future, in 15 or 20 years all the world's commercial seeds would be genetically modified and patented and natural seeds would be virtually extinct. Evil lives on!

2010 Runner-Up: BP (British Petroleum), "for causing the worst environmental catastrophe in U.S. history, devastating the livelihoods of millions across the Gulf Coast and putting profits ahead of safety." You know the rest.

2010 Runner-Up: Chevron, for dumping 18.5 billion gallons of toxic waste into the Ecuadorian Amazon, then doggedly fighting all attempts to make it clean up.

2009 Worst Company in America: Exxon-Mobil, "Big Oil's worst polluter," for spending hundreds of millions of dollars to deceive the public into thinking climate change is not real and for making the largest corporate profits in history while taking government subsidies and externalizing its costs (that is, leaving them for government and taxpayers to pick up.)

2008 Worst Company in America: Blackwater (now Xe Corporation), the largest private mercenary army in the world, "for killing unarmed Iraqi civilians, hiring paramilitaries trained under military dictatorships, and using its close political and financial ties with the Bush Administration to secure lucrative contracts." To clean up their image, they are now called "global stabilization professionals" instead of "mercenaries." Xe is the largest private contractor for the U.S. State Department's "security services" and was recently sold to Monsanto. What a pair.

2007 Worst Company in America: Halliburton, "the nation's leading war profiteer, for systematically shortchanging our troops after exploiting political connections for $20 billion in government contracts, and then attempting to shirk responsibility for its full share of United States taxes."

Comment; All these companies lobby extensively in Washington to get the U.S. administration, Congress, or both to back them. Here's the **"Believe it or Not"** department. The current Secretary of Agriculture, as Governor of Iowa, was a leading advocate for Monsanto, genetic engineering, and factory farming. Vilsack has "promoted the most controversial and dangerous forms of agricultural biotechnology," says an organic farming website. Former Monsanto Vice President for Public Policy Michael Taylor is now a senior advisor to the Food and Drug Commissioner on food safety. And in 2009 Roger Beachy, longtime president of Monsanto's nonprofit arm, the Danforth Plant Science Center, was appointed chief of the U.S. Department of Agriculture's National Institute of Food And Agriculture, which is said to routinely twist the arms of university agricultural research departments to keep them from doing anything that might benefit smaller family farms or organic farming and support only research on procedures and machinery that benefit big time chemical and biotech agribusiness.

What's up here? Why are our leaders not held accountable for their promises? What happened to campaign statements from President Obama like, "I'll tell ConAgra that it's not the Department of Agribusiness. It's the Department of Agriculture;" and also, "If I am elected President of the United States, I will support legislation to require the mandatory

Wal-Mart does not make my list of the worst of the worst, even though I dislike the company for driving thousands of local stores out of business, and for its relentless union-busting and abysmal employee relations (See Barbara Ehrenreich's *Nickel an Dimed: On Not Getting By in America*), because it has also been a leader in environmentally conscious retailing, such as through achieving major fuel savings in transport and building design. On balance it's a crapshoot, terrible in some ways and good in others.

Ever since the 19th century business and the plutocrats have been carrying on a relentless campaign to break unions. In reality, most gains by union members benefit others too. When unions salaries go up, it exerts a pressure that tends to push other salaries up.

The Radical Wrong has succeeded in deceiving millions of hard-pressed working people. Through glib fast talk they have tricked many others into resenting union members due to the latter's generally safer, healthier working conditions, somewhat higher wages, and decent health and retirement benefits. These are all things that they themselves would like. Yet the same working people who have been conned into resenting unions turn a blind eye to the multimillion-dollar salaries and enormous investment portfolios of the plutocrats who don't face the same challenges as working class and middle class people. When union members win a contract with decent health and retirement benefits, it causes other companies and agencies to look bad by comparison and often prods them to improve. Turning others against unions is just another politically unscrupulous method to divide and rule. Instead of getting suckered in by such tactics, *all working people—and those who would like to find work but can't—should join hands and hearts and work together for our common good*. Of course the situation is radically different now that there is competition from offshoring and movement of factories to other countries. But decisions about how to meet our era's new situations need the most thoughtful and creative input possible from all segments of the population. One segment denigrating the other and pushing them down is just the latest example of an oligarchic "divide and rule" philosophy.

You might reasonably wonder why I have not listed the nation's best businesses along with the worst. After all, there is a widely published list of the 500 "greenest" businesses, and I've seen a similar list of the most labor-friendly companies (good healthcare, pensions, positive employee ratings of top executives, etc.) In fact, there are not just hundreds, but tens of thousands (or more) of businesses that serve our country and its people very well, in diverse ways. Kudos to them all. They're part of the solution. May they grow and prosper.

Finally, you may say, "But what about multinationals from other countries? After all, a lot of the items manufactured or sold in the U.S. now are from countries headquartered in Europe or Japan or India or elsewhere. And many of the ultra rich are really more multinational than they are American, if you look at their investment portfolios." You're right! And the potential for "all of the above" to secretly influence U.S. politics skyrocketed with the "Citizens United" (i.e. Corporate Plutocrats United Against the Citizens) Supreme Court decision. Since multinationals did not exist in the 1700s, our founders did not discuss them.

SOLUTIONS

- **Reinstate the mild but useful regulations of Wall Street financial and investment transactions that were in place at the end of the George H.W. Bush administration.**

- **End unnecessary regulations and red tape that make it harder for businesses to get going and operate. Keep regulations that protect the health of people and the environment, rethink them with our latest and best knowledge and rewrite them for maximum clarity, simplicity, and ease of execution.**

- **Set up groups of citizens and experts on banking and investment who owe nothing to big financial institutions, and insulate them from lobbying pressure. These groups should include main street merchants, workers, and people from the academic world and from nongovernment organizations that offer constructive critiques of our financial system. They can be local groups that meet regularly or well-facilitated internet groups. Ask each to carefully analyze what has gone wrong in the way our financial, industrial, and commercial system is working and what can be done to make it right. Get input of original ideas from people and groups all over the country that will issue independent reports that are free from any editing by representatives of big government or business. (Note: These are eminently reasonable, middle-of-the road steps that not even in the same ballpark with the much more thoroughgoing changes advocated by some.)**

- **Require labeling of GMO and Bovine Growth Hormone treated products as such. Stop all U.S. government attempts to influence other countries' agricultural policies—most especially the heavy handed arm-twisting that is being done to get them to accept GMO foods. And don't get suckered in by the word "natural" on food labels or in food advertising. It means nothing. It definitely doesn't mean "is not genetically modified."**

* * *

12. Silk Suits and Work Boots: How Do Wealth and Poverty Affect Us?

(Disclosure: I live a middle-class life. My friends and relatives include multimillionaires at one extreme and those who work for minimum wage or are destitute dumpster-divers on the other. My wife sometimes works for multibillionaires and tells me about their lives and multiple mansions. (Last week she worked at a luxury resort where the dues are half a million dollars a year, for which members get one week in one of the resort's time-share cabins.) She also makes regular supermarket inventory clearance food drop-offs at homeless shelters. With all that, we see much of the income spectrum first hand.)

Were it not for the wealthy, luxury car sales would plunge precipitously, horse trainers and haute couture fashion models would all get pink slips, and country club fairways would soon be overgrown with crabgrass. Also, some of the wealthy support the arts, contribute to charities, and some even keep large acreages as natural ecosystems or working farms and ranches instead of letting them get chopped up for development. (Others, of course, make big bucks by chopping them up for development.)

Nonetheless, warm feelings between rich and poor become strained when the rich are increasing their wealth by actively stepping on those less fortunate, including the destitute who are sleeping on cardboard sheets beneath bridges. Conflict between rich and poor is one of the oldest polarities in political life. In China, there have been *four* revolutions aimed at reducing the gap between rich and poor. The earliest was recorded by Chinese historian Szuma Ch'ien who wrote that Emperor Wu Ti, who reigned from 140 B.C. to 87 B.C., carried out radical changes "to prevent private individuals from "reserving to their sole use the riches of the mountains and the sea in order to gain a fortune, and from putting the lower classes into subjection to themselves." Later, Wang Mang, who ruled from 9 to 21 AD, nationalized the land and divided it into equal small parcels for the peasants. A thousand years later, Wang An-Shih, Premier from 1068 to 1085 A.D., offered low-interest government loans to the working class to stop usurious money-lending, advanced seed to farmers at reasonable rates, carried out engineering works to control floods and provide jobs, provided pensions for the old, the unemployed and the poor, and improved education. But the taxes needed for all this were unpopular. Wang An-Shih was dismissed and his decrees revoked. The most recent rebellion against rule by the rich was Mao ZeDong and Chou En-Lai's Twentieth Century revolution, which helped the poor but was brutal and filled with its own injustices.

On the other side of the world, after its golden age ancient Athens became so polarized between rich and poor that in its divided and weakened state, Philip of Macedon conquered it easily. The gap between rich and poor was also especially great during the decadent later Roman Empire, when the oligarchy had stolen almost all the land from the common people, and the Senate was no more than a fig leaf to cover plutocratic rule. Will and Ariel Durant write, "Antiquity had never known so rich, so powerful, and so corrupt a government." Have we forgotten the effects of such imbalance? The French forgot, and the guillotine of revolutionary France rendered Marie Antoinette's head unable to eat her cake. This historic example once again showed that too great a difference in wealth is a road to disaster.

Now in America the widening gulf between those at the top and bottom of the income ladder is at the center of political firestorms. The Big Lie in this situation is that "the best way to ensure prosperity for everyone is for government policy to help the very rich get even richer, so their surplus cash will 'trickle down' to everyone else. Let's look at some insights that are relevant to our situation.

ARISTOTLE

"Poverty is the parent of revolution and crime. . . The most perfect political community is one in which the middle class is in control, and outnumbers both of the other classes." **Aristotle**

"Content makes poor men rich; discontent makes rich men poor. . . There are two ways of being happy: We must either diminish our wants or augment our means - either may do -- the result is the same and it is for each man to decide for himself and to do that which happens to be easier." **Benjamin Franklin**

Franklin also said, "Money has never made man happy, nor will it, there is nothing in its nature to produce happiness. . . .The more of it one has the more one wants. . . . Who is rich? He that rejoices in his portion." And yet again: "Buy what thou hast no need of and ere long thou shalt sell thy necessities. . . . It is the eye of other people that ruin us. If I were blind I would want neither fine clothes, fine houses or fine furniture."

He that is of the opinion money will do everything may well be suspected of doing everything for money. . . . Money has never made men happy. . . If you desire many things, many things will seem few."
Benjamin Franklin

Despite Franklin's wise philosophy, **Alexis de Tocqueville** remarked, "As one digs deeper into the national character of the Americans, one sees that they have sought the value of everything in this world only in the answer to this single question: How much money will it bring in?"

"An industrious farmer occupies a more dignified place in the scale of beings . . . than a lazy lounger, valuing himself . . . too proud to work, and drawing out a miserable existence by eating on that surplus of other men's labor, which is the sacred fund of the helpless poor. **Thomas Jefferson.** "I have not observed," Jefferson continued, "men's honesty to increase with their riches." And also, "Merchants have no country. The mere spot they stand on does not constitute so strong an attachment as that from which they draw their gains."

Jefferson continued, "I agree. . . that there is a natural aristocracy among men. The grounds of this are virtue and talents. . . . There is also an artificial aristocracy, founded on wealth and birth without either virtue of talents. . . The natural aristocracy I consider as the most precious gift of nature, for the instruction, the trusts, and government of society. . . . The artificial aristocracy is a mischievous ingredient in government, and provision should be made to prevent its ascendancy."

More simply, "Few men have virtue to withstand the highest bidder." **George Washington.** The wealthiest President in America's history, Washington also said, "Let your heart feel for the afflictions and distress of everyone, and let your hand give in proportion to your purse."

"Most of the luxuries and many of the so-called comforts of life are not only not indispensable, but positive hindrances to the elevation of mankind." **Henry David Thoreau**

ALEXANDER HAMILTON

Security and freedom often go together: "In the general course of human nature, A power over a man's subsistence amounts to a power over his will." **Alexander Hamilton**

"Property is the fruit of labor... That some should be rich shows that others may become rich, and hence is just encouragement to industry and enterprise. Let not him who is houseless pull down the house of another; but let him labor diligently and build one for himself, thus by example assuring that his own shall be safe from violence when built." **Abraham Lincoln**.

On the other hand, **Lincoln** also said, "All American citizens are brothers of a common country, and should dwell together in bonds of fraternal feeling."

Comment: Such fraternal feeling comes a little harder when you're either stepping on someone else on your way up, or sleeping on a sheet of cardboard under a freeway.

"He mocks the people who proposes that the government shall protect the rich and that they in turn will care for the laboring poor." **Grover Cleveland**

"Poverty taught me the true value of the gifts useful to life." **Anatole France.**

Anatole France also wrote, "The law, in its majestic equality, forbids the rich as well as the poor to sleep under bridges, to beg in the streets, and to steal bread."

On behalf of materialism, **Mark Twain** noted that: "Clothes make the man. Naked people have little or no influence on society."

"If you legislate to make the masses prosperous, their prosperity will find its way up and through every class that rests upon it." **William Jennings Bryan,** on a "trickle up" rather than "trickle down" theory of prosperity.

Theodore Roosevelt wrote to his son, "This country will not be a permanently good place for any of us to live in unless we make it a reasonably good place for all of us to live in."

Comment: At the end of the Roaring Twenties, an era when the very rich few ran the country to suit themselves, the stock market crashed and the Great Depression began. The Federal Reserve Board tightened the money supply, banks failed, and people lost their life savings. Stores and factories were shuttered. Two million people found themselves homeless. Farmers went bankrupt because people could not afford the food they grew, while lines of the unemployed stretched around the block outside soup kitchen doors. In dust bowl states, problematic farming, overgrazing, and prolonged drought turned millions of acres into savage dust storms that blackened the sky at high noon. Throughout the world, international trade plunged by a third and in some countries unemployment claimed a third of the population. People wanted to work. But the financial and industrial systems had broken down and starvation stalked the land. The times were desperate. On March 4th, 1933, Franklin D. Roosevelt, ranked by almost all historians as one of our four greatest presidents, took the nation's helm. A wealthy man himself, he insisted that rich and poor must cooperate in putting the nation and the world back on the right path. Work needed to be done.

In his inaugural address, Roosevelt declared, "The money changers have fled from their high seats in the temple of our civilization. We may now restore that temple to the ancient truths. . . . . Throughout the nation men and women, forgotten in the political philosophy of the Government, look to us here for guidance and for more equitable opportunity to share in the distribution of national wealth. . . . I pledge you, I pledge myself to a new deal for the American people." **Franklin D. Roosevelt.**

FRANKLIN D. ROOSEVELT

FDR insisted that rich and poor must cooperate in putting the nation and the world back to work: "In our personal ambitions we are individualists. But in our seeking for economic and political progress as a nation, we all go up or else all go down as one people. . . . No government can help the destinies of people who insist in putting sectional and class consciousness ahead of the general weal. . . True individual freedom cannot exist without economic security and independence. . . . These unhappy times call for the building of plans that . . . build from the bottom up and not from the top down, that put their faith once more in the forgotten man at the bottom of the economic pyramid. . . . People who are hungry and out of a job are the stuff of which dictatorships are made."

Comment: Evidence for that last statement lay close at hand in Russia's Bolshevik Revolution and Hitler's rise in Germany. In FDR's first term, his administration created national bank deposit insurance to protect the savings of both rich and poor, a Social Security system to provide for old age, and the immensely popular Civilian Conservation Corps that put 250,000 people to work restoring the land and controlling erosion to stop the dust bowl. And Roosevelt acted on his statement, "Taxes shall be levied according to ability to pay," enacting a graduated income tax that taxed the poor lightly and advanced by small steps from one income level to the next. He included the vital provision that business owners who reinvested in factories or other U.S. businesses could deduct those investments from their income—so that even if their tax rates were high, their investments would help their capital grow and their companies prosper and provide jobs. He recognized that inevitably some people are capable of earning more than others, yet added:

"'The New Deal. . . seeks to cement our society, rich and poor, manual workers and brain workers, into a voluntary brotherhood of free men, standing together, striving together for the common good of all. . . .The ambition of the individual to obtain for himself a proper security has an ambition to be preferred to the appetite for great wealth and great power. . . We are trying to make a country in which no one is left out." **Franklin D. Roosevelt**

> **Comment:** He *partly* succeeded. Blacks were still left out. In 1962, almost two decades after Roosevelt died, in Washington, D.C. and southern cities like Memphis, I drank from fountains and used restrooms that were still labeled "white" and "colored." FDR did not press that issue, because to pass his programs, he needed the votes of Southern legislators.
>
> Looking back, when the Great Depression was history and the nation was prosperous again, Roosevelt replied to his right wing critics, "It was this administration which saved the system of private profit and free enterprise after it had been dragged to the brink of ruin." Like Washington, Franklin, Jefferson, and his cousin Theodore, FDR was a very wealthy man, but rather than working to entrench the privileges of his class, dedicated himself to improving the situations of the less fortunate.

Harry S. Truman, who became president after Roosevelt died in office, echoed one of Roosevelt's themes: "Experience has shown how deeply the seeds of war are planted by economic rivalry and injustice. ' A few years later, his successor said:

"A people that values its privileges above its principles soon loses both." *Dwight D. Eisenhower*

"[Expanding the Social Security System] "would add immeasurably to the peace of mind and security of the individual citizen, . . . reduce both the fear and the incidence of destitution to the minimum, . . . [and] add greatly to the national sense of domestic security." Republican president **Dwight D. Eisenhower**

From one of the great minds of our own era, we hear this: "When I was 25, my net worth was $100 million or so. I decided then that I wasn't going to let it ruin my life. There's no way you could ever spend it all, and I don't view wealth as something that validates my intelligence." **Steve Jobs**

"If this is going to be a Christian nation that doesn't help the poor, either we have to pretend that Jesus was just as selfish as we are, or we've got to acknowledge that He commanded us to love the poor and serve the needy without condition and then admit that we just don't want to do it." Humorist **Stephen Colbert**

"If I had known what it would be like to have it all - I might have been willing to settle for less." **Lily Tomlin**

LILY TOMLIN

Comment: From the mid-1930s through the 1970s, the income gap between working and middle-class Americans and the power elite no longer increased year by year as it had during the 1920s. In response to Eisenhower's expansion of the Social Security system (endorsed by a Republican House and Senate), many who had not been enrolled in it before were included. The numbers of the destitute decreased. But the plutocratic and corporate dominance ideologues poured huge sums of money into right-wing think-tanks that strategized a major reframing of the political dialogue. In 1980 when Ronald Reagan stepped onto the political stage, their moment arrived.

"No one who lived through the Great Depression can ever look upon an unemployed person with anything but compassion. To me, there is no greater tragedy than a breadwinner willing to work, with a job skill but unable to find a market for that job skill. Back in those dark depression days I saw my father on a Christmas Eve open what he thought was a Christmas greeting from his boss. Instead, it was the blue slip telling him he no longer had a job. The memory of him sitting there holding that slip of paper and then saying in a half whisper, 'That's quite a Christmas present,' it will stay with me as long as I live." **Ronald Reagan**

Comment: Reagan, a great orator with a sunny smile, was an expert at telling folksy tales that won his listeners' hearts. He was also a skilled professional actor who sometimes behaved in ways that ran directly counter to the steps that anecdotes like the one just above suggested he would take.

Right – wing think tanks spent immense effort and expense to discredit FDR and put Reagan in his place in the public's affections. Before his presidency, most Americans appreciated the great contributions that government had made to improve their lives, beginning with Franklin D. Roosevelt and continuing through subsequent administrations. It introduced social security for old age and disability, federal bank insurance so that never again would people lose their savings if their bank went under, and built airports and highways all across the country.

But Reagan's rhetoric adroitly demonized the government. He painted it as fundamentally evil (except, of course, for his administration) and portrayed huge national and multinational corporations as fundamentally virtuous. In that script, business was invariably good and government was invariably bad. Reagan hammered at this theme day in and day out, speech after speech, press conference after press conference, year in and year out. This propaganda campaign of anti-government vitriol was something new that began with his presidency. It had not previously existed as a major element in the national consciousness. But his divisive rhetorical barrage marked the beginning of the contemporary era of "business vs. government" acrimony. It also set the stage for such "welfare programs for the rich" as subsidies for agribusiness corporations that owned hundreds of thousands of acres. Some of those subsidies were so structured that they drove many smaller farmers into bankruptcy, because if you were big you got a lot of (taxpayers') money, and if you were small you got little. That "business good, government bad" legacy spread like a toxic cloud, until now it poisons much of the U.S. political climate.

I lived through that transition, and heard it all too clearly. It was the antithesis of Eisenhower's low-key, capable stewardship, and John F. Kennedy's inclusive message of hope. By contrast, Reagan manned the controls of a wrecking ball that smashed much of what Roosevelt had accomplished into oblivion. He scrapped the progressive income tax, cutting the rates on the richest Americans to between 33% and 50% of what they had been. He made a deal with Congress to trade the reduction of income tax rates for elimination of the lower tax rate on investment capital gains, which had been just 15%. (In other words, he agreed to tax investment earnings at the same rate as earnings from the work of your hands and the sweat of your brow instead of at a lower rate—a good and admirable step. But a few years later, Bill Clinton cut the capital gains rate back to 15%, while leaving Reagan's tax cuts on the rich intact.) Reagan's new tax code also demolished Roosevelt's incentives to reinvest in America. That's one of the reasons why "Made in USA" is a less common label now. It's not only that labor is cheaper in China and Bangladesh.

The Reagan administration struck blows that combined with offshoring and automated and robotized production and active repression of labor unions to end the era of rising middle- and working-class prosperity. It began a massive transfer of wealth to the upper class, and changed the nation's political narrative from being about prosperity for all to being about welfare chiselers trying to gyp taxpayers (especially rich taxpayers) out of what was rightfully theirs. The day he took office in 1980 marked start of a new trend toward an increasing gap between the very rich on one hand, and the middle class, working class, and poor on the other hand that is still underway today. At the same time, he oversaw an enormous increase in military spending, even as the Cold War was ending the need for a huge military force. That military buildup, coupled with dramatically lower taxes on the wealthy, tripled the national debt. And now the right wing is orchestrating a systematic campaign to entrench the divisive plutocratic governing philosophy he championed. As we think about all this, we would be foolish to forget Abraham Lincoln's quotation of the Biblical passage that a house divided against itself cannot stand.

"This long and very successful effort over many, man years to get people to focus their fears and angers and hatred on the government has had its effect. We all know there's plenty to be upset about there. The primarily thing to be upset about is that it is not under popular influence. It is under the influence of the private powers." **Noam Chomsky**

"If a free society cannot help the many who are poor, it cannot save the few who are rich." *John F. Kennedy*

Perhaps you think the comments just above are an exaggeration. Consider this: In 1973 the richest 1 percent made 8 percent of the nation's income. Now the top slice makes 25%. CEOs who once made 50 times the average worker's salary made almost 500 times as much in 2001. In most other countries no comparable event occurred. An chart showing the average pay of company CEOs to that of the company's average worker offers these comparisons as of October 2011: (*This is without even including executive perks such as flying around in corporate jets, or the option to by company stock at far below the market price*).

Country	Ratio of pay of CO to average worker
Japan	11:1
Germany	12:1
France	15:1
Italy	20:1
Canada	20:1
South Africa	21:1
Britain	22:1
Mexico	47:1
Venezuela:	50:1
United States	475:1

(from: creativeconflictwisdom.wordpress.com)

Comment: Could the United States be so much less agreeable a place to live than those other countries that such salaries are needed to attract executives? Or might there be another reason? What do you think?

In the U.S. armed forces the highest ranking general or admiral with greatest seniority receives about 14 times the base pay of the lowest ranking enlisted person with least seniority – not millions of dollars more (although the general or admiral has a number of other nice perks). And there is an ample supply of able men and women who are glad to accept those generals' and admirals' jobs. Money is just one of many incentives that appeal to a spectrum of different human motives.

Today, the oligarchy's think tanks that shaped the gap between the relentless rich and the restless rest are still at work. Their agenda has conveniently overlooked the Constitution's goal, "to promote the general welfare."

"It's all right to tell a man to lift himself by his own bootstraps, but it is a cruel jest to say to a bootless man that he ought to lift himself by his own bootstraps." *Martin Luther King*

MARTIN LUTHER KING

"None of us got where we are solely by pulling ourselves up by our bootstraps. We got here because somebody - a parent, a teacher, an Ivy League crony or a few nuns - bent down and helped us pick up our boots." Supreme Court Justice **Thurgood Marshall**

"It's ironic that those who till the soil, cultivate and harvest the fruits, vegetables, and other foods that fill your tables with abundance have nothing left for themselves. . . Children of farm workers should be as proud of their parents' professions as other children are of theirs. . . "When the man who feeds the world by toiling in the fields is himself deprived of the basic rights of feeding, sheltering and caring for his own family, the whole community of man is sick. . . . . Our sweat and our blood have fallen on this land to make other men rich. We have suffered unnumbered ills and crimes in the name of the Law of the Land. Our men, women and children have . . . suffered the desperation of knowing that the system caters to the greed of callous men and not to our needs. Now we will suffer for the purpose of ending the poverty, the misery, and the injustice, with the hope that our children will not be exploited as we have been." **Caesar Chavez**

CAESAR CHAVEZ

"Politics change when people can't pay for their home mortgages and can't afford medical care and can't send their kids to school. It is such a humiliating blow to be the head of a family and be unable to work and provide, that people don't respond entirely rationally all the time. It can explode in politics in a hard-to-understand way." Vice President **Walter Mondale**

Daniel Gilbert's research found that on the whole, richer people are happier than poor people. At lower levels, happiness increases rapidly as income rises, but after about seventy thousand dollars it levels off and increases only very gradually with additional wealth.

How does wealth affect happiness? Zillionaire Steve Jobs said, "My favorite things in life don't cost any money." And research psychologist Daniel Gilbert, in his keynote speech at the 2010 American Psychological Association Convention in San Diego, described research in which he found that after about seventy thousand dollars (U.S. dollars at 2010 values), it increases only very gradually with additional wealth. For the most part, says Gilbert, people with "enough" income have better nutrition, better health care, more security, more toys, more control over their daily schedules, and get to do more things than people who are barely scraping by. After that, As Benjamin Franklin's remarks at the start of this section suggests, there is not a lot more happiness to be gained by more money.

Gilbert's results replicated similar studies carried out earlier by others. They also parallel a major change in economic thinking. In old economic reckonings, the food needed by a starving child and a Cadillac coveted by a driver who wants to trade up are equally valid aspirations. But growing minorities of economists say, "That's garbage." They speak of *the utility of consumption*. We can make this distinction:

Primary goods and services are needs for food, water, warmth, shelter, health care, and the opportunity to explore and discover.

Secondary goods and services are things we think we need that bring us reasonable comfort and pleasure. Most of these are not true needs, but wants, like a classier car. Due to our social comparisons, however, they may function psychologically like needs.

Tertiary goods and services are (1) items we think we "should want," but don't truly care about, and (2) items we know are sheer froth and indulgence, but we want them anyway. (When the going gets tough, the tough go shopping!)

"No amount of compensation to one person can compensate for injustice to another."
Philosopher Alfred Andersen

Comment: A widespread error is "averaging out"—the notion that we can gauge a country's overall economic welfare by average income. That is, if the rich get richer, it makes up for the poor not having enough. It's related to the "bathtub analogy"—the idea that rising prosperity will "raise the water level in the entire tub" and leave everyone better off. But as economist Hazel Henderson points out, most economies are more like bathtubs with many watertight compartments, so that "general prosperity" fills some compartments to overflowing while the water level in some others does not rise at all. When the Gross Domestic Product rises because some get even richer (while many others get even poorer, as has been happening in the United States since that fateful turning point in 1980), it is not progress. If Len gets a Limo while Hannah remains hungry, Hannah is still hungry.

Nancy Pelosi, first woman Speaker of the House of Representatives, herself from a wealthy family, asks "If you make . . . $1 million a year – should you not participate in the sense of community of our country?"

NANCY PELOSI

<<<>>>

SOLUTIONS

- Acknowledge that rich and poor are all in this together. (We are, you know. If it's not obvious to you yet, it will be.)

- As former Secretary of Labor Robert Reich has pointed out in articulate detail, our economy is heading toward collapse because the middle and working classes are shrinking so severely. As events are unfolding now, before long there will not be enough buyers –that is, enough people with enough money and inclination to pay for— the goods and services that the economy needs to produce to keep its wheels turning. Rich people tend to invest a large share of their income in stocks and bonds, while the many of moderate means tend to spend most of their income on goods and services. For the most part, such spending is what makes the economic wheels turn. As a result, rejuvenated middle- and working-class incomes would benefit the rich more than an additional increase in their own already more than adequate incomes. Paradoxical but true.

- Adopt the principle that we ought to restructure our economy so that everyone gets the primary goods and services they need (and contributes to providing them for others) before others start getting large amounts of tertiary goods and services. Figuring out how to do this will, of course, take considerable thought and work. We need to engage in a deep and profound rethinking of the ways our culture and communities and society are organized. And then we need to undertake an economic transformation that will take us beyond the immense current problems of structural unemployment caused by robotization and offshoring, and declining markets resulting from declining wages and personal assets of most people. Neither traditional capitalism nor socialism addresses these problems effectively, nor do any approaches suggested by the Republican and Democratic parties. And hardly anyone in the U.S. and the other rich countries is thinking about how to do these things in the context of the whole world economy in which problems of poverty are even more severe in many other nations than in our own. Meeting these problems creatively and successfully is one of the daunting challenges of our time.

* * *

13. Plutocrats, Proletarians and Pee-ons Duke it Out:
Is "Class War" Myth or Reality?

In recent decades whenever someone suggests a measure to reduce income inequality, it has become fashionable for the billionaires' braying battalions to cry, 'This is a declaration of class war!' George W. Bush was quite fond of the phrase. Several magazines and investment advisory newsletters wrote caustic comments about working people and the poor. "Class war" was their rejoinder when President Obama said that it would help the country to "spread the wealth around." Is the term "class war" appropriate? If so, who is fomenting it?

"Men who look upon themselves as born to reign, and others to obey, soon grow insolent. Selected from the rest of mankind, their minds are early poisoned by importance; and the world they act in differs so materially from the world at large, that they have but little opportunity of knowing its true interests." **Thomas Paine**

"Experience demands that man is the only animal which devours his own kind, for I can apply no milder term to the general prey of the rich on the poor."
Thomas Jefferson

"The mass of mankind has not been born with saddles on their backs, nor a favored few booted and spurred, ready to ride them. . . . An aristocracy of wealth is of more harm and danger than benefit to society." **Thomas Jefferson**

Jefferson also remarked, "Men by their constitution are naturally divided into two parties. 1. Those who fear and distrust the people, and wish to draw all powers from them into the hands of the higher classes. 2dly those who identify themselves with the people, have confidence in them, cherish and consider them as the most honest and safe, although not the most wise depository of the public interests. In every country these two parties exist, and every one where they are free to think, speak, and write, they will declare themselves. . . The bank mania is . . . raising up a monied aristocracy in our country which has already set the government at defiance. and . . . their principles are unyielded and unyielding. . . . These have taken deep root in the hearts of that class from which our legislators are drawn. . . . The . . . appellation of aristocrats and democrats is the true one expressing the essence of all."

"It has ever been my hobby-horse to see rising in America an empire of liberty, and a prospect of two or three hundred millions of freemen, without one noble or one king among them. You say it is impossible. If I should agree with you in this, I would still say, let us try the experiment, and preserve our equality as long as we can." **John Adams**

"The rights of persons, and the rights of property, are the objects, for the protection of which Government was instituted. . . . I have no doubt but that the misery of the lower classes will be found to abate whenever the Government assumes a freer aspect and the laws favor a subdivision of Property."" **James Madison.**

"Who can suffer injury by just taxation, impartial laws, and the application of the Jeffersonian doctrine of equal rights to all and special privileges to none? Only those whose accumulations are stained with dishonesty and whose immoral methods have given them a distorted view of business, society, and government. Accumulating by conscious frauds more money than they can use upon themselves, wisely distribute, or safely leave to their children, these denounce as public enemies all who question their methods or throw a light upon their crimes. Plutocracy . . . . preys upon the nation in time of peace and conspires against it in the hour of its calamity. Conscienceless, compassionless, and devoid of wisdom, it . . . is already sapping the strength of the nation, vulgarizing social life, and making a mockery of morals. . . . In the name of business honor which it has polluted; in the name of the home which it has despoiled . . . in the name of in the name of the people whom it has oppressed, let us make our appeal to the awakened conscience of the nation." Populist leader **William Jennings Bryan**

"There is not a man of us who does not at times need a helping hand to be stretched out to him, and then shame upon him who will not stretch out the helping hand to his brother." *Theodore Roosevelt*

ROBERT F. KENNEDY

"In many ways Wall Street is closer to London than it is to Harlem, a few miles uptown; Scarsdale is often closer to Paris than to Selma, Alabama; and Americans in Appalachia are in many ways closer to Favelas of Rio de Janeiro than they are to society in which you and I live. . . . It is the essence of responsibility to put the public good ahead of personal gain." **Robert F. Kennedy**

"It may be true that the law can't change the heart, but it can restrain the heartless." **Martin Luther King**

"In this world it is possible to achieve great material wealth, to live an opulent life. But a life built upon those things alone leaves a shallow legacy. In the end, we will be judged by other standards." **Caesar Chavez**

David Barsamian: "More on this class war issue. If the Republican right-wing economic initiative which is essentially an attack on the poor . . . "
Noam Chomsky: "Poor" is a funny word for it. It's an attack on maybe three-quarters of the population."
Barsamian: "Might not elites be concerned in that it would result in social instability and uprisings. . .?"
Chomsky: "That's why they have this huge crime bill. . . . They want to criminalize a large part of the population. They have been working on this for some time. . . . If you go back to the 1970s, it began to appear, because of changes in the international economy, as if it might be possible for

real ruling groups to . . . roll back everything connected with the social contract that had been won by working people and poor people over a century of struggle. . . I think they think they can roll it back [and] go right back to the days of satanic mills (to use William Blake's phrase) where they believe they have enough weapons against the population—and it's not implausible—that they can destroy human rights, eliminate the curse of democracy, except in a purely formal way, move power into the hands of absolutist, unaccountable institutions which will run the world in their own interests without looking at anyone else, enhance private power, and eliminate workers' rights, political rights, the right to food, destroy it all. . . . Now I think they think they can carry it off. . . .That means for a sector of the population great wealth and privilege and enormous government protection, because none of these people believe in a free market or anything remotely like it. They want a powerful welfare state, directing resources and protection to them. . . For the rest, those who you need to do the dirty work, you pay them a pittance, and if they won't do it, get somebody else. . . . Here you don't quite send out death squads, so you lock them into urban slums which are ore or less urban concentration camps and make sure they don't have any resources there so it will collapse and deteriorate. If that won't work, just throw them into jail."

"Yes, there is class warfare in America, and my class is winning. [Our government needs to] "stop coddling the super rich. . . .We can rise to any challenge but not if people feel we're in a plutocracy. We have to get serious about shared sacrifice. . . .The market system rewards me outlandishly for what I do, but that doesn't mean I'm any more deserving of a good life than a teacher or a doctor. . . . We need a tax system that essentially takes very good care of the people who just really aren't as well adapted to the market system but are nevertheless doing useful things in society." Investment genius **Warren Buffett**

Comment: Current government policies lead inexorably toward even greater wealth for the favored few and less for the hardworking many and the penurious poor. By contrast, income inequality decreased or stayed pretty much the same during the presidencies and policies of Franklin D. Roosevelt, Harry Truman, Dwight D. Eisenhower, John F. Kennedy, Lyndon Johnson, Richard Nixon, Gerald Ford, and Jimmy Carter, and during those years we heard little braying from the top of the income ladder about "class war."

You're probably familiar with the psychological process of *projection,* in which people seem to see qualities in others that they themselves possess but refuse to acknowledge. Disowning those qualities in themselves, they accuse others of having them. That's the situation with "class war" accusations. Blame the victims!

I think the "class war" the metaphor is a poor one, although conveniently inflammatory for the "divide and conquer" crowd. "Class exploitation and conflict" is more precisely descriptive and more useful.

Today class exploitation and conflict is overwhelmingly carried out by the wealthiest members of society, not by the middle class, the working class or the poor (despite all mystifications to the contrary.) Now the various "flat tax" proposals and other related ideas that are some right wingers' top priority and that were on prominent display in the 2011-12 Republican presidential primary debates would demolish the last remaining populist vestiges of the tax system and favor the already very rich even more, leaving a blackened, scorched-earth no-man's land between the very wealthy and almost everybody else. In short, anything that interferes with upgrading from a Mercedes to a Bentley gets the label "class war" slapped on it by those who aspire to far more that they don't need than they already have.

Perhaps you have wondered, "What will to happen if the U.S. keeps on moving in the increasingly polarized "wrong direction" that 80 percent of our people now say it is moving in? Under such circumstances, democracy typically withers, whimpers and eventually dies. That's what the ruling elite's actions are leading toward.

If the disparity between rich and poor keeps on growing, here's a prediction: More and more people will find themselves with no means of livelihood. Since some of them will inevitably turn to crime rather than watch their families starve, crime will rise. In turn, the rich will hire more guards and more and more of them will live in gated communities (as is already happening), and they will be increasingly reluctant to spend much time mingling with the rabble (i.e. general public.) Pricey investment newsletters are recommending buying stock in corporations that build gated and guarded subdivisions. Society will be more and more sharply divided between the rich and the rest. Police costs will skyrocket to enforce the laws that protect and help the rich. Judicial costs will rise. Rich and poor alike will be increasingly afraid to walk and drive in neighborhoods and shopping centers where mugging rates will be more common. Public services from schools to sewage treatment will keep on deteriorating. Now that the radical right has largely captured the Republican Party and has the rest of its leaders under siege, that's the direction in which the policy proposals of almost every current and recent Republican presidential candidate point, as they try to plaster the erroneous label "socialism" on every other alternative. They much prefer fascism (in pseudo-democratic drag). Do you find that vision of the future attractive?

We have already moved far toward a society filled with a new class of kings and nobles. They have no royal titles, but their wealth and power is so great that in many cases it eclipses that of the kings and nobles of yesteryear.

Reversing that scenario of moving into a new era of blatantly plutocratic rule, so that most people will again say that our country is moving in the "right direction," is what the Radical Wrong crowd is screaming is "class war."

On October 31, 2011, writer **Andrew Sullivan** said in *Newsweek,* "The financial sector and its deregulated leverage binge and the Clinton and Bush years greatly benefited the top 1 percent. Much of this, we now know, was based on obscure mathematical formulas no one fully understood at best and were direct scams against their own customers at worst."

Sullivan continues, "Raising taxes on those who have benefited the most from the past 30 years to help reduce the debt is not class warfare. It's an obviously pragmatic attempt to get some fiscal sanity back. . . The collapse of faith in big government is hard to distinguish from the collapse of support for big business—especially when the tax code reads like a conspiracy between them against the rest of us. . . There is simply a limit beyond which economic inequality threatens democratic life, when the majority suspect that a tiny minority has fixed the system beyond repair through the existing institutions." (I'd say "rigged" is a better word than "fixed.")

Comment: U.S. politics and government economic policies between 2000 and 2008 increasingly resembled brokerage houses "selling short" the very securities they were marketing to their clients (i.e. secretly betting that their price would go down, while their clients hoped they would make money from the price going up). How corrupt can you get? That kind of outrageous white-collar crime sets a terrible example for all the people who look to the nation's elite for guidance about how to live their own lives. Shouldn't the "big swinging dicks," as members of the Wall Street Power crowd like to call themselves (Yes, there is an alternative word that starts with "p"), at Goldman Sachs and other brokerages who were doing that short-selling to such customers as pension funds be in the slammer along with Bernard Madoff? What was the response in the executive suites of high finance to these revelations? A furious attempt by Wall Street to resist any new regulation and eager grasping for taxpayers' money in bailouts paid for in part by their victims. Recently Wall Street has been lobbying furiously to repeal the one of the few regulations that kept it from damaging the economy even more than it did, the Dodd-Frank financial regulation law.

But there is another direction in which we might move. Daniel Gilbert's research found that people reported being happier when they were buying things for others than when buying things for themselves. In that spirit, the legendary Andrew Carnegie "transformed himself from robber baron to secular saint with his hospitals, concert halls, libraries, and university; Alfred Nobel [by establishing the Nobel Prize] ensured that he would be remembered for something other than the invention of dynamite," writes Christia Freeland in *The Atlantic*. In our time, socially engaged investment genius George Soros has spent billions on diverse worthy causes. Rising numbers of the super-rich have found the marginal utility of doing good to be greater than that of making a few million more dollars. They have a sense that the rich, powerful, and well educated have a responsibility to the less fortunate.

And now there is the voice of Warren Buffett, one of the world's richest men. A *Time* magazine profile states that Buffett is "demanding higher taxes on the rich and more government spending on the rest to solve our economic problems. . . . The country that made him rich is lousy with bailout billionaires, a culture of selfishness and a loss of opportunities." *Buffett notes that his personal tax rate is about half that of his office staff, who make a tiny fraction of the money he does – and it should be the other way around.* Time adds, "Bond traders and corporate raiders of the world, take note: your higher taxes should subsidize bridge builders and child-care workers."

SOLUTIONS

- Drop the "class war" metaphor and start talking about specific details of "class exploitation and conflict" instead.

- Carefully examine the voting records of your legislators at all levels and see whether they favor the few, the many, or all the people—and act accordingly. You will find them on websites of *Project Vote Smart*, the *League of Women Voters*, or the *League of Conservation Voters*.

- Insist that Presidents appoint, and Congress approve, officials for Treasury Department and other top economic positions in the government who owe nothing to Wall Street or other giant banking and investment institutions. (Personnel from those sources can be hired as consultants to provide needed information.) Note that these are staunchly middle-of-the-road proposals, not leftist ones. Real leftists would deconstruct and reconfigure the whole government financial economic regulatory apparatus and policy.

- If you are among the privileged few, consider working for the good of the many, as Franklin, Washington, Jefferson, Theodore Roosevelt, Franklin D. Roosevelt, and John F. Kennedy did. You will probably feel better about yourself and your life. (It is intriguing that Franklin was one of the most prolific inventors in American history, yet did not patent his inventions. He wrote that since he

enjoyed great advantage from the inventions of others, he was glad to share his own inventions with others without profit.

* * *

14. How Foxes Guard the Henhouse: Deficits and Taxes

In 2011 the Republican right wing tried to define the deficit as the central issue facing the country, while at the same time opposing the scheduled expiration of the Bush-Cheney "temporary" tax cuts for the super-rich, which would have gone far toward balancing the budget. The Big Lie with this issue is the assertion that "Our huge national debt is all due to entitlements that require paying money to middle class and poor people." In that view, the fact that U.S. military spending is more than half the world's total, and that some investors and corporations get enormous subsidies and tax breaks, should be considered irrelevant to the topic of deficit reduction. Let's take a closer look.

"An election is coming. Universal peace is declared and the foxes have a sincere interest in prolonging the lives of the poultry." Playwright and poet **T.S. Eliot**

"As a private man has a right to say what wages he will give in his private affairs, so has a community to determine what they will give and grant of their substance to the administration of public affairs." **Samuel Adams**

"Friends and neighbors complain that taxes are indeed very heavy. . . We are taxed twice as much by our idleness, three times as much by our pride, and four times as much by our folly." **Benjamin Franklin**

"The purse of the people is the real seat of sensibility. Let it be drawn upon largely, and they will then listen to truths which could not excite them through any other organ. . . . Considering the general tendency to multiply offices and dependencies and to increase expense to the ultimate term of burden which the citizen can bear, it behooves us to avail ourselves of every occasion which presents itself for taking off the surcharge. . . . [I advocate arranging matters so that] no generation can contract debts greater than may be paid during the course of its own existence. . . . Neither the representatives of a nation, nor the whole nation itself assembled, can validly engage debts beyond what they may pay in their own time. . . . Our revenues once liberated by the discharge of the public debt, and its surplus applied to canals, roads, schools, et., and the farmer will see his government supported, his children educated, and the face of the country made a paradise by the contributions of the rich along, without his being called on to spare a cent from his earnings. The path we are now pursuing leads directly to this end." **Thomas Jefferson**

Jefferson also said (arguing for tariffs paid by the wealthy, since there was no income tax back then) "The farmer will see his government supported, his children educated, and the face of this country made a paradise by the contnributions of the rich alone, without his being called on to spend a cent from his earnings."

Finally, he remarked, "We can pay off [Hamilton's] debt in fifteen years, but we can never get rid of his financial system." **Thomas Jefferson**

"An unlimited power to tax involves, necessarily, a power to destroy; because there is a limit beyond which no institution and no property can bear taxation." "An unlimited power to tax involves, necessarily, a power to destroy; because there is a limit beyond which no institution and no property can bear taxation." **John Marshall**

"It is the duty of those serving the people in public place closely to limit public expenditures to the actual needs of the government economically administered, because this bounds the right of the government to extract tribute from the earnings of labor or the property of the citizen, and because public extravagance begets extravagance among the people. . . Those who are selected for a limited time to manage public affairs . . . may do much by their example to encourage. . . that plain way of life which among their fellow-citizens aids integrity and promotes thrift and prosperity."
Grover Cleveland

"I like to pay taxes. With them I buy civilization." Supreme Court Justice **Oliver Wendell Holmes, Jr.**

"Taxes, after all, are dues that we pay for the privileges of membership in an organized society."
Franklin D. Roosevelt

"I'm proud to pay taxes in the United States; the only thing is, I could be just as proud for half the money." Entertainer **Arthur Godfrey**

"Haven't we already given money to rich people? Why are we going to do it again?" *George W. Bush*

(a comment to Vice President Dick Cheney, regarding their administration's second round of tax cuts for the wealthy)

"The expenses of government, having for their object the interest of all, should be borne by everyone, and the more a man enjoys the advantages of society, the more he ought to hold himself honored in contributing to those expenses."
French economist and statesman **Anne Robert Jacques Turgot**

"Where is the politician who has not promised to fight to the death for lower taxes – and who has not proceeded to vote for the very spending projects that make tax cuts impossible?" **Barry Goldwater**

"We're going to close the unproductive tax loopholes that allow some of the truly wealthy to avoid paying their fair share. In theory some of those loopholes were understandable, but in practice they sometimes made it possible for millionaires to pay nothing while a bus driver was paying ten percent of his salary, and that's crazy. It's time we stopped it." **Ronald Reagan** (He did indeed close the capital gains tax loophole, but now it's back.)

Reagan also remarked "I am not worried about the deficit. It is big enough to take care of itself."

"I even had a special stamp made up in the shape of a pig to use for vetoing bills that are full of pork. . . We can't afford to think of government as a bottomless well of money. . . The bigger and more expensive our government becomes, the more of our paychecks it takes and the more of our personal decisions it takes over from us." **Jesse Ventura**

"Of course the truth is that the congresspersons are too busy raising campaign money to read the laws they pass. The laws are written by staff tax nerds who can put pretty much any wording they want in there. I bet that if you actually read the entire vastness of the U.S. Tax Code, you'd find at least one sex scene ("Yes, yes, YES!" moaned Vanessa as Lance, his taut body moist with

moisture, again and again depreciated her adjusted gross rate of annualized fiscal debenture.)"
Dave Barry

"There may be liberty and justice for all, but there are tax breaks only for some."
Martin A. Sullivan

BILL CLINTON

The only presidents in U.S. history to ever pass balanced budgets were Democrats Andrew Jackson and Bill Clinton.

"Conservatives never really believed in shrinking the size and scope of government, at least not when they were running the show. That's why we are $15 trillion in debt." **Nick Gillespie**, editor of Reason.com\.

'How badly do the ultra-rich need those [Bush-Cheney] tax cuts? 'Maybe you want to know who's making out in this economy. . . . The number of people with more than $1 million of investable assets jumped 8.3% last year to 10.9 million, their total wealth booming 10% to $42.7 trillion. That surpassed the previous peak in 2007. Recession? What recession? North American's high net worths own $11.6 trillion, up 9%. Asia's rich have supplanted Europe's to take the second spot. The really rich – those with more than $30 million – are doing even better. Their wealth worldwide jumped nearly 12% last year. It's great news for the rest of us, because it means we can all get jobs as butlers or scullery maids." **MarketWatch, 2011.**

"I find the argument that we need lower taxes to create more jobs mystifying, because we've had the lowest taxes in this decade and about the worst job creation ever." **Warren Buffett**

"Of course, a lot of right wingers are very upset about this because they believe this health care bill will cost a lot of money. You know what I think? Just pretend it's another unnecessary war. You'll feel better about it already."
Jay Leno

"[Occupy Wall Street Demonstrators] blame, with some justification, the problems in the financial sector for getting us into this mess, and they're disappointed with the policy response here in Washington. And at some level, I can't blame them." Federal Reserve Chairman **Ben Bernanke**

Item: The Pentagon now has on order 2.457 F-35 joint strike fighters. The cost of each plane is now estimated at $618 million, and the cost keeps going up. It is estimated to be 42 percent more expensive than an F-16 but that estimate is termed "wildly optimistic." The F-35 "is a gigantic performance disappointment, . . . an unaffordable mediocrity, and the program will not be fixed by any combination of hardware tweaks or cost-control projects." **Winslow Wheeler,** Director of the Straus Military Reform Project at the Center for Defense Information.

Comment: Those on the political right are entirely correct when they say they do not want the present generation to leave future generations in debt for our spending. As it happens, their actions have been quite different from their words. In 2001 Federal Reserve Board chairman Alan Greenspan enthusiastically backed the Bush-Cheney tax cuts for the rich, but he later admitted that they were a mistake. When they were passed, Republican and Democratic legislators alike agreed that they were temporary, and would expire in 2012. But 2012 arrived and Republican legislators, led by screaming and shrieking pawns of the very well to do, including the Senate Minority Leader, refused to allow them to expire as promised and called doing so "raising taxes" – even though letting them expire on schedule would largely solve the current national deficit problem.

It is of at least equal importance that many legislators, especially on the far right, but also neocons on the "left," are unwilling to significantly cut the largest single discretionary cause of the chronic U.S. debt, which is the costs of our huge military force and our elective wars (some large, some small and barely noticed by most people), which just happen to channel enormous profits to the oligarchs and plutocrats. U.S. military spending is currently at least as great as that of all other nations of the world combined.

Oddly, those who are rightly concerned about burdening our children and grandchildren with an enormous deficit do not seem to give a whit about burdening future generations with poisoned lands and waters. And they don't raise objections to the prospect of a world so crowded that it is a cauldron for violence, with catastrophic shortages in resources of all kinds. Nor is there a worthy focus on combating climate change spawned by human impacts on the ecosphere, with the resulting increase in hurricanes, tornadoes, floods, wildfires, droughts, heat waves, and other natural disasters. How strange!

Amid their professed strong commitment to reducing the national debt, we may note that *no Republican administration* (the radical right's preferred party) has *ever* passed a balanced budget. The only presidents in our history to do so were Andrew Jackson and Bill Clinton. Ronald Reagan's budget director David Stockman later admitted that the Reagan administration's "supply side economics" was really a Trojan horse for cutting tax rates on the rich.

Clinton undid much of the havoc Reagan wrought on the budget. He reduced the federal civilian payroll by 377,000 employees—the lowest level since the Kennedy administration, despite the nation's larger population . . . and reduced federal spending as a percentage of GDP from 22.2 percent to just 18.5 percent. Paul Begala writes, "Had we simply continued Clintonomics, we would have paid off the national debt. Not the annual deficit—[Clinton's policies] had already eliminated that—but the entire national debt, in 2009."

Then George W. Bush slashed rates on the top tax brackets again and again, while leaving in place Clinton's 50% reduction in the capital gains tax. And in late 2010, Senate Republican leader Mitch McConnell said the Senate Republicans **would block every single bill** until President Obama approved extension of the Bush-era tax cuts for the rich. (That's mighty big-hearted of you, Mitch.) Only McConnell laid that egg did he begin to cluck loudly about the deficit. Ezra Klein wrote in Newsweek, "It's still Ronald Reagan's world, at least when it comes to taxes. . . Republicans really, really, really care about tax cuts for rich people." We shouldn't be surprised. Trusting plutocrats to balance the budget is like trusting the foxes to care for the hens. Sure they'll do their best to balance it—after their own pockets are full enough. When will that be? Never. Or at least, not until their consciousness rises above their pockets.

Psychologists tell us that immediate reinforcement affects behavior more strongly than delayed reinforcement. The impact of tax cuts comes soon, that of deficits later.

There is also the bottom end of the income spectrum. Taxpayers provide schools, emergency rooms, and welfare payments for people who cannot afford those things themselves – even people who have, like a woman I met last week, nine children. As Jesse Ventura points out, it is irresponsible to start a family before you can provide for the children. We should not reward such behavior through our social policies. And currently, those who can't pay for medical help receive the most expensive help available – emergency rooms. Recently a firefighter-paramedic told me, "Three fourths of my medical calls are for people who have some minor medical problem, like a cut that could be treated with a band-aid. Because they can't afford to see a doctor, they call to have us take them to the emergency room."

Why is this happening? The unfortunate reality is that today most economists and medical planners are on the payrolls of companies or agencies dedicated to the status quo. Any intelligent taxation policy has to take into effect the interests of all the people, its effects on businesses both small and large, its effects on agriculture and the environment. With the huge economic and social problems that face us today (such as government subsidies that help giant agribusiness corporations drive small farmers out of business), the immense environmental problems that are looming on the horizon, and financial situations in more than a few countries that are even more dire than our own, a profound thinking of major structural policies regarding taxing and spending is essential. Such a project is not yet even on the radar of either major U.S. political party. It is time for a next step in the evolution of our culture – a next step that truly restores the vision and ideals of our nation's founders at the same time that it addresses today's realities.

<<<>>>

SOLUTIONS

- **To end the deficit, return to Bill Clinton's tax schedules, with these exceptions: (1) Do not reinstate the historic "marriage penalty." (2) Tax capital gains on investments at the Ronald Reagan level: that is, the same rate as ordinary income, with these exceptions: a 15% rate on the increase of the value of your home and one rental or vacation dwelling, up to a ceiling for the 15% rate of (a specified) several times the median value of homes in your area, adjusted for inflation at the rate of the Consumer Price Index increase in your city or county. (3) Close the loopholes that make it possible for some wealthy individuals and highly profitable corporations to pay nothing.**

- **End policies that are helping the rich get even richer while the poor get even poorer. For example, we could return to Dwight D. Eisenhower's tax schedule, with the same exceptions described just above, adjusted so that inflation does not push people into higher tax brackets.**

- Reduce welfare costs and educational and medical costs required to support welfare recipients (food stamps, etc.) who depend on such revenues for survival. Do this without causing avoidable hardship or suffering. For example, our social welfare system could, like those in some other countries (and in line with Jesse Ventura's comment), aim at reducing the number of children born to parents who cannot themselves support them. One approach would be to provide (1) Full payments for poverty-level families with up to two children and no increase for any additional children beyond two. (2) The opportunity to obtain a green card only for immigrants with zero to two children, with revocation of the card if that number is exceeded before citizenship is attained. (Reason: the average birthrate among immigrants, especially those at poverty level, is much higher than among native-born citizens.)

- To reduce medical costs for people who cannot pay their own way, set up (ideally with local funding) outpatient clinics in which the first person seen is a nurse practitioner, with a doctor available if needed. Return emergency rooms to the role of dealing with real emergencies.

* * *

15. Sleight of Hand with Adam Smith's ideas

ADAM SMITH

To correct widespread misconceptions, this section deals specifically with Adam Smith. An Englishman who lived during the 1700s, Smith is often credited with being the founder of capitalism as we know it today. Actually, as you will see, he disdained its outlook. His economic thinking was concerned with production, consumption, trading and exchange, and markets. All these existed before the economic system called capitalism came into being. In Smith's day capitalism as it exists now did not yet exist. Since this section addresses widespread misunderstandings of Smith's ideas that are often misrepresented as the thinking of America's founders, the quotations below are from him alone.

"Consumption is the sole end and purpose of all production; and the interest of the producer ought to be attended to, only so far as it may be necessary for promoting that of the consumer." **Adam Smith**

"Labour was the first price, the original purchase - money that was paid for all things. It was not by gold or by silver, but by labour, that all wealth of the world was originally purchased." **Adam Smith**

"No society can surely be flourishing and happy, of which the far greater part of the members are poor and miserable." **Adam Smith**

"There can be no proper motive for hurting our neighbor. . . . To disturb his happiness merely because it stands in the way of our own, to take from him what is of real use to him merely because it may be of equal or more use to us, is what no impartial spectator can go along with." **Adam Smith**

"We rarely hear . . . of the combinations of masters, though frequently of those of the workman. But whoever imagines, upon this account, that masters rarely combine, is as ignorant of the world as of the subject." **Adam Smith (Comment:** Think interlocking boards of directors, the national Chamber of Commerce, the Koch Brothers' retreats where the corporate rich and political plutocrats meet and mingle, etc.)

"Our merchants and master-manufacturers complain much of the bad effects of high wages in raising the price, and thereby lessening the sale of their goods both at home and abroad. They say nothing concerning the bad effects of high profits. They are silent with regard to the pernicious effects of their own gains. They complain only of those of other people." **Adam Smith**

"To feel much for others and little for ourselves; to restrain our selfishness and exercise our benevolent affections, constitute the perfection of human nature."
Adam Smith

"The necessaries of life occasion the great expense of the poor. They find it difficult to get food, and the greater part of their little revenue is spent in getting it. The lucuries and vanities of life occasion the principal expense of the rich. . . . It is not very unreasonable that the rich should contribute to the public expense, not only in proportion to their revenue, but something more than that proportion." **Adam Smith**

"The subjects of every state ought to contribute towards the support of the government, as nearly as possible, in proportion to their respective abilities, that is, in proportion to the revenue which they respectively enjoy under the protection of the state. . . It is not very unreasonable that the rich should contribute to the public expence, not only in proportion to their revenue, but something more than in that proportion. " **Adam Smith**

Comment. "Capitalism" refers to an economic outlook and system which has as its end making as much money as possible. In almost any economy, capital is needed to get tools, equipment and materials and to pay workers' wages, but it that context it is a means to production and consumption, not an end in itself. There is a similar confusion with "markets." We unthinkingly use the term "free markets" for economic forms that are no such thing at all. A large share of international trade, for example, is highly regulated by global and regional bodies such as the World Trade Organization. Actually, those who use the term "free trade" usually mean either "unrestricted trade" or "trade according to the rules favored by giant multinational banks and other corporations." Smith, like the founders of the American Republic, lived before any of those arrangements came into being. To claim that he was supportive of them is just plain dishonest. He is best known for writing **The Wealth of Nations,** but his other major work, **The Theory of Moral Sentiments**, tells us at least as much about his attitudes.

"The invisible hand" is Smith's best-known concept is –the idea that when everyone pursues his or her own economic interest (in the contemporary telling, no matter how relentlessly) it will benefit all. In some situations that is true. But the concept suffers from major limitations. First, Smith was referring to a marketplace such as a public market with are many buyers and sellers for each commodity; not to a world where giant enterprises are trying to gain monopolistic or oligopolistic control over products that lets them set prices highly favorable to themselves and disadvantageous to everyone else. Second, Smith's statement was a theory. He offered no empirical evidence for it. But the many who found it advantageous to regard it as established fact overlooked that detail. And while Smith generally favored "free markets," he also described a list of steps that government might reasonably take regarding the economy and trade. These were meant to prevent dishonesty, violence, and fraud, ensure the quality of goods, impose tariffs on imports in order to bargain for reduction of tariffs by other countries, regulate banking, provide public goods like highways, harbors, bridges, and canals, and so on. His real attitudes were quite different from his distorted public image.

In Smith's writing, the pursuit of self-interest is limited by the laws of justice. He disapproved of actions that would harm others. And he said that a person ought not to "throw down any of " his competitors. He carefully distinguished between "self interest" and "selfishness." The latter refers to "issues in harm or neglect of other people." In his view, actions that benefit one group at the expense of others should be avoided.

"What can be added to the happiness of a man who is in health, out of debt, and has a clear conscience?" *Adam Smith*

No one did more to create and spread a false understanding of Smith's ideas than Milton Friedman at the University of Chicago, who even wore an Adam Smith necktie to lend credibility to his spin on Smith's views. Friedman wrote articles with such titles as, "The Social Responsibility of Business is to Increase its Profits." The only ethical responsibility of business to society, he said, is to make more money. He even claimed that a social responsibility other than to generate as much profit as possible for business owners is "a fundamentally subversive doctrine." It subverts his own twisted outlook, but that's all! Although Friedman did indeed say that maximizing profits should be done without deception or fraud, those caveats were a minimal theme in his writing. He was so dedicated to promoting his view that the only social responsibility of business is to make money that most of his readers and listeners heard little else. Since his audience included the writers of most business textbooks, his misrepresentations rather than Smith's real outlook were swallowed by hundreds of thousands of economics and business students. In short, Friedman's view was a myopic, shriveled caricature of Adam Smith's far larger, kinder, and more generous field of thought.

<<<>>>

SOLUTIONS

- The time has come to move on in our thinking about economics. We can integrate the best and most thoughtful of Smith's observations into the reconceptualization that is needed to meet the world's changing conditions, making sure to test them empirically. With a little luck, Friedman's disreputable distortions will one day be visible nowhere but in the footnotes of economic history books.

- Regard both communism and contemporary capitalism as historically interesting perspectives that one day will belong in the history books along with feudalism and other obsolete systems. Capitalism as we know it depends on economic growth, and such growth will one day end, when eventually resources of many kinds decline and finally population stops growing (whether through intelligent worldwide birth control or through catastrophic disasters and population crashes).

- Transform our economies by deeply thinking through new modes of design, production, allocation, distribution, and consumption to: (1) provide primary goods and services for all before some receive large amounts of tertiary goods and services; (2) maintain and resurrect the good health of Earth's ecosphere and local ecosystems; and (3) be viable in an equilibrium economy –which is probably due to arrive within the present century-- rather than a growth economy. The next stage in economics will have to depend not on a single dominant economic model, but on a spectrum of approaches that fit diverse peoples, places, and conditions that exist in dynamic interaction with each other.

* * *

16. Religion and Government: Paine, Jefferson, and Madison Make The Situation Perfectly Clear

Some of today's Radical Wrongers have convinced themselves that our founding fathers held the principle that, "My religion and others that agree with it have the right to get our views made into laws that everybody has to follow or else they should be arrested and get thrown into jail." There is usually a heavy loading of self-righteous energy behind that view. Some state legislatures have actually put laws on the books that are based on that outlook. (To me it smells an awful lot like the energy behind the hangings of so-called "witches" by the Puritans in early Salem.) In reality, that attitude is one of the things the founders fought against most strongly, as you will see below.

"Forced worship stinks in God's nostrils." **Roger Williams**, founder of Rhode Island in 1636, the first colony to hold that no aspect of a Church's doctrine should determine government policy or actions.

"Of all the animosities which have existed among mankind, those which are caused buy a difference of sentiments in religion appear to be the most inveterate and distressing, and ought most to be deprecated." **George Washington**

Thomas Paine wrote, "Persecution is not an original feature in any religion; but it is always the strongly marked feature of all religions established by law." He added, "As to religion, I hold it to be the indispensable duty of government to protect all conscientious professors thereof, and I know of no other business which government hath to do therewith. . . I fully and conscientiously believe that it is the will of the Almighty that there should be a diversity of religious opinions among us." And on a more personal note, he said "My mind is my own church. . . I believe that religious duties consist in doing justice, loving mercy, and endeavoring to make our fellow-creatures happy."

"While we are under the tyranny of Priests, it will ever be their interest, to invalidate the laws of nature and reason, in order to establish systems incompatible therewith." Revolutionary war hero *Ethan Allen*

ETHAN ALLEN

Thomas Jefferson, who studied the New Testament with great care and compiled "The Jefferson Bible" (available free online) that presents his conclusions about which of the statements attributed to Jesus Christ's were truly authentic, commented extensively on the relation between church and state: "Is uniformity attainable? *Millions of innocent men, women, and children, since the introduction of Christianity, have been burnt, tortured, fined, imprisoned*; yet we have not advanced one inch towards uniformity. What has been the effect of coercion? To make one half the world fools and the other half hypocrites. To support roguery and error all over the earth. . . I may recover health by medicines I am compelled to take against my own judgment, but I cannot be saved by a worship I disbelieve and abhor. . . . The impious presumption of legislators and rulers, civil as well as ecclesiastical, who, being themselves but fallible and inspired men, have assumed dominion over the faith of others, *setting up their own opinions and modes of thinking as the only true and infallible, and as such endeavoring to impose them on others,* (my italics) hath established and maintained false religions over the greatest part of the world and through all time."

Along with Ethan Allen, Jefferson was no fan of the doctrines and actions of the leaders and priests of the Roman Catholic Church. **Jefferson continued,** "The priests have so disfigured the simple religion of Jesus that no one who reads the sophistications they have engrafted on it . . . would conceive these could have been fathered on the sublime preacher of the Sermon on the Mount. . . We should all then, like the Quakers, live without an order of priests, moralize for ourselves, follow the oracle of conscience, and say nothing about what no man can understand, nor therefore believe. . . . But a short time elapsed after the death of the great reformer of the Jewish religion, before his principles were departed from by those who professed to be his special servants, and perverted into an engine for enslaving mankind, and aggrandizing their oppressors in Church and State. . . . My opinion is that there would never have been an infidel, if there had never been a priest."

Jefferson also wrote, "To compel a man to furnish contributions of money for the propagation of opinions which he disbelieves is sinful and tyrannical. . . . It behooves every man who values liberty of conscience for himself to resist invasions of it in the case of others. . . . It does me no injury for my neighbor to say there are twenty gods, or no God. It neither picks my pocket nor breaks my leg." And he concludes, much as Paine did, "I have ever judged the religion of others by their lives. For it is in our lives, and not from our word, that our religion must be read."

"The purpose of separation of church and state is to keep forever from these shores the ceaseless strife that has soaked the soil of Europe with blood for centuries. . . . In no instance have... the churches been guardians of the liberties of the people. . . Religion and government will both exist in greater purity, the less they are mixed together." . . . The number, the industry, and the morality of the priesthood, and the devotion of the people have been manifestly increased by the total separation of the church from the state." **James Madison**

"If the liberties of the American people are ever destroyed, they will fall by the hands of the clergy." **Marquis de Lafayette**

"I like the silent church before the service begins, better than any preaching." **Ralph Waldo Emerson**

Commenting on claims that the Bible justifies, or prohibits, slavery, "Both read the same Bible, and pray to the same God; and each invokes His aid against the other. It may seem strange that any men should dare to ask a just God's assistance in wringing their bread from the sweat of other men's faces; but let us judge not that we be not judged. The prayers of both could not be answered; that of neither has been answered fully." **Abraham Lincoln**

"Anyone who knows history, particularly the history of Europe, will, I think, recognize that the domination of education or of government by any one particular religious faith is never a happy arrangement for the people." **Eleanor Roosevelt**

"No woman can call herself free who does not own and control her body. No woman can call herself free until she can choose consciously whether she will or will not be a mother. . . . She goes through the vale of death alone, each time a babe is born. As it is the right neither of man nor the state to coerce her into this ordeal, so it is her right to decide whether she will endure it." Family planning pioneer **Margaret Sanger**

Margaret Sanger

"Woman must have . . . the fundamental freedom of choosing whether or not she will be a mother and how many children she will have. Regardless of what man's attitude may be, that problem is hers - and before it can be his, it is hers alone. . . . When motherhood becomes the fruit of a deep yearning, not the result of ignorance or accident, its children will become the foundation of a new race." **Margaret Sanger**

"I believe in an America where the separation of church and state is absolute – where no Catholic prelate would tell the President (should he be Catholic) how to act and no Protestant minister would tell his parishioners for whom to vote – where no church or church school is granted any public funds or political preference – and where no man is denied public office merely because his religion differs from the President who might appoint him or the people who might elect him. . . . I believe in an America . . . where no public official either requests or accepts instructions on public policy from the Pope, the National Council of Churches, or any other ecclesiastical source --- where no religions body seeks to impose its will directly or indirectly upon the general populace or the public acts of its officials – and where religious liberty is so indivisible that an act against one church is treated as an act against all." **John F. Kennedy**

"Religious factions. . . are trying to force government leaders into following their position 100 percent. . . . I'm frankly sick and tired of the political preachers across this country telling me as a citizen that if I want to be a moral person, I must believe in 'A,' 'B,' 'C,' and 'D.' . . . I will fight them every step of the way if they try to dictate their moral convictions to all Americans in the name of 'conservatism.' **Barry Goldwater,** who was called "Mr. Conservative."

"You don't have to be straight to be in the military; you just have to be able to shoot straight. **Barry Goldwater**

Barry Goldwater

"A lot of so-called conservatives think I've turned liberal because I believe a woman has a right to an abortion. That's a decision that's up to a pregnant woman, not up to the pope or some do-gooders on the religious right." **Barry Goldwater**

"Lord, there's danger in this land. You get witch-hunts and wars when church and state hold hands." Singer and songwriter **Joni Mitchell**

"The price of seeking to force our beliefs on others is that someday they might force their beliefs on us." New York Governor **Mario Cuomo**

"I believe in the separation of church and state. . . We all have our own religious beliefs. There are people out there who are atheists, who don't believe at all. They are citizens of Minnesota and I have to respect that. . . The religious right wants to tell people how to live . . . I hate what the fundamentalist fanatics are doing to our country. . . I have a strong belief that you are in charge of your body, whether male or female. It's the house you are living in for your entire existence – your temple, as the more religious might say." **Jesse Ventura**

'To label family planning and legal abortion programs "genocide" is male rhetoric, for male ears. . . Women know, and so do many men, that two or three children who are wanted, prepared for, reared amid love and stability, and educated to the limit of their ability will mean more for the future of the black and brown races from which they come than any number of neglected, hungry, ill-housed and ill-clothed youngsters. Pride in one's race, as well as simple humanity, supports this view." Black Congresswoman **Shirley Chisholm**

"Any woman should have the right to a safe and legal abortion." First Lady **Betty Ford**

Betty Ford

"A woman's ability to decide how many children to have, and when, without interference from the government, is one of the most fundamental rights we possess. It is not just an issue of choice, but equality and opportunity for all women." **Barack Obama**

"Being pro-choice is trusting the individual to make the right decision for herself and her family, and not entrusting that decision to anyone wearing the authority of government in any regard." **Hillary Clinton**

"I remember those days, when people would go to Mexico to get back-alley abortions. . . I hope every woman in this country, whether they agree with Roe or they disagree with Roe, whether they themselves would make one decision or another, will come together and say, "Pro-choice means that the Government respects the individual, and isn't that really what our country is all about?" Senator **Barbara Boxer**

"If men could get pregnant, abortion would be a sacrament." **Anonymous**

"Christianity has sufficient inner strength to survive and flourish on its own. It does not need state subsidies, nor state privileges, nor state prestige. The more it obtains state support the greater it curtails human freedom." Supreme Court Justice **William O. Douglas**

"The Supreme Court has ruled that they cannot have a nativity scene in Washington, D.C. This wasn't for any religious reasons. They couldn't find three wise men and a virgin." **Jay Leno**

"I'm completely in favor of the separation of Church and State. My idea is that these two institutions screw us up enough on their own, so both of them together is certain death." **George Carlin**

"The overreach of the far right isn't just now entering our pants—it's always been there. . . . After a year of coordinated assaults on Planned Parenthood, "personhood" initiatives that stood to make oral contraceptives illegal, and other attacks on protected sex, we have come to a bizarre moment. . . Welcome to the new war on contraception. The Catholic Church's fight to forbid insurance-provided birth control to employees of religious organizations—and the all-male panel on a House Oversight Committee hearing on contraception—has officially codified this war. But . . . a few questions stand out; namely, how is it in a country where 99 percent of women have used birth control that we are fighting over whether people should have access to contraceptives? How did a position this extreme and alienated from the will of the people enter the mainstream political conversation?" Writer **Sady Doyle.** Doyle continues, "Author **Christina Page** says that she's been recommending since 2008 that reporters ask all GOP candidates about their position on contraception. 'The media wasn't willing.'"

President John Adams and First Lady Abigail Adams would not have been pleased at this turn of events.

Stephen Colbert: "They are holding hearings in Washington right now about women's reproduction. It's five guys up there. . . . Why are women so obsessed with controlling their own bodies, anyway?"

Nancy Pelosi, replying: "It's a women's health issue which is very important to every family. The family's health, a mother's health, and the health of her children. It isn't up to five guys sitting around a table in Washington, D.C. to tell women what to do. It would be wise for the gentlemen to understand."

"Women should not need a permission slip from government to take care of their own reproductive health." Ohio state senator **Nina Turner,** who in response to recent bills that would restrict women's health services and contraception, authored a bill requiring men to see a sex therapist before they could get a prescription for Viagra.

> **Comment:** Believe it or not, many authors of bills that take away women's reproductive rights and restrict their health care options hypocritically mouth comments about "freedom!" Apparently they mean their own freedom to tell others how to live. A national tidal wave of bills like Turner's, with exciting variations such as in Texas requiring sonograms and X-rays of the penis and genitals before prescribing drugs to stiffen drooping male organs, would seem a fitting response to the recent wave of male-authored bills that force government to take away women's rights and their sovereignty over their own bodies. It's time to get the government's and some religions' iron hands out of women's underwear!
>
> Thomas Paine's *The Age of Reason* is an extended treatise on the government-religion nexus. George Washington, who did not attend any church himself but waited outside the church while his wife took communion, made a lengthy statement of inclusiveness regarding Muslims, Hindus, and peoples of every one of the world's religions.
>
> *A key element of religious imperialism is an attempt to forge laws and political institutions that constrain others in ways that promote the beliefs and practices of one's own sect.* Members of some religions try to impose their views on the rest of the people by legislation, by pressuring the state or national administration to issue executive orders that turn their wishes into policy, by court cases, or in some countries by armed takeover.
>
> In the U.S. the Vatican's cause got a boost from Jimmy Carter, who named anti-family-planning zealot John H. Sullivan to head USAID (Agency for International Development.) Then it got a much bigger boost from Ronald Reagan, who mouthed approval of the founding fathers' bedrock principle of separation of church and state, then invited the Pope to decide our nation's contraception and abortion policy. During the Reagan years, the U.S withdrew funding from the International Planned Parenthood Federation, the United Nations Fund for Population Activities, and other family planning groups. "American policy was changed as a result of the Vatican's not agreeing with our policy," explains [Reagan's Vatican ambassador] William Wilson. "AID sent people from [the Department of State] to Rome, and I'd accompany them to meet the president of the Pontifical Council for the Family, and in long discussions they finally got the message."
>
> Why do we have an embassy in the Vatican City and an ambassador to the Holy See, and no parallel representative to the Baptist Church, or the Quakers, or the Episcopal

Church, or Presbyterians, or Unitarians, or the United Church of Christ, or the Assembly of God? That arrangement seemed odd to Protestant groups who protested Harry Truman's nomination of such a representative, which Truman then withdrew. In 1969 Richard Nixon appointed Henry Cabot Lodge as his personal representative to the Vatican, and in 1984 Reagan established formal diplomatic relations, with the result described above.

And why are five male Republicans in the House of Representatives on a committee talking about contraception? Make no mistake: The Vatican is still trying to control U.S. state and federal policy to suit its own wishes, and has managed to drag some unsuspecting Evangelicals along with it. Now a Roman Catholic presidential hopeful has sneered at John F. Kennedy's comments above, which express exactly the sentiments of Franklin, Paine, Washington, Jefferson, Ethan Allen, and Abraham Lincoln. Those wise gentlemen were not leftists—they were American patriots. For the most part they were largely individual libertarians, which is neither a leftist nor a rightest stance. Not a single one of them was a religious authoritarian. (This critique of the high hierarchy of the House of Rome does not apply to most American Catholic citizens, who for the most part stand with our founding fathers and John F. Kennedy in our nation's historic commitment to separation of church and state.)

Stripped to its bare bones, the Radical Wrong's reproductive agenda appears to be to crush such independence and autonomy as women have attained, and throw the advances women have made toward equal of status and opportunity into the garbage can. It looks to me suspiciously like contraception and abortion are the cover stories, barefoot and pregnant is the agenda, and iron-fisted male domination of women's lives and destinies is the goal.

In sharp contrast, the *Religious Coalition for Reproductive Choice* is a nationwide alliance of more than *forty* mainstream Protestant, Jewish, and other religious groups which hold that **"*every woman must have the right to consider all options when she faces a problem pregnancy and the freedom to allow her to come to a decision that is in harmony with her own moral and religious values--without government intrusion.*"** The coalition points out that "At the very heart of the abortion debate are conflicting religious views about when "personhood" begins -- a dispute that has engaged theologians for centuries. . . Any law passed to restrict abortion would impose a religious view held by some citizens, and in effect, prevent all other citizens from freely practicing their own religions. . . . **The abortion debate in America is not a conflict between the 'God-fearing' and the 'Godless' but is instead a struggle between those determined to undermine religious freedom and those determined to preserve it."** These are the spokespersons of 40 denominations saying they don't want to have others' religious doctrines imposed on them, and don't want to impose their religious doctrines on others.

As for the idea that government ought to dictate whether a woman can choose whether to be pregnant is a "conservative" view, forget it. Barry Goldwater's wife Peggy was co-founder of Arizona Planned Parenthood in 1937. "We knew family planning could relieve a great deal of human suffering," wrote Peggy in a local magazine piece. "Still we felt somewhat bold and daring in planning our program. Even among intelligent people, the subject was considered too intimate to be discussed or dealt with openly." Today their granddaughter is a clinic volunteer and Planned Parenthood board member.

In 1964 Harry S. Truman and Dwight D. Eisenhower served together as bipartisan honorary co-chairs of Planned Parenthood. In stark contrast to presidential hopeful Mitt Romney's declaration in March of 2012, "Planned Parenthood, we're going to get rid of that." Amid turbocharged sex in television, magazines, movies and music, does eliminating women's health services make any sense? Those who advocate that path are making themselves mental prisoner in an asylum disconnected from real life values and realities. For example, U.S. HIV rates have remained constant for decades despite the existence of medicines and knowledge of practices that could them down dramatically—at least in part because right wing extremists have opposed making that knowledge widely available.

For the record, Jesus Christ was silent on both contraception and abortion, taking no position about either.

Jesus did not advocate the slightest bit of the Papal or extremist Evangelical agenda toward women. He was a friend and defender of women in his own time. He strongly opposed every attitude and every action that would lead toward unnecessary suffering. By contrast, the present right wing agenda leads directly to substantial needless suffering by women. Today's candidates such as Romney and Santorum who wish to deny women control over their own bodies are completely ignoring Jesus' parable. In this matter, the right wing extremist, Radical Wrong's outlook appears to be, "We don't care if they suffer, as long as we get our ideology written into law."

Have you ever wondered where America's anti-abortion movement began? Prior to 1869, the Roman Catholic Church accepted abortion to end a pregnancy "until the soul entered the body," which was held to occur when the mother feels the fetus starting to move around, usually around the end of the first trimester. The great Catholic theologian St. Thomas Aquinas held that human life begins not at conception but at some point in the second trimester. (And in the old days, priests and popes could marry, which may have allowed at least some degree of a tempering feminine influence on the Church's patriarchal hard line. In 1869 however, Pope Pius IX, who openly and very vocally opposed democracy, freedom of speech, critical thinking, and self-determination --and who sat on a throne, wore a crown, and was said "to have a heart of stone" issued a new edict. But Pius IX banned any termination of pregnancy. With a twist of mystifying linguistic magic, a zygote, embryo, or fetus at any stage was transformed into an "unborn child." That's like saying that a high-school Freshman is "a high school graduate who is still working toward the degree." In Pius IX's view a fertilized ovum, invisible to the naked eye, was held to have a "right to life," with no regard to how much suffering the pregnancy and birth might cause for the mother who might have to drop out of school or lose her job, the father who might have to pay twenty years of child support.

(Please note that this criticism of Pius IX's policy is in no way a criticism of the Roman Catholic Church. Some of the best and kindest people I know are Catholics, including friends and relatives. I consider Pope John XXIII to be one of the great men of the 20th Century, and his encyclical *Pacem in Terris* probably the greatest encyclical in Papal history.).

John XXIII, who by my reading probably exemplifies the true spirit of Jesus Christ's teachings more fully than any other pope in history, established a commission to study birth control, which after great study, voted to allow oral contraception under some circumstances – a sensible move, since a considerable proportion of Catholics were already using "the pill." But in 1968 the hard-line Pope Paul VI vetoed the decision.

Until the mid-1970s, only Roman Catholic organizations had any coordinated opposition to abortion. In fact, before 1980 the Southern Baptist Convention officially advocated **loosening** abortion restrictions. W. Barry Garrett wrote in *The Baptist Press,* "Religious liberty, equality, and justice are advanced by the [Roe vs. Wade] Supreme Court Decision." Ironically, however, more recently many Evangelical Christians who dislike the Catholic Church swallowed the Papal doctrine on abortion lock, stock, and barrel. Apparently they did not read or respect what Washington, Madison, Jefferson, Paine, and Allen said and wrote, and set out to impose their own beliefs on us all.

The comments by Stephen Colbert and Nancy Pelosi above refer to the fact that bizarrely enough, in 2012 contraception resurfaced as a political issue, on the initiative of white male Roman Catholic congressmen carrying the agenda of the Pope and right-wing Cardinals. They tried to block President Obama's ruling that all hospitals and health insurers include contraception among their services and payment items if a woman desired it. The argument was that Catholics would be required to offer a service they disagreed with on religious grounds. Actually, surveys have shown that today, most Catholics thumb their noses at the Pope and Cardinals' policies and use contraception more, on the average, than the general population. In other words, the Pope and Cardinals are trying to force policies on their church's members with which most of their own congregations disagree. And in my county, the largest hospital belongs to the Catholic Church. To allow it, or insurers, to deny contraceptive services or coverage would surely result in more unwanted pregnancies among low-income women who could not afford to pay the costs of seeing a private doctor out of their own pockets. (The county's homeless shelters for women and children are already overflowing—including the one run by Catholic Charities.) In short the Vatican would be imposing its policies on all women who use Catholic hospitals and all who are covered by any health insurance plans that wished to cut costs by denying contraceptive coverage. And then if Mom can't support herself and the child, and Dad happens to skip town, your taxes and mine rise to cover the costs of unwanted births—sometimes until adulthood.

For the record, Jesus Christ was silent on both contraception and abortion, taking no position about either. The Old Testament offers no guidance, since it contains passages that can be considered pro-abortion and others that can be considered anti-abortion. Muslim countries vary in their views and practices. The sensible and honest course of action is to think the matter through for ourselves.

Singapore brought about a radical drop in poverty and an equally radical improvement in living standards by making contraception widely available and promoting smaller families. China, had it not put in place policies to reduce family size, would have about 400 million more people today than it presently has – a difference greater than the entire population of the United States. (Yes, there have been major problems in accomplishing that. It is not easy to balance them against the other problems that would be caused by 400 million extra people, which is the equivalent of 400 new cities of a million people each, causing more pollution and competing for resources from all around the world—translating, for example, into higher oil prices and gas prices for you and me at the pump. In some matters there are no easy answers that have no drawbacks.)

SOLUTIONS

- **In short, return to the founding fathers' clear, succinct principle of complete separation of church and state.**

- **Prohibit the government from interfering in the internal affairs of any religion. (This is not meant to stop it from enforcing laws that protect the life, safety, health and property of members of any sect, or those whom a sect's policies may intentionally or inadvertently harass, or those served by facilities owned by the sect.)**

- **Strike down all the authoritarian and anti-libertarian laws that give any branch or agency of local, state, or federal government any authority over a woman's body and pregnancy.**

- Any and all government deliberation and policymaking related to women's bodies should be made by councils that consist entirely of women members.

- In all matters and cases where some religions advocate a given policy and others oppose it, the government may make neither make any law or policy nor take any action. In accord with Jefferson's principle, it may not contribute to funding schools run by religious organizations.

- Ensure that the government does not impose on the people any law or policy based on sectarian beliefs, wishes, perspectives, or policies.

* * *

17. International Affairs:
From "With Malice Toward None" to Global Empire

Most of this book is concerned with the domestic politics, economics, and other affairs of the United States. Our founding fathers knew well, however, that we live in a world filled with many different peoples and nations that have diverse interests. Today, some on the far right say, "Since the U.S. has more economic and military power than any other country, we ought to be able to do anything we please." That includes replacing regimes our government and multinational corporations do not like with others to its liking. Furthermore, executives and directors of many multinational corporations, and the legislators who work hand in glove with them, seem to see no problem with having the banking and commercial policies that control what our country and others must do hammered out in secret meetings of international organizations that are not elected by or visible or accountable to the people. Yes, today's circumstances are quite different from those when our nation was born. Nonetheless, the observations that Paine, Washington, Jefferson, and others offered about our relations with other nations need to be part of our ongoing reflection and discussion. I suspect that they would not be pleased about much of our foreign policy today. Here are their words.

"It is pleasant to observe by what regular gradations we surmount the force of local prejudices, as we enlarge our acquaintance with the World." **Thomas Paine**

"Observe good faith and justice toward all nations. Cultivate peace and harmony with all. . . . It will be worthy of a free, enlightened, and . . . great nation, to give to mankind the magnanimous and too novel example of a people always guided by justice and benevolence." **George Washington**

Washington also wrote, "The nation which indulges toward another an habitual hatred or an habitual fondness is in some degree a slave. It is a slave to its animosity or to its affection, either of which is sufficient to lead it astray from its duty and its interest. . . . Antipathy of one nation against another disposes each more readily to offer insult and injury; to lay hold of slight causes of umbrage; and to be haughty and intractable, when accidental or trifling occasions of dispute occur. Hence frequent collisions, obstinate, envenomed, and bloody contests. The nation, prompted by ill will and resentment, sometimes impels to war the government, contrary to the best calculations of policy. . . At other times, [the government] makes the animosity of the nation subservient to projects of hostility, instigated by pride, ambition, and other sinister and pernicious motives. The peace often, sometimes perhaps the liberty, of nations has been the victim." And he added, "There can be no greater error than to expect, or calculate, upon real favors from nation to nation. It is an illusion which experience must cure, which a just pride ought to discard."

"Are fleets and armies necessary to a work of love and reconciliation? Have we shown ourselves so unwilling to be reconciled that force must be called in to win back our love? Let us not deceive ourselves, sir. These are the implements of war and subjugation; the last arguments to which kings resort." **Patrick Henry**
(He was speaking of England. Might we now ask whether his words apply to us?)

"My hope of preserving peace for our country is not founded in the greater principles of non-resistance under every wrong, but in the belief that a just and friendly conduct on our part will procure justice and friendship for others. . . . I love peace, and I am anxious that we should give the world still another useful lesson, by showing them other modes of punishing injuries than by war, which is as much a punishment to the punisher as to the sufferer. . . . Commerce with all nations, alliance with none, should be our motto." " **Thomas Jefferson.** And he added, "It is a kind of law of nature that every nation prospers by the prosperity of others."

"If there be one principle more deeply rooted than any other in the mind of every American, it is that we should have nothing to do with conquest." *Thomas Jefferson*

"[America has] respected the independence of other nations while asserting and maintaining her own. She has abstained from interference in the concerns of others, even when conflict has been for principles to which she clings . . . She goes not abroad, in search of monsters to destroy. She is well-wisher to the freedom and independence of all. She is the champion and vindicator only of her own . . . She well knows that by once enlisting under other banners than her own, were they even the banners of foreign independence, she would involve herself beyond the power of extrication, in all the wars of interest and intrigue, of individual avarice, envy, and ambition, which assume the colors and usurp the standard of freedom. The fundamental maxims of her policy would insensibly change form liberty to force . . . She might become the dictatress of the world." **John Adams**

"If there is one thing that we do worse than any other nation, it is try and manage somebody else's affairs." **Will Rogers**

"We have learned that we cannot live alone, at peace; that our own well-being is dependent on the well-being of other nations, far away. We have learned that we must live as men, and not as ostriches. . . We have learned to be citizens of the world, members of the human community." **Franklin D. Roosevelt**

"Let us never negotiate out of fear. But let us never fear to negotiate. . . .Peace is a daily, a weekly, a monthly process, gradually changing opinions, slowly eroding old barriers, quietly building new structures. And however undramatic the pursuit of peace, the pursuit must go on." **John F. Kennedy**

"Today we know that World War II began not in 1929 or 1941 but in the 1920's and 1930's when those who should have known better persuaded themselves that they were not their brother's keeper. . . . Leadership in today's world requires far more than a large stock of gunboats and a hard fist at the conference table." **Hubert H. Humphrey**

"[The Trilateral Commission is] a skillful, coordinated effort to seize control and consolidate the four centers of power: political, monetary, intellectual, and ecclesiastical...[in] the creation of a worldwide economic power superior to the political governments of the nation-states involved." **Barry Goldwater**

Chilean novelist **Isabel Allende** writes, "On September 11, 1973, a military coup ended a century of democratic tradition in Chile and started the long reign of General Augusto Pinochet. Similar coups followed in other countries, and soon half the [South American] continent's population was living in terror. This was a strategy designed in Washington and imposed upon the Latin American people by the economic and political forces of the U.S. right wing. In every instance the military acted as mercenaries to the privileged groups in power. . . Torture, concentration camps, censorship, imprisonment without trial, and summary executions became common practices. Thousands of people 'disappeared,' masses of exiles and refugees left their countries running for their lives." (Isabel Allende is the daughter of democratically elected Chilean President Salvador Allende, who was murdered by Pinochet's troops.)

"There are always politicians and technocrats ready to show that the invasion of 'industrializing' foreign capital benefits the area invaded. In this version, the new-model imperialism comes on a genuinely civilizing mission, is a blessing to the dominated countries, and the true-love declarations by the dominant power of the moment are its real intentions. Guilty consciences are thus relieved of the need for alibis, for no one is guilty: today imperialism radiates technology and progress, and even the use of this old, unpleasant word to define it is in bad taste." **Eduardo Galeano,** Uruguayan journalist and author.

Congressman **Ron Paul,** in *A Foreign Policy of Freedom: Peace, Commerce, and Honest Friendship,* writes, "This work is dedicated to my children and grandchildren and to future generations of Americans in the hope and prayer that wisdom and peace may prevail so that no other American father, mother, son or daughter will ever again be asked to fight and die in another undeclared unconstitutional foreign war."

"Treaties make international law and also they make domestic law. Under our constitution, treaties become the supreme law of the land." *Secretary of State John Foster Dulles*

"All treaties made, or which shall be made, under the authority of the United States, shall be the supreme law of the land; and the judges in every state shall be bound thereby, anything in the constitution of laws of any state to the contrary notwithstanding." *The United States Constitution, Article VI, Clause II.*

Comment: After World-War II, the United States contributed heavily to rebuilding Japan and Germany, and to fostering democracy in those countries. For some time those policies brought great respect worldwide.

The U.S. also led the way in moving to re-order world trading, banking, and finance. The 1947 Bretton Woods General Agreement on Tariffs and Trade (GATT) included *forty five thousand* tariff concessions and a package of trade rules. This was meant to reduce tariffs that countries erected to protect their own industries against outside competition, to speed the flow of goods and services around the globe as big business and some governments wished, and to lower prices. Coincidentally or not, it also made it easier for big multinational corporations to swallow up smaller local companies worldwide.

A companion measure to set up an international trade organization was strongly opposed in the U.S. Congress due to our Constitution's provision that any international treaty to which we have agreed trumps all U.S. and state laws. (This directly contradicts other provisions of the constitution, including those that grant all legislative power, including regulation of foreign commerce, to the Congress.) Presidents Truman, Eisenhower, Kennedy, Johnson, Nixon, Ford, Carter, and Reagan all chose not to pressure Congress to agree to such a treaty. But the troika of George W.H. Bush, Bob Dole, and Bill Clinton made it a top priority and in 1995 the World Trade Organization was formally born. (*It passed by two votes and afterward members of Congress admitted that not a single one of them had read it through.*) Not long afterward the North American Agreement on Tariffs and Trade – NAFTA--followed.) Some hailed the WTO as the bright light of a new dawn, while others saw it as the Creature From the Black Lagoon crawling up out of the muck of a polluted harbor, dripping anti-democratic, anti-environmental, and plutocratic toxic waste wherever it went.

Today neither Congress nor the President can veto laws or regulations made by the

WTO. Decisions are made in secret councils that neither public nor press can witness, with no minutes published. WTO Courts trump national courts—even the Supreme Courts of the U.S. and other nations. A country with regulations that do least to protect human health or the environment can claim "unfair restraint of trade" by nations that do more to protect people and ecosystems. Members of these councils are primarily representatives of multinational corporations (appointed by the administrations of member nations) who are ideologically committed to increasing corporate power and the power of the already-dominant nations. Freedom for the biggest and most powerful global corporations? Yes. Freedom, equality, or democracy for smaller, more local businesses, or governments of less powerful nations? Not much. Transparency in decision making and freedom for the people? Hardly.

For example, in March 2012 a WTO committee banned a 2008 U.S. law that meat sold here must be labeled to show its country of origin, a law that consumer advocates had sought for fifty years. In February you could read where your beef or pork or chicken came from; in April you could not. Freedom for whom? For multinational agribusiness meat producers, but not the people. One more win for corpocracy! Lori Wallach, director of Public Citizen's global trade watch, speaks of "mystery meat." When England had its mad cow epidemic in England, wouldn't you have wanted to know whether you were buying British meat? Wallach says, "An unaccountable international agency should not be able to eliminate our consumer safety policies." The WTO has also struck down "dolphin safe" tuna labeling laws so people would know that the canners weren't netting dolphins together with the tuna and canning them both together. There are so many other laws to protect consumers and the environment that are in danger of being struck down by the WTO that I couldn't begin to list them all here. And it gets worse: Industry is lobbying to apply the same "treaty-supremacy" model to the nine-nation Trans-Pacific Free Trade Agreement that is now being negotiated. *There's* your "secret world government."

For decades some Americans have been concerned about the possible emergence of a "world government" that would tell us what to do. This concern was centered on the United Nations. But it turns out that we were looking in the wrong place. Barry Goldwater's remark about the Trilateral Commission ("a skillful, coordinated effort to seize control and [create] a worldwide economic power superior to the political governments of the nation-states involved") actually ended up as a bizarrely accurate description of the World Bank and the International Monetary Fund, which were established by treaties that invalidate all U.S. laws and those of all other member countries that conflict with its secret deliberations and rulings. *That,* it appears to me, is the "World Government" we need to be most concerned about today.

Meanwhile on the exciting covert operations front, the CIA has demonstrated a strong tendency to overthrow democratic governments of small countries that object to U.S. policies and a peculiar taste for establishing fascist governments. And the U.S. Army has trained armed forces of the dictators and supplied them with weapons. In Latin America such events occurred in Cuba, Guatemala, El Salvador, Nicaragua, Panama, Chile, Argentina, Uruguay, Bolivia, and others. It happened over and over again. The Army's School of the Americas trained officers who went back to their countries and set up death squads, assisted in "disappearances" of democratically oriented politicians such as in Argentina and Uruguay, or carried out campaigns of genocide against indigenous peoples, such as in Guatemala. (For details, see Galeano's *Open Veins of Latin America.)*

In Southeast Asia this tactic backfired again and again, and "elective wars" in Vietnam, Cambodia and Laos, as well as support for Indonesia's Suharto dictatorship, lost America respect worldwide. In the Middle East, in Iran in 1953 the CIA and Great Britain's intelligence agency overthrew the democratically elected government of Prime Minister Mohammed Mosaddegh and teamed up with Tehran mobsters to make Mohammed–Reza Shah Pahlavi the dictator of a puppet government whose abuses were so extreme (notably abuses by the CIA-trained secret police), that at last Islamic fundamentalists overthrew the Shah and established a regime overtly hostile to the West, with which we are still coping today. In Iraq, after Britain left a democratic government in place as its imperial forces withdrew, the CIA selected a sociopath named Saddam Hussein to head up a new government that presumably would do as the U.S. wanted it to. (The agency certainly does have talent for picking character. The Shah in Iran, Hussein in Iraq, Diem in South Vietnam, Pinochet in Chile, Somoza in Nicaragua, , Suharto in Indonesia, -- what a list of luminaries! Is "Intelligence" really the right word for all this?) Had he foreseen its future, Harry Truman would probably have had second thoughts when he set up the CIA.

Nonetheless, the "neocons" (neo-conservatives, which includes some erstwhile social "liberals" who are also international superhawks) have advanced an agenda of a "New World Order" of U.S. dominance for the next hundred years no matter what, or how heavy the burden may be for taxpayers like you and me—and for our youth who end up dead or mutilated. The key idea is that by projecting overwhelming military power throughout the world, the U.S. can maintain a "Pax Americana" that will compel other nations to do as the U.S. government and multinational corporations wish. In the neocon view, strong central government and budget deficits are OK when they're needed to maintain military dominance. (Delusions of being a modern Roman Empire are sometimes mentioned, with careful inattention to the fact that Rome was basically governed by a gang of plutocratic thugs in fancy clothes who had no interest in democracy.) Neocon "godfather" Irving Kristol writes, "If you have the kind of power we now have, either you will find opportunities to use it or the world will discover them for you." He describes the wars from Korea to Iraq II as being events that just sort of happened, while largely ignoring who made them happy and why. In the neocon mindset, whatever the U.S. War Machine costs and however many people die, it is justified, and criticism is unpatriotic. For clarity's sake, "Support our troops" always means "support the war," and never "Bring our troops home."

The neocon view that the United States military can dominate what happens all around the globe for the next century ignores the emerging reality of a world with multiple major powers, each of which sees itself as having primary influence in its own geographical area. We can either learn to live in a multi-centric world or we can maintain such an enormous military establishment that one day our government will get an FFF bond rating from Standard and Poors and collapse.

When George W. Bush flew to South America with the hope of setting up a North and South American free trade zone, he was booed off the continent. Latin Americans knew all too well that U.S. meddling in their countries usually meant that U.S. troops would soon be on their soil, or that the CIA or the Army would soon be instructing their military in how to kill the best and brightest of their democratic leaders. (Skeptical? See the CIA Assassination Manual reprinted in Jesse Ventura's *63 Documents the Government Doesn't Want You to Read*). The Latin American countries wanted no part of such a "trade" association, and no one who knew much about the U.S. role in Latin American history could blame them. "Would that Ben Franklin, Thomas Paine, John Adams, and Thomas Jefferson were here to set us on the straight and narrow path now.

While they opposed alliances and entanglements on principle, however, they were not doctrinaire. In the Revolutionary War, the American Colonies' alliance with France was an indispensable aid. French warships and troops alike aided the revolutionary cause in the war to throw off British rule. Therefore we can learn both from their general principles and from their practical response in a specific situation.

<<<>>>

SOLUTIONS

- Release the fantasy that we are a modern Rome that can control the world indefinitely, and recognize that trends and events move far faster in our jumbo-jet and internet world than in Rome's horse and chariot age. Also remember that Rome spent most of its history as an imperial dictatorship.

- Strive to understand the different psyches, perspectives, and cultures of peoples around the world, and stop trying to make others think and act as we do.

- Consider what the global dominance ideology looks like from the other side of the fence. So long as U.S. diplomatic and military policy is based on a neocon mindset (by whatever label), others such as some militant Muslims will view the United States and their allies as greedy, brutal countries bent on world domination who are willing to crush anyone and anything in their path. Therefore, in their view the Western imperialist powers should be harassed and attacked whenever and however possible. Not good.

- Repudiate and abandon policies at the World Bank and other such institutions that allow secret decisions and agreements by unelected agents of our government and others. Establish new international laws or treaties that cannot overrule national laws meant to protect peoples and ecosystems. Or shut down the Bank.

- Change international economic institutions so that they work toward fair wages and working conditions all around the world. Strengthen economies of all nations rather than enriching and empowering some at the expense of others.

- Acknowledge that diplomacy is a million times cheaper than war, and return to once again regarding war and covert activities against other governments, as a last, worst resort.

*   *   *

18. Eisenhower's Nightmare: From Defending Our Shores To Endless War?

In few ways has the United States moved farther from the thinking and sentiments of our founding fathers than in regard to war. This magical transformation in our national policies has resulted in part from the semantic smokescreen that now calls all wars and military activities "defense," even when they are nothing of the sort. Here is what our founders said:

"The Congress shall have Power to lay and collect Taxes . . . To raise and support Armies, but no Appropriation of Money to that Use shall be for a longer Term than Two Years."
Article I, Section 8, the United States Constitution

Benjamin Franklin and **George Washington** made conflicting statements about war. On one hand Franklin said, "All wars are follies, very expensive and very mischievous ones. . . Do good to your friends to keep them, to your enemies to win them." But he also declared, "Even peace may be purchased at too high a price." And Washington said,

"My first wish is to see this plague of mankind, war, banished from the Earth." *George Washington*

> **Comment:** Despite this remark, Washington was America's commanding general during the Revolutionary War. Did Washington and Franklin hold internally contradictory attitudes? It appears not, but rather that their apparently opposite statements and actions referred to dramatically different historical circumstances. The British navy and army constituted a brutal imperial power that systematically employed extreme violence. That violence provoked the American Revolution.

"No man was a warmer wisher for reconciliation than myself, before the fatal nineteenth of April 1775, but the moment the event of that day was made known, I rejected the hardened, sullen tempered Pharaoh of England for ever; and disdain the wretch, that with the pretended title of FATHER OF HIS PEOPLE, can unfeelingly hear of their slaughter, and composedly sleep with their blood upon his soul. . . . The laying a Country desolate with Fire and Sword, declaring War against the natural rights of all Mankind, and extirpating the Defenders thereof from the Face of the Earth, is the Concern of every Man to whom Nature hath given the Power of feeling; of which Class, regardless of Party Censure, is the AUTHOR. . . I make the sufferers case my own, and I protest, that were I driven from house and home, my property destroyed, and my circumstances ruined, that as a man, sensible of injuries, I could never relish the doctrine of reconciliation, or consider myself bound thereby." **Thomas Paine**

Continuing this theme, **Paine** also wrote, "But if you say, you can still pass the violations over, then I ask, hath your house been burnt? Hath your property been destroyed before your face? Are your wife and children destitute of a bed to lie on, or bread to live on? Have you lost a parent or a child by their hands, and yourself the ruined and wretched survivor? If you have not, then are you not a judge of those who have. But if you have, and can still shake hands with the murderers, then are you unworthy the name of husband, father, friend or lover, and whatever may be your rank or title in life, you have the heart of a coward, and the spirit of a sycophant."

Comment: It appears to me that more than a few Iraqis could justifiably quote this very passage in relation to the American bombing and invasion of their country. In both the early American case and the Iraqi case, the local inhabitants were defending themselves against a foreign invading power. To be sure, the prophet Muhammad made no statement that would justify killing innocent civilians. On the other hand, he did say, much as Thomas Paine suggested in our own case, that Muslims are duty bound to protect their home and country. For us to ignore that reality is both rash and reckless.

"If we desire to avoid insult, we must be able to repel it; if we desire to secure peace, one of the most powerful instruments of our rising prosperity, it must be known, that we are at all times ready for War." **George Washington**

Comment: We cannot reasonably expect people in other countries to feel differently than Paine described when we are the ones who invade or threaten them. Paine advocated creating an American navy to protect the young American nation against the British. Patriots in every country are likely to feel similarly when the United States takes on a role that resembles that of England toward the American colonies.

"In point of safety, ought we to be without a fleet? We are not the little people now which we were sixty years ago; at that time we might have trusted our property in the streets, or fields rather, and slept securely without locks or bolts to our doors and windows. The case is now altered, and our methods of defence ought to improve with our increase of property. A common pirate, twelve months ago, might have come up the Delaware, and laid the city of Philadelphia under contribution for what sum he pleased; and the same might have happened to other places. . . If America had only a twentieth part of the naval force of Britain, she would be by far an over-match for her; because, as we neither have, nor claim any foreign dominion, our whole force would be employed on our own coast, where we should, in the long run, have two to one the advantage of those who had three or four thousand miles to sail over before they could attack us, and the same distance to return in order to refit and recruit. To unite the sinews of commerce and defense is sound policy; for when our strength and our riches play into each other's hand, we need fear no external enemy." **Thomas Paine**

Comment: Except in the matter of genuinely defending our own nation, the founders of our country resolutely opposed war. Today's American left and right and center agree that it is only sensible to defend our borders and people against foreign armies that try to invade our country. (As it happens, due to the protection of two oceans that is not a frequent event.) Note also that Paine unequivocally says, "because, as we neither have, nor claim any foreign dominion, our whole force would be employed on our own coast." Never did he advocate invading another country. Here right wing politicians are divided. Some favor spending even more on arms and armies than we do today, while a vocal minority declares that our nation has no business conducting war in and against other nations. Lately I have seen more and more young people with artificial arms and legs. Our government has sacrificed young peoples lives and limbs in military adventures. On this issue, the radical wrong's minority is right.

"Over grown military establishments are under any form of government inauspicious to liberty, and are to be regarded as particularly hostile to republican liberty." **George Washington**

"That there are men in all countries who get their living by war, and by keeping up the quarrels of Nations is as shocking as it is true." **Thomas Paine.** And Paine also wryly noted that, "To establish any mode to abolish war, however advantageous it might be to Nations, would be to take from such Government the most lucrative of its branches."

"Great is the guilt of an unnecessary war." *John Adams*

"Never was so much false arithmetic employed on any subject, as that which has been employed to persuade nations that it is in their interest to go to war. Were the money which it has cost to gain, at the close of a long war, a little town, or a little territory, the right to cut wood here, or to catch fish here, expended improving what they already possess, in making roads, opening rivers, building ports, improving the arts, and finding employment for their idle poor, it would render them much stronger, much wealthier and happier. This I hope will be our wisdom. . . . Believing that the happiness of mankind is best promoted by the useful pursuits of peace, that on these alone a stable prosperity can be founded, that the evils of war are great in their endurance, and have a long reckoning for ages to come, I have used my best endeavors to keep our country uncommitted in the troubles which . . . assail us on every side. . . . The care of human life and happiness, and not their destruction, is the first and only legitimate object of good government."
Thomas Jefferson

Jefferson also remarked, "Breaking men to military discipline, is breaking their spirits to principles of passive obedience." **Thomas Jefferson**

"When the sword is once drawn, the passions of men observe no bounds of moderation."
Alexander Hamilton (who died in a duel with Aaron Burr).

"Of all the enemies of public liberty, war is perhaps the most to be dreaded, because . . . the means of defense against foreign danger historically have become the instruments of tyranny at home." *James Madison*

"No nation could preserve its freedom in the midst of continual warfare. . . War is the parent of armies; from these proceed debts and taxes [which are] known instruments for bringing the many under the domination of the few." **James Madison**

ALEXIS DE TOCQUEVILLE

"All those who seek to destroy the liberties of a democratic nation ought to know that war is the surest and shortest means to accomplish it. . . No protracted war can fail to endanger the freedom of a democratic country." **Alexis de Tocqueville**

"War will disappear only when men shall take no part whatever in violence and shall be ready to suffer every persecution that their abstention will bring them. It is the only way to abolish war." **Anatole France**

"I spent 33 years and four months in active military service and during that period I spent most of my time as a high class muscle man for Big Business, for Wall Street and the bankers. In short, I was a racketeer, a gangster for capitalism. I helped make Mexico. . . safe for American oil interests in 1914. I helped make Haiti and Cuba a decent place for the National City Bank boys to collect revenues in. I helped in the raping of half a dozen Central American republics for the benefit of Wall Street. I helped purify Nicaragua for the International Banking House of Brown Brothers in 1902-1912. I brought light to the Dominican Republic for the American sugar interests in 1916. I helped make Honduras right for the American fruit companies in 1903. In China in 1927 I helped see to it that Standard Oil went on its way unmolested. . . . I might have given Al Capone a few hints. The best he could do was to operate his racket in three districts. I operated on three continents." **Marine Corps Major General Smedley Butler**, the most decorated Marine in U.S. history.

"War is just a racket. A racket is . . . something that is not what it seems to the majority of people. Only a small inside group know what it is about. It is conducted for the benefit of the very few at the expense of the masses."
Marine Corps Major General Smedley Butler

GENERAL SMEDLEY BUTLER

Butler also noted that, "At least 21,000 new millionaires and billionaires were made in the United States during [World War I]. That many admitted their blood gains in their income tax returns. How many other war millionaires falsified their tax returns no one knows. . . .The general public shoulders the bill. . . . Newly placed gravestones. Mangled bodies. Shattered minds. Broken hearts and homes. . . . Depression and all its attendant miseries. Back-breaking taxation for generations and generations. . . . It pays high dividends. . . The sky is the limit. . . . Uncle Sam has the money. Let's get it. . .. Of course, it isn't put that crudely in war time. It is dressed into speeches about patriotism, love of country, and 'we must all put our shoulders to the wheel.' **Smedley Butler**

During World War II, Republican Presidential candidate **Wendell Willkie said, "**I have noticed, with much distress, the excessive wartime activity of the investigating bureaus of Congress and the administration, with their impertinent and indecent searching out of the private lives and the past political beliefs of individuals." (Neither party has a monopoly on this kind of malicious mischief.)

At least one remark from India's great nonviolent liberator **Mohandas Gandhi** is in order: "What difference does it make to the dead, the orphans, and thehomeless, whether the mad destruction is wrought under the name of totalitarianism or the holy name of liberty or democracy?"

"We seek peace, knowing that peace is the climate of freedom." President **Dwight D. Eisenhower,** who served as Supreme Commander of Allied Forces in Europe during World War II.

DWIGHT D. EISENHOWER

"I like to believe that people in the long run are going to do more to promote peace than our governments. I think that people want peace so much that one of these days governments had better get out of the way and let them have it." *Dwight D. Eisenhower*

There is also the matter of when and how war can be initiated. "The constitution vests the power of declaring war in Congress; therefore *no offensive expedition of importance* (my italics) can be undertaken until after they shall have deliberated upon the subject and authorized such a measure." **George Washington**

"War should only be declared by the authority of the people, whose toils and treasures are to support its burdens, instead of the government which is to reap its fruits. . . . The executive has no right, in any case, to decide the question, whether there is or is not cause for declaring war." **James Madison,** primary author of the Constitution.

"Allow the President to invade a neighboring nation whenever he shall deem it necessary to repel an invasion, and you allow him to do so whenever he may choose to. . . If to-day he should choose to say he thinks it necessary to invade Canada to prevent the British from invading us, how could you stop him? . . He will say to you, "Be silent: I see it, if you don't. . . . The provision of the Constitution giving the war making power to Congress was dictated, as I understand it, by the following reasons: Kings had always been involving and impoverishing their people in wars, pretending generally, if not always, that the good of the people was the object. . . Our [constitutional] convention . . .resolved to so frame the Constitution that no one man should hold the power of bringing this oppression upon us." **Abraham Lincoln**

Comment: I grew up on and around Army posts and Air Force bases. My parents were both civilian employees of the military. My father, a decorated Army Ranger who spied behind German lines during World War II, was lucky to come home at all. He wanted to become an officer but got shot up too badly in the war. In college I enlisted in Air Force ROTC, but when we took a test that measured how accurately we could drop bombs on photographs of targets—well, that was not my cup of tea and I resigned. I had wanted to be a pilot but my eyesight was too poor. The most I managed was to wear the uniform and a chrome plated helmet and carry the American flag in the color guard at the head of parades and in drill team competitions. Later I served in the Peace Corps.

Eisenhower was President during my later childhood and teens. He had spent most of his adult life studying war, participating in it, directing it, and seeking to prevent it. In his presentation to the American Society of Newspaper editors on April 16, 1953, he spoke of the possibility of a future world permanently at war or on the edge of war: "humanity hanging from a cross of iron." His grim prophecy has come to pass. The United States now has a permanent wartime economy.

In order to invade other countries, some presidents have sidestepped the Constitution by making such statements as "This is not a war, but just a 'police action', so no Congressional permission is necessary.'" This violates the intent of the Constitution. In our country policemen don't use tanks and artillery, lay land mines, or drop bombs. In response to the U.S. invasion of Vietnam, in 1973 Congress passed the War Powers Resolution, which defines just three cases in which the president can use force: "(1) a declaration of war, (2) specific statutory authorization, or (3) a national emergency created by attack upon the United States, its territories or possessions, or its armed forces." The resolution has been widely ignored. So has the Constitutional limit of two years for "appropriations of monies to raise and support armies." George W. Bush did obtain a congressional declaration of War for Iraq War II, but did it with lies and deception that horrified even my loyally Republican father-in-law when the truth came to light.

In **War is a Racket**, General Smedley Butler lists the sky-high profits of major companies involved in World War I before the war and during the war. A similar accounting could be made for every war since. Between 2001 and 2010 – the Iraq and Afghanistan war years, U.S. military spending rose by **83%**. Profits at the five biggest U.S. defense contractors grew from $6.7 billion to $24.8 billion. Those companies' profits grew twice as fast as their income, and stock prices of the Daddy Warbucks companies in the S&P 500 jumped 67% while those of most other industries were flat or up just a few points. The price of those huge profits for the few is incredible and avoidable suffering for others.

During the Carter Administration and again during the Clinton Administration military spending declined. (In the former case, due to Pentagon politics some of the cuts were not the wisest. Some forces lacked the equipment, supplies, or spare parts they needed. A properly equipped smaller force is better than a poorly equipped larger one.) Under Reagan and G.W.H. Bush the arms budget jumped dramatically, and under G.W. Bush it did so again.

You can look online at pages that list companies with U.S. military contracts (which includes some foreign companies in Canada and elsewhere) from A to Z. By my count, the "A"s alone come to 116 companies. That leaves "B" through "Z." You can count them if you like. See: (http://www.militaryindustrialcomplex.com/companies.asp).

Some are arms manufacturers; others are communication companies, military clothing suppliers, and a multitude of other kinds of companies. Moreover, the U.S. now sells more guns and bombs, missiles and warplanes than all other nations combined. If you look again at the Star Wars movies, perhaps you will notice how much some of today's military gear and police riot gear resemble Darth Vader.

"Wait a minute," you might say. "A lot of jobs will be lost when the U.S. starts seriously cutting its military budget" (which we have to do if we wish to avoid becoming a bankrupt nation). Indeed. That's why careful planning of military budget reductions is needed. Employment can be shifted to other areas like protecting the environment where we get a lot more job creation bang for the buck.

Butler points out that when young people were put into the ranks "they were remolded; they were made over; they were made to . . . regard murder as the order of the day. . . . Through mass psychology, they were entirely changed. We used them for a couple of years and trained them to think nothing at all of killing or being killed. Then, suddenly, we discharged them and told them [that] this time they had to do their own readjustment." There was no training program to prepare them for re-entry into living and working in peaceful society. Today, still, the rate of suicides and mental illness is far greater among ex-soldiers than among other people. The soldier pays the largest part of the bill for war.

The tragic reality is that whether we are talking about an American, an Afghani, or an Iraqi, every person killed or maimed in war is someone's father or mother, husband or wife, sister or brother, daughter or son. The loss, pain and grief of some unknown family in a far-off land is no less than your loss and pain and grief would be if it were a member of your own family.

"I have seen war on land and sea. I have seen blood running from the wounded. I have seen men coughing out their gassed lungs. I have seen the dead in the mud. I have seen cities destroyed. I have seen 200 limping, exhausted men come out of line—the survivors of a regiment off 1,000 that went forward 48 hours before. I have seen children starving. I have seen the agony of mothers and wives. I hate war." **Franklin D. Roosevelt,** president of the United States during World War II

"The work, my friend, is peace. More than an end of this war – an end to the beginnings of all wars." Undelivered address by **Franklin D. Roosevelt,** scheduled to be given the day after he died.

"We are fighting for peace, and for the welfare of mankind. We are not fighting for conquest. There is not one piece of territory or one thing of a monetary nature that we want out of this war. We want peace and prosperity for the world as a whole." **Harry Truman,** in Berlin at the end of World War II.

Comment: Whether we send soldiers to invade another nation or have some kid on an air base in Nevada guiding a cruise missile to its target in the Middle East makes no difference to those who lose arms or legs or family members in the war. A recent *Time* magazine article featured an Iraqi whose arms had been blown off and his entire family killed when his home was hit by some kind of bomb or missile intended for a target three miles away. Asked about casualties among the Iraqi people, former head of the U.S. Central Command, General Tommy Franks replied, "We don't do Iraqi body counts." I will repeat one of Eisenhower's oft-quoted lines:

"Every gun that is made, every warship launched, every rocket fired, signifies in the final sense a theft from those who hunger and are not fed, those who are cold and are not clothed. I hate war as only a soldier who has lived it can, only as one who has seen its brutality, its futility, its stupidity.

When people speak to you about a preventive war, you tell them to go and fight it. . . War settles nothing. . . Though force can protect in emergency, only justice, fairness, consideration and cooperation can finally lead men to the dawn of eternal peace. . . *The problem in defense is how far you can go without destroying from within what you are trying to defend from without."* (my italics) **Dwight D. Eisenhower**

"This conjunction of an immense military establishment and a large arms industry," **Eisenhower continued**, is new in the American experience. The total influence. . . is felt in every city, every Statehouse, every office of the Federal government. . . We must not fail to comprehend its grave implications. Our toil, resources, and livelihood are all involved; so is the very structure of our society."

OMAR BRADLEY

"Man is stumbling blindly through a spiritual darkness while toying with the precarious secrets of life and death. The world has achieved brilliance without wisdom, power without conscience. Ours is a world of nuclear giants and ethical infants. We know more about war that we know about peace, more about killing that we know about living." Five-star General and Chairman of the Joint Chiefs of Staff **Omar Bradley**

Bradley also remarked, "Wars can be prevented just as surely as they can be provoked, and we who fail to prevent them, must share the guilt for the dead. . . . Armed forces can wage wars but they cannot make peace. For there is a wide chasm between war and peace—a chasm that can only be bridged by good will, discussion, compromise, and agreement. [But] disillusionment can come from expecting too much, too easily, too soon. In our impatience we must never forget that fundamental differences have divided this world; they allow no swift, no cheap, no easy solutions. While as a prudent people we must prepare ourselves to encounter what we may be unable to prevent, we nevertheless must never surrender ourselves to the certainty of that encounter. For if we say there is no good in arguing with what must inevitably come, then we shall be left with no choice but to create a garrison state and empty our wealth into arms. The burden of long-term total preparedness for some indefinite but inevitable war could not help but crush the freedom we prize."

"Each generation should be made to bear the burden of its own wars, instead of carrying them on, at the expense of other generations." **James Madison**

Will Rogers said succinctly, "I have a scheme for stopping war. It's this - no nation is allowed to enter a war till they have paid for the last one."

James Madison and Will Rogers were actually echoing the far more restrictive provision of the Constitution, quoted at the beginning of this section, which has seldom been observed in practice.

"War involves in its progress such a train of unforeseen circumstances that no human wisdom can calculate the end; it has but one thing certain, and that is to increase taxes." *Thomas Paine*

Regarding military procurement, "Why does the Air Force need expensive new bombers? Have the people we've been bombing over the years been complaining?" **George Wallace**

"Whenever you drop bombs, you're going to hit civilians." **Barry Goldwater**

"Fighting for peace is like screwing for virginity." **George Carlin**

"When I lost my rifle, the Army charged me 85 dollars. That is why in the Navy the Captain goes down with the ship." **Dick Gregory**

"My hope is that gays will be running the world, because then there would be no war. Just a greater emphasis on military apparel." **Roseanne Barr**

"It is our duty as Americans to use the military to go into the world and make the world like us." **George W. Bush**

"This war had been advanced on lie upon lie. Iraq was not responsible for 9/11. Iraq was not responsible for any role al-Qaeda may have had in 9/11. Iraq . . . did not try to acquire nuclear weapons technology fom Niger. This war is built on falsehood." Congressman **Dennis Kucinich**

Jesse Ventura, a former Navy SEAL, said, "War isn't civilized. War is failure. It's the ultimate result of a breakdown in public policy." Of Iraq War II, he wrote, "Bush is responsible for the deaths of hundreds of thousands of people—our troops and Iraqis. . . We were not in any imminent danger and the Bush administration knew it, yet did everything to make us think we were, all based upon lies. Why is it that they were allowed to get away with it? Where is the spine of our country today?"

Congressman Ron Paul says, "Another term for preventive war is aggressive war - starting wars because someday somebody might do something to us. That is not part of the American tradition. . . . Setting a good example is a far better way to spread ideals than through force of arms." Continuing on, Paul says, War is never economically beneficial except for those in position to profit from war expenditures. . . .The most important element of a free society, where individual rights are held in the highest esteem, is the rejection of the initiation of violence."

If you don't find the comments above persuasive, listen to this one by **Hermann Goering**, Hitler's close confidante, head of the *Luftwaffe,* and most senior military commander: "Why of course the people don't want war. Why should some poor slob on a farm want to risk his life in a war when the best he can get out of it is to come back to the farm in one piece? Naturally the common people don't want war. . . It is the leaders of the country who determine the policy and it is always a simple matter to drag the people along, whether it is a democracy or a fascist dictatorship or a Parliament or a Communist dictatorship. . . . The people can always be brought to the bidding of the leaders. That is easy. All you have to do is tell them they are being attacked and denounce the pacifists for lack of patriotism and exposing the country to danger. It works the same in any country." Apparently, judging by the last half century, it works in ours.

"Every one of my successors has been in gratuitous wars. I think we could have resolved most of those conflicts in a peaceful way. And we share very little of our wealth with other people. These are a violation of the teachings of the Prince of Peace." **Jimmy Carter**, a former naval officer who kept the United States out of war during his administration.

"We as a nation must undergo a radical revolution of values. We spend far too much of our national budget establishing military bases around the world rather than bases of genuine concern and understanding." *Martin Luther King*

Comment: Despite the present budget crisis, and the huge contribution that our war and other military expenses make to the deficit, arms industry spokesmen talk in doomsday terms about the effects of cutting the U.S. military budget. What's the reality?

In 2010 U.S. military spending was somewhere between 43% and more than half of the world's total, depending on whether you count only what is in published budgets or supplemental and secret spending as well. For instance, "budget requests for U.S. military spending do not include combat figures, which are supplemental requests that Congress approves separately. The budget for nuclear weapons falls under the Department of Energy." And a large share of CIA spending is hidden in budget categories that keep everyone clueless about how much it is. Veterans' health care may also be counted under other departments. The Center for Defense Information concludes, "Few [military spending] numbers will be accurate; many will be incomplete, some will be both. Worse, few of us will be able to tell what numbers are too high, which are too low, and which are so riddled with gimmicks to make them lose real meaning."

The Friends Committee on National Legislation calculates that, all military costs considered, 39% of U.S. taxes go to pay for current military spending and past, present and future wars. Even more amazing, the so-called "national defense" spending category is typically more than half of the discretionary budget—that is, the money that the Presidential Administration and Congress have direct control over (in contrast to mandatory spending like interest on the debt, Social Security, and so on.) A substantial share of that military money is mislabeled "defense." It's really "spending on foreign wars."

All this is from a nation that enjoys the geographical and geopolitical security of facing no military threat along our own borders. By one accounting, next in spending after the U.S. were China (7.3 % of world military spending), the U.K. (3.7%), France (3.6%), and Russia (3.6%). India is ramping up its spending to float a blue-water navy to counter China's naval influence in the Indian Ocean.

Why do we spend so much of our tax money on the armed forces? According to General Smedley Butler, it is to provide enormous profits for the arms manufacturers, who of course make major campaign contributions to legislators who give them the contracts to build the weapons. There is also another reason. The craving for security, which includes food and water, adequate clothing and shelter, good health, and protection from attack by others, is the most fundamental human motive. When our government or a war industry company brandishes a gun aloft and says, "They're gonna get you," we all too easily give in to whatever policies and spending that we're told are needed to keep *them* from getting us—like giving up basic constitutional freedoms, as in the "Patriot Act." Ongoing U.S. policy of attempted global domination, in complete violation of the intentions of our nation's founders, provokes "blowback" in the form of terrorist attacks. Beyond that highly negative outcome of the "neocon" ideology, the U.S. just cannot afford to continue its self-appointed role as, in our eyes, the world's policeman, and in the eyes of many others, an imperial bully. These days the government carries a tin beggar's cup to China and to its own Social Security Trust Fund to borrow more deficit-financed funds in order to maintain our 737 military bases around the world. For more information, see,

<visualeconomics.creditloan.com/**military-spending-worldwide**/> or http://en.wikipedia.org/wiki/List_of_countries_by_military_expenditures)

Diplomats can sit around in grand councils and bray like hounds until they fall on the floor from hyperventilation and it will not affect the basic problem that General Butler identified. He maintained **that the only way to prevent war is to take the profits out of it.** To do this, he suggested that starting one month before the war, "Let the officers and the directors and the high-powered executives of our armament factories. . . as well as the bankers and the speculators be conscripted – to get . . . a total monthly income not to exceed that paid to the soldiers in the trenches. . . They aren't running any risk of being killed or of having their bodies mangled or their minds shattered. . . Give capital and industry and labor thirty days to think it over and . . . there will be no war."

Butler also suggested that government be prohibited from going to war without a limited election, in which only young people who have been found acceptable for induction into the armed forces would be allowed to vote. Short of that, I suggest that at the very least, congress be required to vote on any military action, and that to be eligible to vote, every congressperson must either agree to be inducted into the armed forces or supply a member of his or her family or a close relative to be inducted.

What about the Afghan war? **Lt. Colonel Daniel Davis,** who spent two tours of duty in Iraq and two in Afghanistan, wrote in January 2012, "Senior ranking US military leaders so distorted the truth when communicating with the US Congress and American people in regards to conditions on the ground in Afghanistan that the truth has become unrecognizable. This deception has damaged America's credibility among both our allies and enemies, severely limiting our ability to reach a political solution. . . . It has likely cost American taxpayers hundreds of billions of dollars Congress might not otherwise have appropriated . . . The single greatest penalty our Nation has suffered, however, has been that we have lost the blood, limbs and lives of tens of thousands of American Service Members with little to no gain to our country as a consequence of this deception."

Why are we still in Afghanistan?" The initial attacks were to disable Al Quaeda and capture Osama Bin Ladin. That has been done. **Joe Klein** writes in *Time,* "We kicked out the Taliban regime that protected al-Quaeda. We successfully used special operations and drone attacks to destroy most of the al-Quaeda hierarchy and infrastructure, including Osama Bin Ladin." The Taliban the U.S. is fighting now, according to Klein, have nothing to do with al-Quaeda, who were Saudi Arabians whom they consider foreign invaders.

Comment: I abhor the Taliban's reported attitude toward women. I have seen no evidence, however, that the U.S. allies in the northern provinces are better in that regard.

We ought to remember history. No one has ever beaten the Afghanis on their own ground. They have beaten back everyone who has tried, including the Soviet Army, which was based far closer to Afghanistan, with far shorter supply routes Every day there is an enormous flow of cash from the U.S. treasury into Afghanistan, and U.S. soldiers are coming back in coffins or without arms, legs, or eyes. So why are we there? I see three reasons.

First, as General Butler noted, the war ensures brisk business and high profits for the U.S. war industry, so congresspersons with such companies in their districts vote your tax money to continue it.

Second, writes Lt. Colonel Daniel Davis, "According to Bob Woodward's 2010 book *Obama's Wars,* there were five powerful advocates for sending another large contingent of troops into Afghanistan: Chairman of the Joint Chiefs of Staff Admiral Michael Mullen, Secretary of Defense Robert Gates, Secretary of State Hillary Clinton, General Stanley McChrystal and Iraq war hero General David Petraeus. How could the President, barely a year into his first term and with no independent military experience, go against this formidable fivesome?

. . . Obama's top National Security Council advisor, Lieutenant General Douglas Lute, said, "Mr. President, you don't have to do this." Lute ran down the list of risks, but the tally was five to one. (Sociologist C. Wright Mills pointed out in the mid-twentieth century that the U.S. military establishment has now become one of the principal power centers in the American oligarchy) General Petraeus declared several years ago, "Every army of liberation has a half-life after which it turns into an army of occupation." We are far past that point in Afghanistan.

According to Davis, as more U.S. troops poured into Afghanistan, more U.S. soldiers were killed and wounded, and more Afghanis were killed and wounded. The casualties directly tracked the size of the U.S. force. It appears that General Lute was right.

Third, there is The Great Game," an ancient contest among Western and Eastern powers for control of the resource-rich Central Asian countries to the north of Afghanistan and their fuel and mineral reserves. But nobody mentions that. Given the strategic disadvantage of U.S. supply lines that stretch around the world, it seems more sensible to get at those resources through commerce than through warfare. Let the corporations that want those resources pay to get them, not U.S. taxpayers and military families. Joe Klein concludes, "For the life of me, I can't see the rationale for the loss of even one more American life or limb there."

That war is not a partisan issue. Most Republicans except Ron Paul, support it, while many Democrats oppose it. In a March 2012 interview with Jay Leno, Republican Mitt Romney criticized President Obama for not sending *more* troops in. And Romney says he thinks the U.S. should *increase* the size of our military establishment (which would also increase its already astronomical costs), while at the same time reducing the country's total spending. Who would be the losers? You figure it out.

SOLUTIONS

- Base our national defense policies from this time onward on the thoughts and attitudes of Paine, Washington, Jefferson, Madison, Lincoln, Eisenhower, Butler, and Bradley.

- Enlist all nations in continuing to reduce the world's still-huge stockpile of nuclear weapons.

- Immediately stop producing and using depleted uranium warheads, which on explosion create radioactive dust that cause birth defects and major health problems, for our own troops while at war and for a country's people for decades or even centuries. (Pictures of Iraqi babies born dead and deformed are not featured in U.S. media, but the exist and are sobering.)

- Work vigorously with other nations to eliminate land mines and cluster bombs from all countries' military arsenals, since they pose a hazard for many decades after a conflict ends. (Every week people still get blown up by old land mines in Vietnam.)

- Return the Department of Defense to the task of defending our country, and end its present mission as a Department of War to further corporate interests.

- Institute a systematic plan to reduce the size and scope of the armed forces, to reduce military spending to a level the nation can reasonably afford. (Reduce force levels, while maintaining excellent equipment and preparedness of the forces that remain.)

- Limit the National Guard and the Coast Guard to protecting our nation and prohibit their deployment in foreign wars. Most men and women in the National Guard did not sign up to invade and occupy other countries.

- Begin transforming much of the mission of the military-industrial complex into one of conserving and restoring the ecosystems we depend on for survival.

* * *

19. Two Gentleman Farmers
and the Natural Environment

For some Radical Wrongers, getting all the resources we can as fast as we can is the only important thing. Concern about taking care of the natural environment is seen as a bunch of wimpy hooey. "Drill baby, drill, and never look back" is the mantra. If that's not the true attitude of most Radical Wrongers, it's certainly what it sounds and looks like. It was encouraged by the Reagan administration's "supply side" mentality, which meant, "Forget about conservation and doing more with less—just increase the rate at which we extract resources." That outlook may be overrepresented in the media, however, because of all the money the big oil and coal and mineral interests spend to promote it.

In some circles it is the custom to use the Bible to justify whatever one wishes to do. Those who stand to gain from treating nature carelessly often cite these lines: "Be fruitful, and multiply, and replenish the earth, and subdue it: and have dominion over the fish of the sea, and over the fowl of the air, and over every living thing that moveth upon the earth." (Genesis. 1:28) In those days, "subduing the earth" to bring forth crops meant something quite different than it means with today's giant machines.

At this point we have more than carried out the ancient instructions. We *have* filled the earth and subdued it. We rule over other creatures with such a heavy hand that our efforts sometimes look like a scorched-earth war against nature. The Old Testament, however, did not instruct us to *kill* the fish, the birds, the wild beasts, and the crawling things.

Genesis, Chapter 2, Verse 15, says, 'The Lord God took man and put him in the Garden to till it and to keep it.' 'Till' means to help make it fruitful and productive. 'Keep,' in Hebrew, means to guard and protect, as in "The watchman keeps the city.' As I read the Old Testament, the purpose of human creation is to exercise our dominion in such a way that nature stays healthy," says **Reverend Michael Moore** of the United Church of Christ.

George Washington and Thomas Jefferson understood that. Neither the imperial English who ravaged American forests to build Britain's fleet nor most of the revolutionaries who rebelled against British rule and founded the United States said much environmental politics. They were not concerned, for the land was vast and unspoiled. Washington and Jefferson, however, were both avid farmers, acutely sensitive to the turning of the seasons and the condition of the land. Washington's notebooks are full of jottings about agriculture. Early on he planted a tobacco monoculture, but soon saw that it impoverished the soil and then started sowing a wide variety of crops. He planted several varieties of wheat that ripened throughout the year to keep his mill operating year round, and turned his flax crop into homespun textiles to avoid the high prices of English cloth. Jefferson was always experimenting with different cultivars, he developed new agricultural machinery, and he and Washington corresponded often about good farming practices and caring for the land. But most European settlers lacked the sensitivity to nature displayed by Jefferson and Washington. For twenty thousand years the Native American peoples had made a right relationship to the land the central element of their culture, but when the Europeans came, the land, the game, and the trees seemed "free" for the taking, and most settlers saw no need to care for them. Heedless exploitation, pollution, and ugliness are the result. Our grandchildren will reap the bitter harvest of our ancestors' and our own neglect.

"All things are parts of one single system, which is called Nature; the individual life is good when it is in harmony with nature." **Zeno of Citium,** founder of the Greco-Roman Stoic school of philosophy.

"The moral duty of man consists of imitating the moral goodness and beneficence of God, manifested in the creation, toward all His creatures." **Thomas Paine**

"When the well's dry, we know the worth of water." **Benjamin Franklin**

"I consider [agriculture] to be the proper source of American wealth and happiness." **George Washington**

"There is not a spring of grass that shoots up uninteresting to me. . . .The greatest service which can be rendered in any country is to add a useful plant to its culture." Also, "We must use a great deal of economy in our wood, never cutting down new, where we can make the old do." **Thomas Jefferson**

Of people's relationship to the land, **Jefferson** also wrote, "I am conscious that an equal division of property is impracticable. But the consequences of this enormous inequality producing so much misery to the bulk of mankind, legislators cannot invent too many devices for subdividing property. . . . The earth is given as a common stock for man to labour and live on . . . . It is not too soon to provide by every possible means that as few as possible shall be without a little portion of land. The small land holders are the most precious part of a state."

"He who knows what sweets and virtues are in the ground, the waters, the plants, the heavens, and how to come at these enchantments, is the rich and royal man." **Ralph Waldo Emerson**

"What's the use of a fine house if you haven't got a tolerable planet to put it on?" **Henry David Thoreau**

"I am in favor of animal rights as well as human rights. That is the way of a whole human being." **Abraham Lincoln**

Comment: Lincoln established Yosemite Valley as a public trust, which created a precedent for the national parks system, and he established the Department of Agriculture and the National Academy of Sciences.

"Optimism is a good characteristic, but if carried to an excess, it becomes foolishness. We are prone to speak of the resources of this country as inexhaustible; this is not so." **Theodore Roosevelt**

"There can be no greater issue than that of conservation in this country. . . Unless we solve that problem it will avail us little to solve all others."
Theodore Roosevelt

"The conservation of natural resources is the fundamental problem. . . . We of an older generation can get along with what we have, though with growing hardship; but in your full manhood and womanhood you will want what nature once so bountifully supplied and man so thoughtlessly destroyed; and because of that want you will reproach us, not for what we have used, but for what we have wasted. . . So any nation which in its youth lives only for the day, reaps without sowing, and consumes without husbanding, must expect the penalty of the prodigal son whose labor could with difficulty find him the bare means of life." **Theodore Roosevelt**

At greater length, he said, "To waste, to destroy our natural resources, to skin and exhaust the land instead of using it so as to increase its usefulness, will result in undermining in the days of our children the very prosperity which we thought by right to hand down to them amplified and developed. . . I hate a man who skins the land. . . . Defenders of the short-sighted men who in their greed and selfishness will, if permitted, rob our country of half its charm by their reckless extermination of all useful and beautiful wild things sometimes seek to champion them by saying the 'the game belongs to the people.' So it does; and not merely to the people now alive, but to the unborn people. The 'greatest good for the greatest number' applies to the number within the womb of time, compared to which those now alive form but an insignificant fraction. Our duty to the whole, including the unborn generations, bids us restrain an unprincipled present-day minority from wasting the heritage of these unborn generations. The movement for the conservation of wild life and the larger movement for the conservation of all our natural resources are essentially democratic in spirit, purpose, and method." **Theodore Roosevelt**

Comment: Together with John Muir, Teddy Roosevelt laid the foundations for the national parks and national forests systems, ideas that have since spread around the world. And his nephew FDR put a vast army of people to work in the Civilian Conservation Corps and other agencies planting trees, battling soil erosion to end the dust bowl, and improving parks and trails. He created the Soil Conservation Service and the Federal Aid in Wildlife Restoration Act.

Today thinking people are starting to realize, as they have not done since before Europeans invaded America, that we depend on the entire living fabric of the ecosphere and its uncounted local ecosystems. As we degrade ecosystems, we are killing the ultimate source of our survival.

"A nation that destroys its soils destroys itself. Forests are the lungs of our land, purifying the air and giving fresh strength to our people." **Franklin D. Roosevelt**

"The oldest task in human history: to live on a piece of land without spoiling it. . . . A land ethic . . . reflects the existence of an ecological conscience, and this in turn reflects a conviction of individual responsibility for the health of the land. Health is the capacity of the land for self-renewal. Conservation is our effort to understand and preserve this capacity." Forester and ecologist **Aldo Leopold**

"The supreme reality of our time is the vulnerability of our planet." **John F. Kennedy,** whose work to establish a national wilderness preservation system prepared the way for Lyndon Johnson to sign the bill that actually did so.

RACHEL CARSON

""To stand at the edge of the sea, to sense the ebb and flow of the tides, to feel the breath of a mist moving over a great salt marsh, to watch the flight of shore birds that have swept up and down the surf lines of the continents for untold thousands of year, to see the running of the old eels and the young shad to the sea, is to have knowledge of things that are as nearly eternal as any earthly life can be." **Rachel Carson**

"For the first time in the history of the world, every human being is now subjected to contact with dangerous chemicals, from the moment of conception until death." **Rachel Carson**

"Water and air, the two essential fluids on which all life depends, have become global garbage cans." **Jacques-Yves Costeau**, underwater pioneer.

"A thing is right when it tends to preserve the integrity, stability, and beauty of the biotic community. It is wrong when it tends otherwise." *Aldo Leopold*

"A finite world can support only a finite population; therefore, population growth must eventually equal zero." Ecologist **Garrett Hardin**

"Inanimate objects are sometimes parties in litigation. A ship has a legal personality, a fiction found useful for maritime purposes. . . . So it should be as respects valleys, alpine meadows, rivers, lakes, estuaries, beaches, ridges, groves of trees, swampland, or even air that feels the destructive pressures of modern technology and modern life. The river, for example, is the living symbol of all the life it sustains or nourishes — fish, aquatic insects, water ouzels, otter, fisher, deer, elk, bear, and all other animals, including man, who are dependent on it or who enjoy it for its sight, its sound, or its life. The river as plaintiff speaks for the ecological unit of life that is part of it." **William O. Douglas.** In another Supreme Court ruling, a dissenting opinion in *Sierra Club v. Morton*, he wrote,

"The critical question of "standing" would be simplified and also put neatly in focus if we fashioned a federal rule that allowed environmental issues to be litigated before federal agencies or federal courts in the name of the inanimate object about to be despoiled, defaced, or invaded by roads and bulldozers and where injury is the subject of public outrage. Contemporary public concern for protecting nature's ecological equilibrium should lead to the conferral of standing upon environmental objects to sue for their own preservation. This suit would therefore be more properly labeled as *Mineral King v. Morton*." **William O. Douglas**

"The planet has a fever. If your baby has a fever, you go to the doctor. . . If the crib's on fire, you don't speculate that the baby is flame-retardant." **Al Gore**

"The science is clear and compelling. We humans are changing the global climate." **Bill Clinton**

"Everyone except the far right wing of the Republican Party realizes that oil, gas and coal burning are the main activities that have sent the climate into bigger floods, droughts, hurricanes, and El Ninos." Environmental scientist **Donella Meadows**

"I ask people why they have deer heads on their walls. They always say because it's such a beautiful animal. There you go. I think my mother is attractive, but I have photographs of her." Humorist **Ellen DeGeneres**

In the late 1700s **Thomas Paine** wrote, "Were the Continent crowded with inhabitants, her sufferings under the present circumstances would be intolerable. The more seaport-towns we had, the more should we have both to defend and to lose."

Comment: Paine was talking about loss of seaport towns to pirates and the British. Now we are looking at losing them to rising seas. A recent comprehensive study by the state of California concluded that almost the entire state coastline from Oregon to Mexico is at risk. The East Coast and Gulf Coast are even more vulnerable. Anyone who says the climate is not changing or that human activity is playing no role in the changes is either lying for political advantage or denying what every reputable scientist says is happening.

No task facing the nation, its public and private sectors alike, is more important or more daunting than reducing pollution of air, land, and waters; ending ecosystem-annihilating activities such as trawling (a fishing method that essentially drags a bulldozer blade along the seafloor), stabilizing population both In the U.S. and in the world, and restoring damaged ecosystems.

Washington's and Jefferson's consciousness of the importance of the natural environment was resurrected by Theodore Roosevelt. It was strengthened under FDR during the dust bowl years, and in response to extreme pollution of the nation's waters, became widespread under the nation's excellent first Environmental Protection Agency administrator William Ruckelshaus, appointed by Richard Nixon. Jimmy Carter was a strong environmental president. But Ronald Reagan explicitly campaigned on an anti-environmental platform. He tore Carter's solar collectors off the White House roof and scrapped the gas mileage standards Carter had worked to put into place. And he appointed an avidly anti-environmental figure to head the EPA, the notorious James Watt, instructing him to cripple the agency's work in every way he could. Later that scenario was to be repeated under George W. Bush. (Bush's father, George W.H., was environmentally far better than either Reagan or his own son.) America could have been a shining light leading the world into an environmentally conscious future. Recently that light has been growing dim

The proposal by Justice William O. Douglas to pass "rights of nature" laws that give environmental beings, objects, and ecosystems legal standing so that people can sue in their behalf for their protection has recently been taken up by dozens of communities in Vermont, Massachusetts, and Pennsylvania, including the city of Pittsburgh.

In the most recent revision of its constitution, the nation of Ecuador took a similar tack. It has given legal standing to beings of nature: to forests, rivers, mountains, and wildlife. Concerned citizens can now act as advocates for natural beings that have legal standing. For the sake of the seventh generation, we can hope it works out.

A prime source of higher taxes and disappearing countryside is rising population. In my lifetime I have watched two-lane country roads turn into twelve-lane freeways, one-bore two-lane tunnel get three more bores through the mountain, hundreds of thousands of acres of prime farmland and orchards turn into cities and suburbs, and jail populations soar. Densely populated areas need more police per capita than thinly populated ones, more sophisticated sewage treatment systems, more school classrooms, more highway lanes, more costly public transportation systems, and so on *ad infinitum*. Yes, in Genesis God says, "Be fruitful and multiply." We've already done that—in spades. If you have a son, you may want him to grow tall and strong—up to a point. Maybe even seven feet would be all right (sort of like 7 billion people on earth), but eight would be a bit much and nine a real problem. Population growth in some parts of the world, such as Africa, the Middle East, and parts of Latin America, is so rapid that it foretells immense suffering from lack of basic necessities. I have seen it from Central America to India, but I will spare you the tragic details. Every few years some do-gooder comes along and promises to "end hunger in the world." It's a great goal, but it won't happen as long as population grows faster than agricultural production. And at this point, both population growth and increased food production also increase pollution and cause more rapid exhaustion of nonrenewable resources.

In our nation and numerous others, high population growth is an "elephant beneath the rug" that makes many other problems worse. In addressing it, we need to avoid confusing *growth rate* with *total growth*. The latter number is the more important one.

Paradoxically (but true), if a region's total population has grown larger, **the growth rate can decline, but there can still be greater population growth every year than there was in the past an when the growth rate was higher** but based on a smaller total population.

   Understanding this is crucial, since some people say, "Oh, look—the growth rate is declining. We don't have a problem any longer." Writers who make such remarks are ignoring the near-universal demographic predictions that –barring cataclysmic disaster-- the world is headed toward adding at least another two billion people this century. Their mistake lies in confusing *growth rates* with *total growth*. In the real world, *as the population base gets bigger, the rate of growth can drop, yet produce a larger total increase*. For example: Suppose you own three cows and one has a calf. Your herd has increased by 33%, and now you have four cows. Rancher Fred Jones next door has a hundred cows and ten give birth. His herd has increased by only 10%, but now it has 110 cows. Your herd's growth rate is 23% greater than Fred's, but his herd has grown by ten cows while yours has grown by just one.

   Next year, concerned that his cows are overgrazing the pasture, Fred, resorting to the most basic of birth control methods, has several heartfelt discussions with his herd in which he warns them about the wicked allure of passionate trysts on moonlit nights, and preaches abstinence. At the cost of some grumbling among the cows, he reduces his herd's increase to just eight calves, a growth rate of about 7%. Meanwhile, your four cows produce one more calf, causing a decline in your growth rate to 25%. So even though the growth rate of your herd has dropped by 8% and that of Fred's herd has dropped by just 3%, his herd still grows by eight cows while yours grows by just one.

   Maybe it's happening in your neighborhood. Suppose a city near you with 100,000 people grows by 30% in ten years. Now there are 130,000 people, or 30,000 more. In the following ten years, the growth rate drops to 25% for the decade, but the total number of new people added is 32,500, because it's 25% of a larger base. That's what's happening in high-growth countries around the world. The growth *rate* has been dropping, but the *total annual increase* is high and relentless. Since growth rates work like reinvested compound interest, just as interest itself earns interest, the population increase itself has children. (Economists, big business, and investors don't want to hear this, because our whole economic system is based on growth. As this growth slows, our economies will require profound rethinking.)

   Even when some countries have declining total populations, that doesn't counterbalance other countries with rising populations unless people in the latter countries move to where population is declining. And while some countries with declining populations (such as in Europe) welcome immigration, others don't, because they're afraid that unique qualities of their own culture will be lost, or they think their country is too crowded already, or they don't want the problems that a rising population brings. Moving to a stable population makes dealing with many problems easier. (And yes, it also brings some problems of its own.)

   Most U.S. population growth results from immigration. The United States' current reality of *taking in half of the world's total immigration every year* pushes up taxes to pay for classrooms, health care for the indigent, and other services such as police protection, because on average, immigrants' earnings and payments of taxes are lower than those of other residents. The historic desire to have as large a U.S. population as possible is now counterproductive. It not only raises our taxes, but causes crowding, deterioration of services by hard pressed states and municipalities, and greater difficulty in getting away from twelve-lane freeways into more-or-less unspoiled nature. Also, in many nations from which people want to emigrate, the gap between the ultra rich and ultra poor is even worse than in the U.S. or Europe, so that people at the bottom of the income ladder make less in a day there than in an hour here—so of course many want to come here. The right wing would very reasonably like to see lower illegal immigration levels to reduce such problems. But they're overlooking huge parts of the problem. A narrow focus on illegal immigrants overlooks the larger problem of total immigration, including grave problems with our legal immigration system, which needs a major overhaul.

This is one of the most difficult and complex of all political questions and all issues facing the nation. Some people want more immigration (to bring in their friends and relatives, or to recruit employees with skills they need) while others want less (to reduce taxes, crowding, and social and environmental impacts.) In this complicated and difficult problem, one person's easy answer is completely unacceptable to the next person. Developing the best policies and making the best decisions will require our most careful and creative thought-- and perhaps experimentation, trying something for a specified period to see how it works out.

Some starting points for addressing all this are these:

1. Regard immigration not as an isolated question, but as part of population policy as a whole. We need nothing a well thought-through, coherent national population policy.

2. Dealing with problems of people who already live in the United States should be clearly separated from the question of policies toward those in other countries who would like to move here. Past half-hearted attempts at treating these two questions separately have failed both because we had no control over how many people came in illegally and because Congress and some presidents had basically an "anything goes" attitude about legal immigration. And there are probably other reasons too.

3. There is a also difference between those who come with a wish to stay, and those who come temporarily to work in jobs that are unpopular with native-born citizens, such as agricultural labor, or teaching university physics and mathematics. Many agricultural workers who would like to return to their home countries in the off-season remain here because of the dangers of illegal entry and the high cost of hiring a guide (coyote) to bring them in illegally. Legal entry of an appropriate number of such workers is a better path, if illegal entry can truly be minimized. That's a big "if."

4. A central element of an intelligent national population policy is a *single immigration ceiling,* so that when, for any reason, Congress or the President makes an exception to let extra people from some group or country in, quotas for all other groups are reduced proportionally to stay below the ceiling.

5. Family planning is essential to both population and immigration policy. In this country, family planning instruction should be mandatory for all immigrants because the average birthrate of their families is significantly higher than that of native-born families. And family planning assistance for other countries that send

many immigrants our way could reduce immigration pressures from those nations. This is the exact opposite of what some shortsighted recent administrations have done.

6. Both pro-immigration and anti-immigration advocates should be included in grappling with the issue. Any conclusions and policies that are completely one-sided, and that entirely exclude opposing views, are recipes for trouble.

The widely discussed "anchor baby" problem is real. If citizens of another country come to the U.S to work or vacation and have a child while here, the baby becomes a U.S. citizen. (Many argue that its citizenship should be that of its parents.) Under present "family reunification" law, if it is a U.S. citizen, the infant then becomes entitled to bring in its relatives, and then they are entitled to bring in theirs, and so on, and the thing has no end. Senator Eugene McCarthy, who co-authored that law, eventually concluded that it was a major mistake and regretted that he had done so. "Needed skills" is an alternative entry criterion that would sidestep the "anchor baby" issue even if automatic citizenship for everyone born in the U.S. continues. (But in turn, it raises the "brain drain" issue. One country's gain can be another's loss.)

There is also the problem of people who were born elsewhere but were brought here as young children, so that they have grown up in the U.S. and never known another country (the "Dream Act" issue.) I find myself torn between two conflicting inner voices. One says, "If we give them legal status now and the same drama will be played out yet again in another twenty years." The other voice replies, ""That's only true if we don't gain control over our borders and other entry points. If people have never known another country, they ought to be able to become citizens, or at least permanent residents, coupled with a clear policy *that no such exception will be made again.*"

Now here's a nasty and totally unacceptable situation: A recent court decision released immigrants who had committed major crimes of aggression and robbery whose native countries would not take them back. I view that as an inexcusable crime against the American people. Surely we can figure out a better way to handle such a situation.

Energy and Resources. On a very different environmental matter, not so long ago the United States was the world's leader in new clean energy technologies. But big oil, big coal, and their right-wing allies have fought a two-fisted fight against these initiatives. At this writing, they have won. Despite all rhetoric to the contrary, they are writing 90% of our nation's energy policy. As a result the U.S. has lost its leading edge. Europe, China, and even India have leapfrogged the United States. These countries are producing far more energy from wind, solar, and other green sources and are developing new technologies that are likely to give them worldwide domination of tomorrow's markets for energy production. Other countries from Denmark to Cuba are developing or have developed cellular electric grids that can survive hurricanes or terrorism, while the U.S grid remains so vulnerable to disruption that top officials say the question is not whether the grid will crash, but when.

The American people have the brains and the ingenuity to move beyond present early bio-solar technologies and develop new next generation technologies. But only with public policy support as well as private corporate support, instead of the strong opposition now coming from coal and oil producers, can this happen on a major scale. What we collectively decide to do will affect our children and grandchildren. Which direction do we choose—up or down? If corporate money can keep buying legislators' votes, the answer is probably "down."

A related concern is the condition of the world's ecosystems. Mother Nature has grown angry at our continuing abuse of her, and now is expressing her wrath in unparalleled hurricanes, floods, and tornadoes (and now, maybe even earthquakes caused by lubricating rock layers with fracking fluids, and possibly also cancer caused by the chemicals they contain.) These events shout at us that it is time for a revolution in our attitudes and actions; time to heal and restore the world's life-support systems instead of injuring and stealing from them as we have been doing. And as we turn our attention to healing the gravely wounded world of nature, that action can remind us to heal our own wounded spirits and social fabric.

WILLIE NELSON

Singer and songwriter **Willie Nelson,** and **Anna Lappe** of the Rainforest Action Network, write "Our food is under threat. It is felt by every family farmer who has lost their land and livelihood, every parent who can't find affordable or healthy ingredients in their neighborhood, every person worried about foodborne illnesses thanks to lobbyist-weakened food safety laws, every farmworker who faces toxic pesticides in the fields as part of a day's work. . . When our food is at risk we are all at risk. . . . Over the last thirty years, we have witnessed a massive consolidation of our food system. Never have so few corporations been responsible for more of our food chain. Of the 40,000 food items in a typical U.S. grocery store, more than half are now brought to us by just 10 corporations. . . . More than 90 percent of soybean seeds and 80 percent of corn seeds used in the United States are sold by just one company: Monsanto. [Isn't that a monopoly? It's certainly not Adam Smith's "free market."] Four companies are responsible for up to 90 percent of the global trade in grain. What does this matter for those of us who eat? Corporate control of our food system has led to the loss of millions of family farmers, the destruction of soil fertility, the pollution of our water, and health epidemics including type 2 diabetes, heart disease, and even certain forms of cancer. More and more, the choices that determine the food on our shelves are made by corporations concerned less with protecting our health, our environment, or our jobs than with profit margins and executive bonuses."

Michael Ableman, farmer and founder of the Center for Urban Agriculture says, "We need to focus on what we are for as much as what we are against; occupying our land, our soils with life and fertility, our communities with good food. We need to work to rebuild the real economy, the one based on seeds and sunlight and individuals and communities growing together."

Comment: At this writing, coal companies have blown up more than **five hundred mountains** in West Virginia, Virginia, and Kentucky and then strip mined the coal blasted loose by the explosion. In the process of this apocalyptic strip-mining of the Appalachian mountains more than a million acres of forest have been clear-cut and more than a thousand miles of streams have been buried beneath the rubble from the mountaintops. The ecosystem is annihilated, the drinking water polluted, and the health and safety of everyone in the region is threatened. *Each week, detonations throughout the region add up to the power of a Hiroshima A-bomb.* Then bulldozers shove the debris off the mountain and into streams and valleys below. Such a "valley fill" can be 1,000 feet wide and a mile long. This is happening now. The G.W. Bush administration "streamlined" the permitting process and put the "regulated" the Army Corps of Engineers in charge of "regulating" operations. If Washington and Jefferson could see what's going on, they would not be pleased.

The machinery used is so huge that few miners are needed, so that mining jobs account for less than 1% of jobs in the region. (Best estimates are that developing renewable energy in the region would generate nearly 70,000 new jobs, compared to the present 14,000 mining jobs.

And that's in the United States, where there is more oversight of resource extraction than in many countries. This is just one example of the kinds of damage to ecosystems that are occurring all over the world. You saw another horrible example in the Deepwater Horizon Gulf oil spill. The Gulf of Mexico now has the world's largest "dead spot" where no plants or fish can live. It's not just oil: The "dispersants" used to break up the oil are toxic to most life forms, and now cover a huge area of the ocean bottom.

Details of ecosystem annihilation all over the world fill not just an entire book, but an enormous computer database. We do well to recall **Jefferson's** words that " **If one link in nature's chain might be lost, another and another might be lost, till this whole system of things should vanish by piece-meal.**" In other words, the loss of a crucial plant or animal could take a whole ecosystem down with it (like the honeybees that pollenate so many of our crops). If we want our grandchildren to have a world to live in, we need to start protecting instead of destroying ecosystems all over the world.

Hurricanes, floods, and tornadoes tell us that it is time to heal and restore the world's life-support systems instead of injuring and killing them as we have been doing.

During the Communist era in Eastern Europe, at a Polish Economic Society dinner in 1958, someone remarked to economist John Kenneth Galbraith, "Under Capitalism man exploits man. And under Communism it is just the reverse." *Both exploit nature.* If humankind is to survive, we will have to learn to live in a mutually supportive relationship with nature and protect her from human greed.

<<<>>>

SOLUTIONS

Acknowledge thatsome of the gravest dangers facing us today are not those from other peoples and nations, but from the deterioration of the environmental life-systems that we depend on for survival.

* **Stop letting businesses that poison the air and land and water from walking away and letting government clean them up. They're getting a free ride at taxpayers' expense. Like every dog owner, every business needs to have its own pooper-scooper department.**

* **Adopt Amory Lovins' blueprint for getting off oil and coal by 2050 and achieving national energy independence and energy security.**

Make environmental security the centerpiece of our national security policy. This means ending activity that pollutes and degrades our air, land, forests, and waters and move rapidly into both large- and small-scale ecosystem restoration throughout our nation, and to the degree that we can, throughout the world.

- Transform much of our military-industrial complex into an environmental-industrial complex.

- Develop a national population policy that aims at achieving stable numbers. It would include a single immigration ceiling, so any exceptions that would otherwise increase total immigration would cause all other quotas to be reduced to keep total immigration within the ceiling. Change entry criteria from "family reunification" to skills the country seeds. Secure the borders.

- Quit giving out both federal and state subsidies that help corporate agribusiness wipe out family farms. For example, a California water project sells water below cost for less than it costs to maintain the water system, without limit on how many acres are watered. So if Farmer John has 1000 acres and Agribonanza Inc. has 85,000 acres, taxpayers are subsidizing Agribonanza eighty-five times more than Farmer John. The huge profits that result make it easy for Agribonanza to drive Farmer John out of business, and we are left with one fewer family farm and an even bigger Agribonanza. The same occurs with many crop subsidies. The simple step is to put a cap on the acreage or amount of crop covered by any subsidy that is low enough to encourage family farming.

- Sack the whole crew at the top of the Department of Agriculture (as of 2011) and replace them with an unbiased cross-section of farmers, ranchers, and agriculture experts who have no ties to GMO companies and will allocate research monies as much to encouraging small family farming and true organic farming as to projects that benefit only big time corporate agribusiness, pesticide and herbicide manufacturers, and seed monopolies—which is what the government does now.

- In short, protecting Earth's ecosystems and restoring degraded ones instead of continuing to damage them will need to become the central priority of this present century. *Your life* depends on the health of Mother Earth—or the Lord's Earthly Kingdom, as you prefer.

* * *

PART III:

HEAL YOURSELF, HEAL THE NATION, HEAL THE WORLD

Here we look at connections among our politics, our social relations, and our inner selves. Doing so can us go into our own depths so that, in storyteller Carolyn Casey's words, our souls can speak more deeply to us, and we can connect our small finite stories to the infinite story of which we are all part. Restoring our political institutions to forms consistent with the intentions of the great thinkers of our past can help restore the clear-mindedness and integrity of our people. At the same time, looking inward with an unflinching eye can help us heal psychological wounds that cause ongoing personal suffering, and reverse the disintegration of our communities and ecosystems.

20. How Your Politics Affects You

Your beliefs are tied to attitudes. Your attitudes lead to electrochemical events in your brain and to tension or relaxation in your body that produces or reduces stress. Your attitudes and somatic reactions lead to actions. Repeated again and again, all these personal events shape your personality and character, affecting who you are and who you become. This also works in the other direction. Who you are on the outside--that is, how you act and what you say, affect who you become on the inside, both just below the surface of your self-presentation and at deeper levels. If your usual political stance is hostile, judgmental, and reactive, you become a more hostile, judgmental, reactive, shallow human being. If your political stance is caring, compassionate, and constructive, those qualities grow in your character.

"Give to every other human being the right that you claim for yourself – that is my doctrine." *Thomas Paine*

"He that is good for making excuses is seldom good for anything else," said **Benjamin Franklin**. Also, "He that composes himself is wiser than he that composes a book."

"Pride costs more than hunger, thirst and cold." **Thomas Jefferson**

"Do not go where the path may lead, go instead where there is no path and leave a trail." **Ralph Waldo Emerson**

"Nearly all men can stand adversity, but if you want to test a man's character, give him power." **Abraham Lincoln.**

"Twenty years from now you will be more disappointed by the things that you didn't do than by the ones you did do. So throw off the bowlines. Sail away from the safe harbor. Catch the trade winds in your sails. Explore. Dream. Discover." **Mark Twain**

"If this world of ours is ever to become what we hope some day it may become, it must be by the general recognition that the man's heart and soul, the man's worth and actions, determine his standing." **Theodore Roosevelt**

"In the long run, we shape our lives, and we shape ourselves. The process never ends until we die. And the choices we make are ultimately our own responsibility." She also said, "The giving of love is an education in itself;" and finally, "The future belongs to those who believe in the beauty of their dreams." **Eleanor Roosevelt**

ELEANOR ROOSEVELT

"The enlightenment builders of society, [including] the originators of America, were spiritual thinkers or they were nothing . . . in that they, and none more than Jefferson, envisioned the aim of human life as the dwelling in a reality beyond the world of personal gain and loss, the world of physical satisfaction and pleasure. . . . Our Founding Fathers were artists and masters of building a social order. That was their milieu, their instrument, their art form." **Jacob Needleman**

> **Comment:** When you have acted in a way that has caused some kind of harm, you don't have to consider yourself a bad person because of it. But neither do you have to justify having acted in that harmful way. You are not destined to "moral and spiritual doom." You can acknowledge your mistakes, and improve your actions from now on.

<<<>>>

SOLUTIONS

From time to time it is wise to ask yourself, how a given act or course of action affects (or would affect) who and what you are becoming. You might ask, for instance,

- **Will this help me act and feel friendly and respectful toward others or hostile, antagonistic, hard-hearted, and unforgiving?**

- **Does thinking, feeling, and acting in this way help me become more autonomous and more fully myself, or does it lead me toward depending on others' views and outside authority?**

- **Will this bring greater joy and love into my heart, the lives of those around me, and the world? Or will it cause greater darkness and sadness for both me and others?"**

- **Will it contribute to healing or to wounding my psyche and that of others around me? Will it bring inner peace or inner agitation?"**

As you ask, listen inwardly. Learning to notice, moment by moment, what you and others are actually doing, with few labels or judgments, is a major positive step. The truest answers will usually come not from your mind, but from your heart. If you choose to listen to your inner wisdom instead of to judgments borrowed from others,

your life is likely to be lighter and brighter. If not, good luck—you'll need it.

* * *

21. From the "Attitude Trap" to Finding Your Inner Light

We can address any matter in ways that make us and others feel better or feel worse, and that are more effective or less so. It is easy enough to get stuck in a negative attitude, such as one of self-proclaimed importance, hunger for power, or chronic anger or antagonism. While there can be various short term gains in such attitudes, not one of them leads to a deeply fulfilling life. Fortunately, we can choose the attitude with which we go through life. And we can choose the attitude with which we try to bring about the changes we want to see in our home, community, town or city, or even our country. We create our attitudes through our decisions about what we think and feel and do. We can choose to be big-minded, open hearted, compassionate, perceptive, friendly, or even loving. Or none of the above. Below are some perspectives on the attitudes we bring into our politics, economics, and other community affairs.

PERICLES

"What you leave behind is not what is engraved in stone monuments, but what is woven into the lives of others." Ancient Athenian statesman **Pericles**

"You were born with wings, why prefer to crawl through life?" **Jallaludin Rumi**

"In the following pages I offer nothing more than simple facts, plain arguments, and common sense: and have no other preliminaries to settle with the reader, than that he will divest himself of prejudice and prepossession, and suffer his reason and his feelings to determine . . . the true character of a man, and generously enlarge his views beyond the present day." **Thomas Paine**

"I am determined to be cheerful and happy in whatever situation I may find myself. For I have learned that the greater part of our misery or unhappiness is determined not by our circumstance but by our disposition." **Martha Washington**

"Any fool can criticize, condemn and complain and most fools do." *Benjamin Franklin*

"The worst wheel of the cart makes the most noise. . . . Speak ill of no man, but speak all the good you know of everybody. . . . If you would be loved, love, and be lovable." **Benjamin Franklin**

DOLLEY MADISON

"It is one of my sources of happiness never to desire a knowledge of other people's business."
First Lady **Dolley Madison**

"The succession to Dr. [Benjamin] Franklin, at the court of France, was an excellent school of humility. On being presented to any one as the minister of America, the commonplace question used in such cases was. . . 'It is you, Sir, who replace Doctor Franklin?' I generally answered, 'No one can replace him, Sir: I am only his successor.'" **Thomas Jefferson**

"The sound of a kiss is not so loud as that of a cannon, but its echo lasts a great deal longer."
Oliver Wendell Holmes Jr.

"Our language is the reflection of ourselves. A language is an exact reflection of the character and growth of its speakers." **Caesar Chavez**

> **Comment:** You probably want to keep doing what experience has shown you to be reliable. If so, don't let yourself get conned into letting go of what works for you. Here's a useful principle: *You can depend on the truth of your personal experience as it unfolds, but not necessarily on your old ideas and attitudes (some of which are probably borrowed from people who know less, or have poorer judgment, than you do.)*
>   This is a partly a book about freedom, about liberating your mind and spirit from the oppression of limited and limiting beliefs. In exploring the option of thinking thoughts that are distinctly different from those you've thought before, you literally enlarge your mind. That's not a metaphor. Brain scientists have discovered that opening your mind actually causes the growth of new cortical neurons that help you process new information and rethink the implications of old information. Holding on tightly to what you always thought you knew does not stimulate such growth. Your mind remains "smaller," confined within past mental patterns. The outlook offered here challenges us all to sharpen our mind and our ability to discern what is real and what is not, what works and what does not. We can learn to awaken our responsiveness to life, and to describe events so precisely (and sometimes also so poetically) that few can disagree. As we do this, we unify disconnected sides of our selves that need to be re-owned and embraced.
>   Inner conflicts that are suppressed instead of consciously examined and worked through can result in burying our compassion. This causes people to become mentally and emotionally robotized and unable to experience a deeper humanity. When we lose touch with our inner self, then when our country's bombs kill innocent people in another country, we are detached from our sense of brotherhood, and those innocents are only our "enemies." When someone starves and freezes to death in the midwinter cold, it is only

happening to a "welfare chiseler," not someone's child or friend, brother or sister. Soulfulness and sensitivity conveniently fly out of town.

An especially dangerous quality of many militant extremists is that they do not think beyond their conditioning. They are intolerant of anyone or anything that does not fit their views and attitudes. Such intolerance leads to prejudice and to being **impervious** – that is, unwilling to see, hear or consider anything they disagree with. This all too easily leads to the worst kinds of antidemocratic behavior.

I always wondered why somebody doesn't do something about that. Then I realized I was somebody. **Lily Tomlin**

Instead of working for the survival of the fittest, we should be working for the survival of the wittiest - then we can all die laughing. **Lily Tomlin**

"It isn't until you come to a spiritual understanding of who you are . . . deep down, the spirit within - that you can begin to take control. . . . If you want to accomplish the goals of your life, you have to begin with the spirit." **Oprah Winfrey.** Oprah also says, "I believe that everyone is the keeper of a dream - and by tuning into one another's secret hopes, we can become better friends, better partners, better parents, and better lovers."

OPRAH WINFREY

"Go ahead. Fall down. The world looks different from the ground." **Oprah Winfrey**

<<<>>>

SOLUTIONS

- **Be present in this moment. Notice what is going on in your own mind, emotions, and body (muscular tensions, etc.). Become aware of when you tell yourself something that causes you to react with physical tension. Then breathe deeply, let go of that tension, and think with a clearer, calmer, deeper mind about how you can best handle your situation.**

- **Give yourself a chance to dream, to foresee, to imagine possibilities. Notice what's missing in this moment that you would like to make a part of your life, your community, your culture.**

- **Listen with your heart as well as your mind.**

- **In difficult situations, look for the positive opportunity that may be present then that is not present when everything is going well.** (For example, Franklin D. Roosevelt was able to pass Social Security and national banking insurance to protect people's deposits during the Great Depression. In better times he might not have succeeded in doing so.)

- **Be cheerful rather than gloomy whenever possible (but don't pretend that you feel differently than you do).**

- **Do the best you can.**

- **Use your own inner light to help illuminate the paths and lighten the troubles of others.**

* * *

22. A Mind of Your Own – Or Are You Just Another Parrot?

Ask yourself right now: What have other people told you, or what have you read or watched on TV, that you have repeated to yourself or to others a hundred times or more? Then stop, and fully appreciate that in each moment of your life you choose anew whether to languish in the lazy loops of those well-worn mental grooves, or to truly respond to what is actually happening right now in this new situation. Conditioned responses, whether they are mental, emotional, bodily, or behavioral, are no substitute for thinking and feeling for yourself. But it takes effort to look for the uniqueness of every situation. (Just as, for example, it usually takes considerably more effort to figure out how to do something new on your computer or cell phone than to go through a well-learned sequence of actions that you've gone through many times before.) As a result, most of us usually react automatically. It's easier. It's faster. It gives us a sense of knowing how things are and how they ought to be, and of being in control. Even when we're wrong. Even when our mistaken choices cause unnecessary suffering for us, for others, or both.

It takes effort to produce new thoughts. It also takes effort to act in a way that truly fits a new situation instead of doing as someone else tells us to, in response to their definition of events. Often it requires not only effort but also courage. As a result, most of us passively stick to some old party line that we've previously followed, without thinking through its various effects and feedback loops.—which can be much more complicated than we might imagine. The life of a parrot is easier than that of a responsive and responsible human being—and much of the time it works just fine. But not always. And when it doesn't, it can mean big trouble. The nation's founders saw that reality, and described it in their own ways. Patrick Henry was among them:

"I have but one lamp by which my feet are guided, and that is the lamp of experience." *Patrick Henry.*

> **Comment:** Henry saw that beliefs, attitudes, and what we think is "knowledge" even when it's flat out wrong (and everybody has at least a little of that) can all interfere with accurate perception and wise action. By emphasizing direct experience rather than a belief system as his central guide, he avoided that trap.

Thomas Paine linked clear and careful thinking—and experience-- with freedom: "When men yield up the privilege of thinking, the last shadow of liberty quits the horizon. . . He also pointed that for most people, "A long habit of not thinking a thing WRONG, gives it a superficial appearance of being RIGHT, and raises at first a formidable outcry in defense of custom. . . . Attempting to debate with a person who has abandoned reason is like giving medicine to the dead."

Paine also remarked, "It is necessary to the happiness of man that he be mentally faithful to himself. Infidelity does not consist in believing, or in disbelieving. It consists in professing to believe what one does not believe."

"A house is not a home unless it contains food and fire for the mind as well as the body."
Benjamin Franklin

"Being ignorant is not so much a shame, as being unwilling to learn. . . Who is wise? He that learns from everyone."
Benjamin Franklin

Thomas Jefferson advised, "Think as you please and let others do so; you will then have no disputes." Amid intense partisan conflict, he wrote in a private letter, "I have sworn upon the altar of God eternal hostility against every form of tyranny over the mind of man." He also pointed out that, "He who knows nothing is closer to the truth than he whose mind is filled with falsehoods and errors."

"It is not best that we should all think alike; it is a difference of opinion that makes horse races." On another occasion he added, "It ain't what you don't know that gets you into trouble; it's what you know for sure that just ain't so." **Mark Twain**

"If a million people say a foolish thing, it is still a foolish thing." **Anatole France**

"Lincoln . . . saw things always with his own eyes. . . Most men see things with other men's eyes. And that is the pity of the whole business of the world." **Woodrow Wilson**

"Every real thought on every real subject knocks the wind out of somebody or other." **Oliver Wendell Holmes Jr.** On another occasion he said, "If there is any principle of the Constitution that more imperatively calls for attachment than any other it is the principle of free thought, not free thought for those who agree with us but freedom for the thought that we hate."

"Too often we enjoy the comfort of opinion without the discomfort of thought." **John F. Kennedy**

"The best ideas come, not from edict and ideology, but from free inquiry and free experiment." **Robert F. Kennedy**

"We need to be bold and adventurous in our thinking in order to survive." **William O. Douglas**

"If you are sure you understand everything that is going on, you are hopelessly confused." Vice President **Walter F. Mondale**

"[Accepting uncritically what others say invites people] to conform, to passivity and resignation. . . The method is . . . to distort subtly the sense of great teachers, prophets, and educators so that words and ideas which have been designed to be flaming legends upon the banners of humanity's progress are twisted . . . to bank the fires of protest. . . . Whatever the act, there is for it an accepted mode, and if in the doing the act departs from the mode, there follows proscription, excommunication, and exile into the company of the damned. This passage to Utopia is open to everyone who is willing to be sold into slavery: the fee is a bent knee and a bowed back. There is no waiting, no queuing up, no forms to be filled, no questions to be answered. All may come aboard the barge that sails to the City of the Dead." Psychiatrist **Robert Lindner**

"The corruption of individualism we now so often see in our culture is a species of arrogance that confirms itself by excluding others and begets conflict." Philosopher **Jacob Needleman**

"People are designed to tell the best story possible. So. . . we use the information we have as if it is the only information. We don't spend much time saying, 'Well, there is much we don't know.' We make do with what we do know. There is a very nice example of this, and it's actually the thing that

impressed Malcolm Gladwell when he wrote the book *Blink*. We form an impression of people within less than a second of meeting them, in some cases. We decide whether they're friendly, hostile, or dominant, and whether we're going to like them. [These impressions] are better than nothing. . . but . . . you form them immediately in the absence of adequate information."
Psychologist **Daniel Kahneman**

> **Comment:** Sometimes those first impressions are right and sometimes they're not. I know of one couple who couldn't stand each other when they first met. Now they've been married for thirty years. To truly think for yourself requires questioning what your friends and authorities affirm. It requires observing yourself as you react with the socially learned responses that automatically pop into your mind as if they were your own thoughts. I still remember standing on the front porch the day I graduated from high school and saying something to a friend. Then suddenly the realization struck me like a thunderbolt: "I don't actually think that at all." Instead, I had been repeating a statement that I had heard my father make many times, and I had never before stopped question it. Suddenly at that moment, I realized that I disagreed. We are all walking around with many automatic responses, and many complex sequences of habits, that we need in order navigate our way through daily life—like stopping at a red light. And almost all of us are also walking around with many programmed beliefs and attitudes that we have introjected from parents, teachers, friends, bosses, coworkers, other authority figures, or some media know-it-all who may actually be mostly out to lunch. On the whole, such introjected attitudes tend to be far less accurate than the habits that guide us through our everyday activities. We become full human beings, with our own inner freedom, only when we start to question and think such matters through for ourselves. In some cases, this even means facing conditioned fears learned long ago in childhood, such as "I will be punished, or will not get the caring I need, unless I do and think as I am told to." Such learnings are not undone overnight.

SOLUTIONS

- Watch vigilantly for party-line thinking, both in yourself and in others. You may hold some general principle, but if you hope to act effectively or even wisely, look carefully at, and think carefully about, each unique situation.

- What may and may not be done, who metes out the rewards or punishment, and who is in control of rewarding and punishment all involve power issues. Since conditions sometimes change faster than our rules about how to behave in them, sometimes rules have to be broken, so long as no one is harmed.

- Be watchful of your own exercise of power. Make a habit of asking yourself *what motive each important action is serving*. Are you willing, for example, to transform your inclinations to exercise power into inclinations to act kindly, to render service, and when you're willing, even to love? In so doing, you educate your heart and move toward the next step on the path to greater consciousness.

- If you have children, or are a teacher of any kind, be careful what you pass on to them. Children need both appropriate limits, and freedom to explore and learn and grow. They also need plenty of attention. They learn by imitating you, by your guidance in giving them appropriate appreciation when they venture and when they succeed, and when they follow your appropriate instructions. But avoid power struggles in which you get caught up in "who wins." That can be a way to break a child's tender spirit, if you feel compelled to always be the winner. Children need to learn both how to relate, and how to be autonomous and think for themselves.

* * *

23. Ben Franklin's Flexibility of Mind

In personal life, politics, business, or religion, nothing is easier than to keep on repeating to yourself and others the same old phrases, myths, mental photographs, and mind-movies that you have said and thought so many times before. You can exercise every outer freedom that the Bill of Rights guarantees you, but if you seldom get out of the well-practiced routes and ruts of your customary neural circuits, you have no inner freedom. By contrast, you may find that it helps you to develop your inner freedom by remembering the line, "Up until now I . . . , but now I'm realizing that. . . ." or ". . . now I can. . ." The present moment and the future are where you live. What you have thought, felt, and done in the past is a sometimes-useful advisor whose perspective is limited to what you knew then. Don't ignore or forget what's valuable in it. But if you depend only on what you thought and did yesterday to fill in tomorrow's blank spots on the map of your life, you'll be wearing blinders. Tomorrow is a clean slate, a great empty space waiting for you to give it form. Here's how others saw the matter:

BENJAMIN FRANKLIN

"Our conscience is not the vessel of eternal verities. It grows with our social life, and a new social condition means a radical change in conscience." **Benjamin Franklin.** He also said, "The doorstep to the temple of wisdom is a knowledge of our own ignorance. . . Observe all men, thyself most."

"Inquiry is human; blind obedience brutal. Truth never loses by the one but often suffers by the other." **William Penn**

"I do not believe that any two men, on what are called doctrinal points, think alike who think at all. It is only those who have not thought that appear to agree." **Thomas Paine**

"I receive reproof when reproof is due, because no person can be readier to accuse me, than I am to acknowledge an error, when I have committed it." **George Washington**

"Men often oppose a thing merely because they have had no agency in planning it, or because it may have been planned by those whom they dislike." **Alexander Hamilton.**

"Facts are stubborn things; and whatever may be our wishes, our inclination, or the dictates of our passions, they cannot alter the state of facts and evidence." **John Adams**

"A foolish consistency is the hobgoblin of little minds, adored by little statesmen and philosophers and divines." **Ralph Waldo Emerson**

"Do I contradict myself? Very well, I contradict myself. I am large. I contain multitudes." **Walt Whitman**

"The dogmas of the quiet past are inadequate to the stormy present. . . As our case is new, so we must think anew, and act anew." *Abraham Lincoln*

"Loyalty to petrified opinion never yet broke a chain or freed a human soul." **Mark Twain**

"Let's be honest with ourselves and not take ourselves too serious, and never condemn the other fellow for doing what we are doing every day, only in a different way." **Will Rogers**

"People who honestly mean to be true really contradict themselves much more rarely than those who try to be 'consistent'. . . . Don't be 'consistent' but be simple true." **Oliver Wendell Holmes, Jr.**

And **Marilyn Monroe** thoughtfully observed, "A sex symbol becomes a thing. I just hate to be a thing."

> **Comment**: Any symbol can become a thing. In politics beliefs become things. Metaphors become things. And the things become idols like unto graven images before which we bow down in mindless obedience, and myths that we come to believe are eternal verities. Politics easily degenerates into idol worship. It appears to me that this is what has happened with many in the "Tea Party," some talk show hosts, and other right wing extremists. Their ideas come between them and reality so that, with their minds immobilized and swaddled in a cocoon of their entrenched ideas, they can no longer see or hear what is real.

"An error doesn't become a mistake until you refuse to correct it." **John F. Kennedy**

"We will not find answers in old dogmas, by repeating outworn slogans, or fighting on ancient battlegrounds against fading enemies long after the real struggle has moved on." **Robert F. Kennedy**

"To mature is to go on creating oneself endlessly." Philosopher **Henri Bergson**

"The next step in the evolution of intelligence [is] the transition from amassing knowledge to developing wisdom." **Peter Russell,** computer scientist

> **Comment:** By actively developing our capacity to notice, moment by moment, what we are thinking, feeling, sensing, and doing we become more able to choose whether to continue what we are doing or to do something else instead. This is as true of politics as of everyday life. It is useful to watch our own projections—especially any fault we perceive in others that we may deny in ourselves. Accepting our less-than-admirable thoughts, feelings, and actions rather denying that we have them and projecting them onto others helps us to become more honest, and to mature and grow.

<<<>>>

SOLUTIONS

- Each time you hear a metaphor (a thing or a mental picture that represents something else), let a red light flash in your brain ("a red light flash" was a metaphor!) to remind you that it is a picture-story of some reality that is meant to cause you to respond in a certain way. Then try to "see through it" —that is, look at or listen to the real event(s) the metaphor supposedly represents.

- Whenever you hear a belief that sounds familiar, ask yourself, "How can I test that against my own experience?" And when you hear yourself repeating an old line that you've repeated many times before, ask, "Can I think about this in a new way?"

- I do not exalt thoughtless rebellion above thoughtless conformity. Many social rules contribute to the safety and well-being of most people, and depend on a shared fabric of mutual cooperation. On the other hand, some rules are arbitrary, unilateral, and destructive. In that case it may make sense to break a rule, or to work to get the rule changed so that it becomes realistic and appropriate. This includes your rules about your own behavior.

* * *

24. Beyond Moral and Ethical Black Holes: Virtue in the People

Morals and ethics are very tricky matters in part because so many people self-righteously assume that their own are correct and everyone else whose moral and ethical views differ from their own is not only wrong but sinful as well. And then they shut their eyes and ears and become impervious to anything that may call their views into question. At the same time, some people who do truly terrible things and cause immense suffering have cover stories to convince themselves and others that what they're doing is right or sensible. They may even unconsciously manufacture false memories of events in their past and then "remember" those pseudo-memories as if they are reality. Sigmund Freud called these "screen memories." There are, however, some moral and ethical principles upon which of the world's great saints and sages have agreed. Brief statements of such principles are discussed below in astute reflections from Franklin and Washington's time and others from incisive thinkers in our own.

The temptations in show business are well known. **Marilyn Monroe** said, "Hollywood is a place where they'll pay you a thousand dollars for a kiss and fifty cents for your soul."

> **Comment:** Much the same can be said of politics, but there often it's a million dollars for your vote and nickel for your soul. A recent President remarked, "You can fool some of the people all the time, and those are the ones you want to concentrate on." Supposedly he was joking but it could serve as the headline for his policies. We need to pay more attention to the integrity of both our politicians and the CEOs who run great corporations. In both places we let some real turkeys rule the roost for life.
>
> Be careful to acknowledge your own and others' moral opinions as such rather than assuming that they are facts. When you pile up pseudo-facts on top of pseudo-belief systems you gradually become dumber and dumber (while you delude yourself into thinking you're getting smarter and smarter. What a deal!) That is, your mind has less capacity for direct awareness, for sorting out truth from falsehood, for recognizing faulty "information," and for reasoning accurately.

"We are what we repeatedly do. Excellence, then, is not an act, but a habit." **Aristotle**

"I expect to pass through this world but once. Any good therefore that I can do, or any kindness or abilities that I can show to any fellow creature, let me do it now. Let me not defer or neglect it, for I shall not pass this way again."**William Penn**

Benjamin Franklin wrote, "The absent are never without fault, nor the present without excuse. And he astutely noted, "How few there are who have courage enough to own their faults, or resolution enough to mend them." He added, "A man wrapped up in himself makes a very small bundle." And, "Many a man thinks he is buying pleasure, when he is really selling himself to it."

"The sacred rights of mankind are not to be rummaged for among old parchments or musty records. They are written, as with a sunbeam, in the whole volume of human nature." *Alexander Hamilton*

"Labor to keep alive in your breast that little spark of celestial fire called conscience," advised **George Washington.** He added, "The foundation of our national policy will be laid in the pure and immutable principles of private morality." And also, **"**As our nation's first President, he astutely noted, "I walk on untrodden ground. There is scarcely any part of my conduct which may not hereafter be drawn into precedent."

"To suppose that any form of government will secure liberty or happiness without any virtue in the people, is a chimerical idea. . . . The circulation of confidence is better than the circulation of money." **James Madison**

"The only foundation of a free Constitution is pure Virtue, and if this cannot be inspired into our People in a greater Measure, than they have it now, they may change their rulers and the forms of Government, but they will not obtain a lasting liberty. . . If 'Thou shalt not covet' and 'Thou shalt not steal' were not commandments of Heaven, they must be made inviolable precepts in every society before it can be civilized or made free." **John Adams**

"The true rule in determining to embrace or reject anything is not whether it have any evil in it, but whether it have more of evil than of good. There are few things wholly evil or wholly good. Almost every thing, especially of government policy, is an inseparable compound of the two, so that our best judgment of the preponderance between them is continually demanded," said **Abraham Lincoln.** He also remarked, "It has been my experience that folks who have no vices have very few virtues." And he added, "You cannot escape the responsibility of tomorrow by evading it today."

JANE ADDAMS

"The good we secure for ourselves is precarious and uncertain until it is secured for all of us and incorporated into our common life. . . . The essence of immorality is to make an exception of myself." **Jane Addams**

"Kindness is the language which the deaf can hear and the blind can see." Mark Twain

"Laws control the lesser man... Right conduct controls the greater one," **Mark Twain**.

"It's not what you pay a man, but what he costs you that counts." **Will Rogers.** He also said, "We will never have true civilization until we have learned to recognize the rights of others."

MAE WEST

"You only live once, but if you do it right, once is enough." **Mae West**

"We have always known that heedless self-interest was bad morals. We know now that it is bad economics." **Franklin D. Roosevelt**

"Washington is a very easy city for you to forget where you came from and why you got there in the first place." **Harry S. Truman**

"As we express our gratitude, we must never forget that the highest appreciation is not to utter words, but to live by them." **John F. Kennedy**

"Ethical behavior is doing the right thing when no one else is watching – even when doing the wrong thing is legal. . . That land is a community is the basic concept of ecology, but that land is to be loved and respected is an extension of ethics. . . . Cease being intimidated by the argument that a right action is impossible because it does not yield maximum profits, or that a wrong action is to be condoned because it pays." **Aldo Leopold**

"Every time you set out to love, something keeps pulling on you, trying to get you to hate. . . . The human personality is like a charioteer with two headstrong horses, wanting to go in different directions. Or sometimes we even have to end up crying out with Saint Augustine as he said in his Confessions, 'Lord, make me pure, but not yet.' . . .There's a tension at the heart of human nature." **Martin Luther King**

"Who wants to be well-adjusted to injustice? What kind of human being do you want to be? Philosopher **Cornel West**

"Government . . . is a terrible social regulator. And morals and values aren't things that legislation can even touch. You can't legislate morality." **Jesse Ventura**

"When morality comes up against profit, it is seldom that profit loses." Congresswoman **Shirley Chisholm**

"It is the language of values that people use to map their world. It is what can inspire them to take actions, and move them beyond their isolation. . . The broader question of shared values . . . should be the heart of our politics. . . . Instead, we either exaggerate the degree to which policies we don't like impinge on our own most sacred values, or play dumb when our own preferred policies conflict with important countervailing values." **Barack Obama**

"Middle-class families "are getting *hammered* and you know Washington doesn't get it. G.E. doesn't pay any taxes and we are asking college kids to take on even more debt to get an education, and asking seniors to get by on less. These aren't just economic questions. These are *moral* questions." **Elizabeth Warren**, consumer advocate and Harvard Law professor

"The obsession among Catholic and evangelical leaders with an issue like contraception stands in stark contrast to their indifference to, for example, the torture in which the last administration engaged." *Newsweek* writer **Andrew Sullivan** (Comment: See the first item in "References.")

> **Comment:** Most of the founding fathers were of a single mind in wishing to create political forms that would not only foster outward freedom and equality, but also create the conditions for people to advance in their inner ethical and moral development.
> I would amend Lincoln's second statement to ". . .**think they** have no vices," for I have yet to meet a person who has none. Truly righteous behavior is humble, while self-righteous behavior is arrogant. As Martin Luther King points out above, living a moral and ethical life is not a simple task. We all face inner conflicts.
> Most dictionary definitions of "ethics" and "morality" are almost synonymous. In popular usage, however, the term "morals" is most often used for sexual matters—even mutually consenting relationships. Oddly enough, it is seldom used for aggression and violence, even when one person's behavior severely injures another. A movie in which consenting adults make love may be viewed as immoral while one in which many people are violently murdered is not. This aspect of our culture requires deep rethinking.
> Many people, groups, and cultures are convinced that their ethics and morals are right while those of others are wrong. Many other people, groups, and cultures think similarly but have very different rules of right and wrong. These rules are typically generalizations at a high level of abstraction, but many people hang onto them like gospel even when they have little or no bearing on truth or reality in a specific situation. And that's occasionally the case with almost everyone. By contrast, **Mae West** offered no pretense: "I generally avoid temptation unless I can't resist it."
> While the founding fathers were unanimous and steadfast in their opposition to the state offering assistance to any particular religion, or enshrining any religion's beliefs in law, they also recognized the omnipresence of, in Alcoholics Anonymous' words, "a power higher than ourselves." They knew that anyone tightly caught in his or her egotism or egocentrism is inevitably a morally and ethically crippled human being. They recognized that dedicating

oneself, in some way and to some degree, to the welfare and service of humankind and of the living world that supports us is essential to moral and ethical development. Manipulating others for one's own selfish purposes ends in a degradation of morals, and often also in self-deception to justify it.

Regarding values, the word "conservative" used to mean, "We ought to keep our present ways where and when possible. Where change is necessary, small or gradual changes to address specific problems are best." That was sensible. But today, many people who call themselves "conservatives" are actually ideological fanatics who want to impose their ways on others and turn the wheel of life in their own direction. And some so-called "conservatives" are turning the world upside down with bulldozers, dynamite, or even bombs. I call that "linguistic insanity." In my view, anyone who uses language insanely is also apt to be at least a little crazy in their thinking and their acting. Always remember that "normal" does not mean "sane." It just means "average" –like the norm—i.e. like most other people, even if they're all nuts.

A different usage of the word "conservative" means "Family values are disappearing. Strict patriarchal, authoritarian firmness and old time morality are the solutions." In that case, the question is **which** family values. Ironically, more than a few who profess this outlook have gotten caught in exciting venues like romantic airport bathroom stalls performing acts that , well . . . demonstrate anything *but* family values. Some others who laud family values are just plain mean and punitive. Recent news stories featured a so-called "Christian" school principal who has large numbers of ex-students who are now adults claiming that he beat them mercilessly with a heavy wooden paddle again and again and again. I wonder how he'd like getting beaten as viciously as he beat all those children?

Many people who want to make laws that impose their own values on others are regular working people who have been lured into an alliance with those who foster the corporate dominance – ("business libertarian") ideology. They have been taken in by the cover story that "free market economics" will fix all the problems they're concerned about. Or they may be worried about the alternative story that unless they support the corporate dominance outlook they'll soon be fired. Many are getting screwed by this unholy alliance as the great corporations wipe our their family businesses, robotize and offshore their jobs, and then blame the resulting unemployment on "the liberals."

Much of that confusion disappears when we use the following basic yardstick of ethical behavior. In every situation, and with every issue, ask,

"Who or what is being –or will be-- helped or harmed, in what ways, how, when, and under what specific circumstances, by doing this or that?"

I have concluded that this question is the foundation of moral and ethical life. Of course, we have to answer the question honestly instead of lying to ourselves to support our preconceptions or prejudices. And we have to realize that the answer is sometimes, "I don't know. Let's do our best to find out." And of course there is also the corollary principle,

"How can we minimize, and do nothing to contribute to, unnecessary and avoidable suffering?"

I call asking and answering these two questions "*The moral and ethical Rock of Gibraltar*," because I know of no other principle that seems as widely applicable as these two taken together.

In relation to the Roman Catholic religion, I believe that most lay Catholics are ethically more advanced than their own Church's present leadership, which is stuck in an obsolete self-serving authoritarian worldview. The tsunami of priest-and-altar-boy sexual abuse scandals in recent decades, and the present pope's history of dragging his feet when he was in charge of investigating them, removes all claims to the to-moral high ground that the Church's current top hierarchy might presume to make. At this point in history it is presumptuous for them to try to instruct anybody about anything regarding sex and sexual morality. Let them clean their own house first.

SOLUTIONS

- Despite all difference among the cultures, ethnic groups, nations, religions, and political parties, there are two criteria for making ethical judgments that are universal in their reach.

- First, we can ask, "Who or what is helped or harmed, in what ways, and under what specific circumstances? For whom is the help or harm greater, and for whom is it less?"

- Second, we can ask, "What course of action will minimize the amount of unnecessary suffering that occurs to all involved?"

- These questions bring ethical and moral judgments from the abstract level to the level of specific events in which you do your very best to find out what is actually happening to the real people and other beings involved, and what the effects are.

- Also, when change is truly needed, moving slowly enough to avoid upsetting people needlessly is usually wise when possible. So is trying out new measures or policies on a small scale before applying them system-wide. Some problems, however, are large enough and urgent enough that once solutions have been debugged, broad applications is needed.

- Let your conflicting inner voices have a conversation with each other. Truly listen to both or all of them, while minimizing your preconceptions about which is right. Let it go on until you've heard each of them thoroughly, instead of immediately siding with one and refusing to hear what the rest of you has to say. Maybe both –or all—of them have something valuable to say that you need to take into account.

* * *

25. Truth and Freedom are Intertwined

Today when I hear a politician or executive ramble on about freedom, my first thought is often, "How does he (or she) want to hoodwink us now? What con job is he (or she) trying to run? How does this person actually want to *take away* my freedom?

In 1883, the Italian writer Carlo Collodi published the story of Pinocchio, whose nose grew longer when he was telling a lie. Today most politicians, political parties, rabble-rousers, and corporate executives (and for that matter many of the rest of us) have Pinocchio noses if you use your "third eye" to see them. They tell a multitude of large and small lies about politics and society. (When you listen to someone you can ask yourself, "How long is this person's Pinocchio nose?") Sometimes, lost in a trance of illusions, we may not even realize that we're mouthing others' fabricated falsehoods, or that many of our leaders and pundits are lost in the very same trances as their followers. They are part of that ancient parade of the blind leading the blind that stretches back into prehistory.

To be free to act intelligently and effectively, I need to know the facts about what's going on -- not some corrupt half-true story. "Truth" is not a fact, but the quality of a statement about a fact. A statement or concept is true if it is a clear and accurate representation of the thing or event it refers to. In general, knowing the truth increases my freedom (although in some cases, knowing the truth reduces my freedom, in the sense of showing clearly just what needs to be done). If I lie to myself about myself, or about another person, or a situation, I impair my ability to choose wisely. If I lie to you, I impair yours. Others have said,

"We are apt to shut our eyes against a painful truth, to avoid listen to the song of that siren till she transforms us into beasts. Is this the part of wise men, engaged in a great and arduous struggle for liberty?" **Patrick Henry**

"The liberties of a people never were, nor ever will be, secure, when the transactions of their rulers may be concealed from them. . . For my part, whatever anguish of spirit it may cost, I am willing to know the whole truth; to know the worst and provide for it." *Patrick Henry*

"Tricks and treachery are the practice of fools, that don't have brains enough to be honest." **Benjamin Franklin**.

"I hope I shall possess firmness and virtue enough to maintain what I consider the most enviable of all titles, the character of an honest man," said **George Washington.** He also said, "It is better to offer no excuse than a bad one," and optimistically stated, "Truth will ultimately prevail where there is pains to bring it to light."

"He that would make his own liberty secure must guard even his enemy from oppression; for if he violates this duty he establishes a precedent that will reach to himself." **Thomas Paine**

"No face which we can give to a matter will stand us so well at last as the truth. This alone wears well." **Henry David Thoreau**

"How many legs does a dog have if you call the tail a leg? Four. Calling a tail a leg doesn't make it a leg. . . Let the people know the truth and the country is safe," said **Abraham Lincoln.** He went on to state, "He who makes an assertion without knowing whether it is true or false, is guilty of falsehood; and the accidental truth of the assertion does not justify or excuse him."

"Honesty is not a quality. Honesty is the manifestation of character. Lincoln was honest because there was nothing small or petty about him, and only smallness or pettiness in a nature can produce dishonesty. Such honesty is a quality of largeness. It is that openness of nature which will not condescend to subterfuge, which is too big to conceal itself. Little men run to cover and deceive you. Big men cannot and will not run to cover, and do not deceive you. Of course, Lincoln was honest. But that was not a peculiar characteristic of him; that is a general description of him. He was not small or mean, and his honesty was not produced by any calculation, but was the genial expression of the great nature that was behind it." **Woodrow Wilson**

"Facts are stubborn, but statistics are more pliable," said **Mark Twain**. " He added, "A man is never more truthful than when he acknowledges himself a liar," and finally, "If you tell the truth you don't have to remember anything."

"Political language. . . is designed to make lies sound truthful and murder respectable, and to give an appearance of solidity to pure wind." **George Orwell.** And also, "In a time of deceit, telling the truth is a revolutionary act."

"Richard Nixon is a no good, lying bastard. He can lie out of both sides of his mouth at the same time, and if he ever caught himself telling the truth, he'd lie just to keep his hand in." **Harry S. Truman.** On another occasion Truman said, "It's plain hokum. If you can't convince 'em, confuse 'em. It's an old political trick. But this time it won't work."

Adlai Stevenson made this offer: "I will make a bargain with the Republicans: If they will stop telling lies about the Democrats, we will stop telling the truth about them."

John F. Kennedy said, "No matter how big the lie; repeat it often enough and the masses will regard it as the truth." He also commented, "The great enemy of the truth is very often not the lie – deliberate, contrived, and dishonest, but the myth, persistent, persuasive, and unrealistic."

"Why is our government so secretive? . . . How come they insist upon keeping us in the dark as much as possible. . . . Nothing we're paying people in public office to do should go on behind closed doors. . . . We've got to have a more open government. Why can't those 10,000 documents on Able Danger be released? The old excuse of 'national security? Shouldn't there be some elected board that would say, 'Okay, tell us why this falls under national security and we'll make the decision whether it truly does, or is this simply a political cover-up?" **Jesse Ventura**

(To open up the doors of government and make it more accessible to the people, Jesse Ventura held town hall meetings over the internet that people could join from their computers.)

MARILYN MONROE

"I'm selfish, impatient and a little insecure. I make mistakes. I am out of control and at times hard to handle. But, if you can't handle me at my worst, then you sure as hell don't deserve me at my best." **Marilyn Monroe**

Comment: I appreciate the honesty of Marilyn Monroe's statement. No self-righteousness. No attempt to seem other than she is.

Many politicians lie. So do many Wall Street and other corporate executives. Patrick Henry's statement above finally saw light in the Freedom of Information Act. Yet far too much that the public should be allowed to know is still "classified" and unavailable. For a democratic government to survive, the people need to be told the truth—or at least be able to find it out. The truth can, of course, be twisted into words and phrases that conceal its meaning. And deceptive labeling can also be a kind of lying. A recent gubernatorial candidate ran ads that lied about her opponent's record, and even after Fact Check publicly announced that the truth was just the opposite, she kept on running the ads—and after she lost the election, was rewarded with a position as CEO of a major corporation. Go figure.

I think that for the most part the government should be required to truthfully tell what it is doing and why. For example, the recent sharp escalation in enforcement of anti-marijuana laws by the Food and Drug Administration would be posted with wording such as "The FDA has stepped up enforcement of anti-marijuana laws as a result of re-viewing the movie "Reefer Madness" and the need to see the Prison-Industrial Complex's jail cells filled." (Politics would become far more interesting.)

<<<>>>

SOLUTIONS

- **Extend the Freedom of Information Act so that the governments and government agencies at every level have to actively show cause why something must be kept secret in order to do so.**

- **Stop harassing, prosecuting, and jailing whistleblowers who reveal secret that embarrass the government or its contractors.**

- Make all contacts with lobbyists by any legislator, from the City Council and local agencies like the Water Agency to the Federal Government, easily visible to anyone who's interested.

- Require government agencies to announce any significant change in policy or procedure and the reason for it in an easily accessible public forum such as a well-known website.

- When a candidate, legislator, or government employee lies, do not support them even if you agree with their positions. Following Jesse Ventura's example, lay out policy decisions for public input and hold internet meetings so that concerned citizens can speak even when they can't make it to city hall.

*   *   *

26. The Mind Control Police

Imagine that you have a tiny patrol car in your head that drives around in the streets of your mind looking for uncomfortable thoughts and feelings. When it finds one, it tells you to push it out of your waking consciousness. All this happens automatically The disturbing thoughts are still there, hiding behind mental bushes and under emotional hedges, but every time one of them starts to bubble up into your awareness, your mind-police siren goes off and distracts you into thinking about something else. Self-deception includes your personal mind-police force that keeps you from acting in ways that you yourself would not approve of if you saw clearly what you were doing. It also includes maneuvers to make sure you're a properly compliant member of your family, community, party, peer group, or culture, in order to gain the rewards for acting in such ways or avoid punishment for not doing so. These mental screening and distracting processes are headquartered in the shadows and back alleys of our consciousness. They are our internal FBI, CIA, and KGB that keep us thinking as our self-image, our neighbors, our party, or our church wants us to think—at least at the conscious level. They are our intrapsychic Departments of Defense. In their own language, the founders recognized all that.

"Who has deceiv'd thee so oft as thy self? . . . It's the easiest thing in the world for a man to deceive himself," said **Benjamin Franklin.** He added, "How few there are who have courage enough to own their Faults, or resolution enough to mend them! . . . Search others for their virtues, thy self for thy vices." And Franklin also observed that "A man is never so ridiculous by those Qualities that are his own as by those that he affects to have." **Benjamin Franklin**

"Self-deceit, this fatal weakness of mankind, is the source of half the disorders of human life. If we saw ourselves in the light in which others see us, or in which they would see us if they knew all, a reformation would generally be unavoidable. We could not otherwise endure the sight." **Adam Smith**

Expanding on that theme, **Adam Smith** also wrote, "It is so disagreeable to think ill of ourselves, that we often purposely turn away our view from those circumstances which might render that judgment unfavourable. . . . He is . . . bold who does not hesitate to pull off the mysterious veil of self-delusion, which covers from his view the deformities of his own conduct. Rather than see our own behaviour under so disagreeable an aspect, we too often, foolishly and weakly, endeavor . . . by artifice to awaken our old hatreds, and irritate afresh our almost forgotten resentments. . . and thus persevere in injustice, merely because we once were unjust and because we are ashamed and afraid to see that we were so."

RALPH WALDO EMERSON

"People only see what they are prepared to see. . . . There are as many pillows of illusion as flakes in a snowstorm. We wake from one dream into another dream." **Ralph Waldo Emerson**

"People respect you because they feel you've survived hard times and endured, and although you've become famous, you haven't become phony." **Marilyn Monroe**

"As the now fully grown child of an alcoholic put it, 'In our family there were two very clear rules: the first was that there is nothing wrong here, and the second was, 'Don't tell anyone.'" Former *Psychology Today* editor **Daniel Goleman.** These two rules also apply to more than a little of what goes on behind closed doors in business and politics.

Goleman also offers an example of collective (widely shared) self-deception:

"The Pentagon's "perception theory," which is described in detail in Pentagon policy papers, boils down to this:

1. In an age of overkill, with plentiful and redundant weaponry . . . no new weapon system offers a significant military advantage.

2. However, if naïve groups—the American public, and other world leaders, for example— believe that the weapons matter militarily, then those weapons will be consequential psychologically and politically.

3. Thus those among the inner circles of military strategists should act as though new weapons systems. . . actually matter militarily, so that they will matter psychologically.

At Stanford's Center for International Security and Arms Control, **Steven Krull** says, "The situation resembles nothing so much as a drawing-room comedy. All of the key characters know a certain secret—that strategic asymmetries are militarily irrelevant in an age of overkill—but because they think that others do not know the secret they act as if they do not know the secret either."

> **Comment.** Almost all of us have at least a small mind control police force that usually does a pretty good job of keeping us from realizing how the ways we really behave differ from our illusions and delusions about ourselves. Most people want to maintain a self-image of being a decent, discerning, and reasonable person. You don't want to think of yourself as a scummy jerk or backbiting bitch. Or if due to unfortunate experiences you do feel "less than," you identify with something bigger and supposedly better than yourself so some of the glory will rub off and improve you a bit. For instance, we feel big when we identify with a powerful corporation, or political party or movement, or nation, and try to think and feel and act as others in it do. If we realize that we have reservations about some of its actions or policies, we are apt to feel diminished, so we suppress those doubts.
> In Goleman's example above, they want to go along with the secret, want to be deceived. We cling to the illusion that there is some new security system or weapons system that will keep us safe. The tragic irony is that due to the illusion that better weapons will suffice, often we ignore potent nonmilitary steps that could realistically contribute toward our safety.
> Over time your mind-police develop routines. You avoid feelings of danger (whether there is any real danger now or not) that you learned when you were punished for telling unwelcome truths or doing things that others didn't like back when you were a child. You may even learn to believe two messages that contradict each other without noticing any opposition between them at al. (In 1984, George Orwell called this "doublethink.") You learn

to accept whatever a given authority tells you. Thereafter you believe everything your authority says, unconsciously being careful to avoid noticing contradictions. For example, at a rally your favorite political hero says, "We need to reduce taxes and shrink government." Everyone cheers wildly (including you). He goes on, "We need a strong national defense, and tomorrow I am introducing a bill to fund five new nuclear aircraft carriers and fifteen new attack submarines." Everyone cheers wildly (including you). Somewhere deep inside you a tiny voice protests, "Those actions directly contradict each other." But the frenzied screams of the crowd drown out that still small voice.

Why does it matter that we deceive ourselves? First, because you become alienated from yourself. You lose track of your own deep sense of who you are, mentally, emotionally, and often spiritually. You become less of a thoughtful human being and more of a puppet whose reactions are jerked back and forth by whoever holds the strings. Second, because you become less adept at perceiving what's real, and at creatively and critically thinking through which course or action is actually best in a given situation.

How does all this come about? At some points in life, most often in childhood, powerful people in your environment have told you that you are not as you think yourself to be. Things are not as you think they are, and only **they** know the truth. Children who receive such messages must either give up the approval, protection and love of their parents or other adult protectors, or must disown their own ability to tell that is real and instead accept what they are told is so. Adults sometimes face a similar choice. Accept what everyone around you believes and give up your inner self, or think for yourself and give up your friends. You are not told that you **should** think and feel differently than you do, but rather that you **do** think and feel as others say you do. As this occurs, we lose our ability to tell what is real and what is not—in regard to both our inner realities and the world around us. When you question programming that conflicts with who you thought you were and what you thought you felt and believed, others invalidate your thoughts and feelings. "C'mon, Jack, you're confused. Only a socialist would say that. Get real."

This can occur nonverbally. A squeeze of your hand or shoulder, a smile, or scowl, or curl of your lip at a crucial moment, may be enough to send the message. I don't even have to speak. In such social contagion, we respond automatically. There is no reality testing, no logic, no reason. As the Great Leader finishes his or her lines the crowd rises to its feet, screaming in adulation and identification, "Yes, Forward!" (toward the Great portal of the Temple of Doom and Death—conveniently renamed the Temple of Truth and Freedom.)

When we are lying to ourselves, we cannot speak the truth to others. The platforms of ALL the parties may be insane but no one realizes it. Your **group** may engage in political or economic dissent, but **you** are not allowed to dissent from **the group's** views. WELCOME TO THE INSANE ASYLUM, RECENTLY RENAMED THE TABERNACLE OF TRUTH AND LIGHT AND WISDOM! ps. -- anyone who points any of this out will be considered crazy and shunned by all the nuts who think that they and others in their group are sane—which in some cases is almost everybody.

<<<>>>

SOLUTIONS

- **If you actively seek to become more deeply honest with yourself, and to find your own truths, keep in mind that you can't do it by mouthing slogans and shuffling along with the crowd. It is an inward journey. But in following that path you develop your own *inner freedom*. (For the most part, both "leftists" and "rightists" are concerned with outer freedom---with what other people, society, and the laws will let them do. *But true outer freedom depends on*** *attaining inner freedom.*

- Be on the alert, moment by moment, to discover and notice the tricky tactics that Big Media, Big Advertising, Big Business and Big Government use to manipulate your thoughts, emotions, and actions. You'll increase your ability to recognize how you use your personal mind-control tactics, and to stop doing so when you wish. Discovering your ways of distorting ideas about yourself and the realities around you is like turning on a car's windshield wipers in a rainstorm. As a result, you can come to know the deeper, richer reaches of your heart and mind. You'll travel fewer wrong roads, and reach more of your desired destinations.

- Watch your own mind in action. Scan your body for muscle tensions and let go of them, take a few minutes to notice yourself breathing, breath by breath. Then when your mind feels clear enough, watch it in action as if you were a spectator sitting behind it. Yes, this is a basic meditation practice. It's a good way to watch your own mind. The key is bringing yourself back to watchfulness when you notice yourself drifting into reverie. The benefit is discovering more about yourself.

- As you watch your mind in action, be especially alert for these three mind-police tactics:

- *Distraction,* or "jumping from one thing to another." Often we do this *just before the item we don't want to think about comes into our consciousness. The clue: Very suddenly you're thinking or talking about something quite different than you were the moment before. People also intentionally do this to each other, as in the use of a "red herring" – dragging a fish across a trail to throw a dog off the scent of what it was tracking.*

- *Selective Inattention,* or "I don't see what I don't like." Instead, I look at something else. Or I may see what I don't like, but perceive it through distorting "lenses" –a screen of transformative concepts or metaphors, so that what's right in front of me doesn't register. For example, a simple act of kindness by someone I dislike can't be genuine—it must have some kind of manipulative intent.

- *Rationalization.* You know this one: *I give myself a cover story.* I find an explanation for my nasty action or that of a friend or group that makes me, or us, look more admirable or less despicable than is really so. This is pervasive in both politics and business.

* * *

27. Helpful vs. Harmful Disagreement

Personal and political disagreements alike can take place with some measure of mutual respect and appreciation for the humanity of those with whom we disagree, or who oppose our interests. (Even in a football game, after one player has knocked another from the opposing team down, often he helps him back up.) Or they can be steeped in antagonism and enmity, and filled with hostility, contempt, and prejudice toward on "the other side." In the former case, finding solutions to conflicts and disagreements that both or all can accept is a real possibility. In the latter case, an endless road of trouble that stretches to the horizon is more likely. The choice of which of these scenarios will unfold is almost always at least partly ours. Blaming "the other" for everything almost always steers us onto the darker path. Hatriots are not patriots. Patriots have at least some sense of common purpose with their fellow citizens. If you're inciting people to hate those in the other party, the other race, the other country, you can sing the anthem as loud as you like and wrap yourself in the flag so tightly that you can't see out, but you're no patriot. If you're inciting hate, you're "part of the problem—not part of the solution."

"A general dissolution of principles and manners will more surely overthrow the Liberties of America than the whole force of the common enemy." **Samuel Adams**

"I have always strenuously supported the right of every man to his own opinion, however different that opinion might be to mine. He who denies to another this right, makes a slave of himself to his present opinion, because he precludes himself the right of changing it." **Thomas Paine.** In addition, Paine said, "He that would make his own liberty secure must guard even his enemy from oppression; for if he violates this duty he establishes a precedent that will reach to himself.

"The boisterous sea of liberty indeed is never without a wave. . . . I tolerate with the utmost latitude the right of others to differ from me in opinion. . . . I know too well the weakness and uncertainty of human reason to wonder at its different results. Both of our political parties, at least the honest part of them, agree conscientiously in the same object—the public good; but they differ essentially in what they deem the means of promoting that good. One side. . . fears most the ignorance of the people; the other, the selfishness of rulers independent of them. . . My anxieties on this subject will never carry me beyond the use of fair and honorable means, of truth and reason; nor have they ever lessened my esteem for the moral worth, nor alienated my affections from a single friend, who did not first withdraw himself." **Thomas Jefferson**

Enemies can be stimulating. Anger can motivate us to take needed action. Yet also, as **Mark Twain** pointed out, on the other hand "Anger is an acid that can do more harm to the vessel in which it is stored than to anything on which it is poured."

"Never let your opponent pick the battleground on which to fight. If he picks one, stay out of it and let him fight all by himself." **Franklin D. Roosevelt**

"Controversy equalizes fools and wise men – and the fools know it." **Oliver Wendell Holmes Jr.** Holmes also said, "Don't flatter yourself that friendship authorizes you to say disagreeable things to your intimates. The nearer you come into relation with a person, the more necessary do tact and courtesy become."

HARRY S. TRUMAN

"It is understanding that gives us an ability to have peace. When we understand the other fellow's viewpoint, and he understands ours, then we can sit down and work out our differences." **Harry S. Truman**

"Freedom is hammered out on the anvil of discussion, dissent, and debate." **Hubert Humphrey**

"To disagree, one doesn't have to be disagreeable." **Barry Goldwater**

"[George Washington] deplored the adversary theory which sees government as a tug of war between the holders of opposite views, one side eventually vanquishing the other. Washington saw the national capital as a place where men came together not to tussle but to reconcile disagreements. . . . Washington's own greatest mental gift was to be able to bore down through partial arguments to the fundamental principles on which everyone could agree." Historian **James Thomas Flexner**

"Washington's great gift of allowing opposition to exist within his administration or under his command, and to bring to this opposition the non-intervening look that is the reconciling force. . . can help us regenerate our image of the democratic process and correct our fantasies that a marketplace of egoistic impulses somehow miraculously produces intelligence and harmony, both in the self and in the society. Washingtonian democracy is not the freedom to try to destroy each other physically or philosophically or morally, but the freedom to bring one's own best thought together with one's best effort to listen and attend to the other. The aim is not to reach the pale and crooked version of mutual accommodation that we call "compromise" . . . but to discover a more comprehensive intelligence that allows each part and each partial truth to take its proper and necessary place in the life of the whole." **Jacob Needleman**

"Congresswoman [Gabrielle] Giffords' message of bipartisanship and civility is one that all in Washington and in the nation should honor and emulate. . . . [She] has brought the word 'dignity' to new heights by her courage." **Nancy Pelosi** (Rep. Giffords was shot in the brain by a gun-toting rightist wingnut who besides shooting Giffords murdered a little girl, a judge, and others in the vicinity.)

BARACK OBAMA

"Most people who serve in Washington have been trained either as lawyers or as political operatives—professions that tend to place a premium on winning arguments rather than solving problems. . . . [But] when we dumb down the political debate, we lose. For it's precisely the pursuit of ideological purity [and] the rigid orthodoxy . . . of our current political debate that keeps us finding new ways to meet the challenges we face as a country." **Barack Obama**

> **Comment:** Political and economic affairs inevitably involve some disagreements, often based on conflicts of interest. Some people become addicted to the subsequent anger, or even rage. They live off it, and provoke situations in which they have more excuses to get angry. The result is that much of the rest of their emotional life tends to become unavailable to them, and their social reality becomes dominated by hostile relations. The downside for their community or nation is that their commitment to anger and negative thinking provokes antagonism and meanness in others, poisoning political dialogues and destroying potential opportunities for improvements. George Washington warned against any demagogue who 'agitates the community with ill-founded jealousies and false alarms, [and] kindles the animosity of one part against another."
>
> The behavior Washington warned against has been the modus operandi of the Radical Wrong. For example, when Newt Gingrich was Speaker of the House of Representatives, he gave all the congresspersons of his party a list of derogatory adjectives that ran from A to Z, with several negative words for each one and suggested that they use these adjectives to characterize their Democratic opponents at every opportunity. (He was also trying to impeach Bill Clinton for lying about a sexual encounter while he himself was cheating on his wife, whom he later divorced in order to marry his mistress who was twenty years his junior. Good 'ol Mr. Morality.) Another right-wing activist, Grover Norquist, told the Denver Post, "We are trying to change the tones in the state capitals—and turn them toward bitter nastiness and partisanship." It is an ancient tactic.

"This is not a case of Democrats vs. Republicans. It's sentient beings vs. the Lizard People." **Bill Maher**

"When will mankind be convinced and agree to settle their difficulties by arbitration?" **Benjamin Franklin**

"The greatest compliment that was ever paid me was when one asked me what I thought, and attended to my answer." **Henry David Thoreau**

"Have you learned the lessons only of those who admired you, and were tender with you, and stood aside for you? Have you not learned great lessons from those who braced themselves against you, and disputed passage with you?" **Walt Whitman**

"Am I not destroying my enemies when I make friends of them? . . . We should be too big to take offense and too noble to give it." *Abraham Lincoln*

Lincoln further stated, "Let us at all times remember that all American citizens are brothers of a common country, and should dwell together in bonds of fraternal feeling. . . . We must not be enemies. Though passion may have strained, it must not break our bonds of affection. The mystic chords of memory, stretching from every battlefield and patriot grave, to every living heart and hearth-stone, all over this broad land, will yet swell the chorus of the Union when again touched, as surely they will be, by the better angels of our nature." Himself a lawyer, **Lincoln** advised, "Discourage litigation. Persuade your neighbors to compromise whenever you can. Point out to them how the nominal winner is often a real loser — in fees, expenses, and waste of time. As a peacemaker the lawyer has a superior opportunity of being a good man. There will still be business enough. Never stir up litigation. A worse man can scarcely be found than one who does this. . . A moral tone ought to be infused into the profession which should drive such men out of it. . . . Resolve to be honest at all events; and if in your own judgment you cannot be an honest lawyer, resolve to be honest without being a lawyer. Choose some other occupation, rather than one in the choosing of which you do, in advance, consent to be a knave."

"Let us not be blind to our differences – but let us also direct attention to our common interests and to the means by which those differences can be resolved. *John F. Kennedy*

Kennedy also said, "If we cannot end our differences, at least we can help make the world safe for diversity."

"Others may hate you but those who hate you don't win unless you hate them. And then you destroy yourself." **Richard M. Nixon**

"I've had a lot of adversaries in my political life, but no enemies that I can remember." **Gerald R. Ford**

WALTER F. MONDALE

"[When I served in the Senate in the 1970s], debates were always heated. But I don't think they had the kind of nastiness they do today. We need to lighten it up . . . to find a way of talking with each other. I've won and I've lost. And I like winning better. [But] when you run for office in a democracy . . . one person wins and one person loses. I think it's important that we do it with civility, with respect." Vice President **Walter F. Mondale**

"I found that I could generally win these arguments [with my grandfather, but] I realized that sometimes he really did have a point, and that in insisting on getting my own way all the time, without regard to his feelings or needs, I was in some way diminishing myself." **Barack Obama**

"I will fight against the division politics of revenge and retribution. . . I will work to lift people up, not put them down." **Hillary Clinton**

HILLARY CLINTON

"My husband and I are in good health. We have laid an exceptionally strong foundation for the campaign and I have no doubt I would have won re-election. . . . I remain deeply passionate about public service. I do find it frustrating, however, that an atmosphere of polarization and 'my way or the highway' ideologies has become pervasive in campaigns and in our governing institutions. . . . . It is time. . . to return to an era of civility in government driven by a common purpose to fulfill the promise that is unique to America." **Maine Senator Olympia Snowe (Rep.),** announcing that she would not seek re-election in 2012.

> **Comment:** A tactic long used by ruling elites is that of turning the various social classes and interests against each other: *Divide and Conquer.* This approach is consciously used by the ruling elite today. The rest of us do not have to get caught in their trap.
>
> Since 1990, scientists have shown that we all have "mirror neurons" that mimic the emotional tone that others express toward us. Love and caring tend to beget love and caring in others. Hostility tends to beget hostility. But we don't have to respond like programmed robots. One path to resolving conflicts is to listen for, hear deeply what is in the other person's heart and what motives underlie their "position," and how their hopes and fears are much like your own. Even if we don't love each other, we can at least show some measure of mutual respect – even when we express our fervent opposition to what others are doing.
>
> Do you think the present polarization could not get worse? In Greece in 366 B.C. Isocrates wrote that, "The rich have become so unsocial that those who own property had rather throw their possessions into the sea than lend aid to the needy, while those who are in poorer circumstances would less gladly find a treasure than seize the possessions of the rich." Members of some oligarchic organizations, reports Aristotle, took a solemn oath: "I will be an adversary of the [common] people . . . and in the Council I will do [them] all the evil

that I can." Later, much of Europe was devastated by wars centered on conflicts about religious beliefs. Washington, Jefferson, Franklin, and Paine knew all that and resolved to do all they could to keep such conflicts from infecting the United States. Now the infections have broken out and have turned into an epidemic. It is up to us to cure them.

In all conflict resolution, clarity of perception is essential. You don't want to misperceive another's hostile intention so that you fail to protect yourself. On the other hand, you want to act in ways that will not evoke or encourage the other's hostility. We can draw aside the smoke, mirrors, and veils of mystification in order to perceive clearly what each party and interest is saying and doing. Attaining that clarity of perception, and reaching into our own hearts for wise counsel, allows us to work together.

<<<>>>

SOLUTIONS

- Beware of every kind of effort by those who serve the interests of the power elite to divide the rest of the people into factions and turn them against each other. Search for common ground and stand together with environmentalists, union members, the unemployed, and all others who are part of the 99%. For that matter, search for common ground with the 1%. You just may find some.

- Criticize actions and policies, not people. Avoid name-calling. Avoid demeaning your opponents. Focus on their actions, ask for change in those which appear necessary, and be civil in your dealings even with those with whom you disagree most.

*   *   *

28. Oh, No – Not the Alpha Complex again!

Personal and political tendencies often go hand in hand. Psychiatrist Alfred Adler coined the now well-known term, "inferiority complex." It means that you feel "less than" others around you. Adler's concept emerged from his personal experience. Due to a case of rickets, he could not walk until the age of four. At five he was hit by a car. As a child, he was skinny, weak, and sickly. Physically, he really was inferior to most others.

When we are tiny children, we are all physically and mentally inferior to the adults around us. They are all-powerful giants who can do almost anything. A small child can't even reach the doorknob or light switch. It makes things even worse when an adult or older kid, in order to feel like a big shot at the child's expense, puts the latter down: "Can't you even do that?" It takes a wise and sensitive parent to encourage children's initiatives and praise their successes instead of criticizing their shortcomings.

In childhood and adulthood alike, there are those who like to think they are bigger and "better than," and do their best to belittle others to make them feel small by comparison. And there are those who are driven to "get to the top" regardless of whom or what they have to crush or destroy to get there. I find it useful to group such patterns together as the opposite of Adler's "inferiority complex" and label them *the Alpha Complex.* To some degree it characterizes everyone who belittles or steps on others in order to feel okay within him- or herself.

Among all the reckonings of advantage and disadvantage, wealth and poverty, power and powerlessness, one item stands out as central. The polarity of *domination vs. respect* is like a sun around which all these other considerations orbit like planets. Anyone who is committed to domination suffers from an alpha complex as described here. (I am not speaking of domination in sports contests where it is appropriate, or situations such as self-defense, where you want to dominate the attacker.)

Do not misunderstand: This does not refer to the extraordinarily able person who excels and achieves great things as a result of unusual natural ability, development of his or her talents, good judgment—and often, at least a little good luck. Such a person is an "alpha" in his or her field, but feels no need to show others up or put them down, no compulsive urge to power, and does not have an alpha complex as defined here.

Some of our nation's founding fathers acknowledged what I call the alpha complex, the trouble it can cause, and ways to deal with it:

"Humility makes great men twice honourable." **Benjamin Franklin**

"In view of the Constitution, in the eye of the law, there is in this country no superior, dominant, ruling class of citizens. There is no caste here. Our Constitution is colorblind, and neither knows nor tolerates classes among citizens. . . . The humblest is the peer of the most powerful." **John Marshall**

"A great man is always willing to be little." **Ralph Waldo Emerson**

"Be curious, not judgmental." **Walt Whitman**

"The strongest and most effective force in guaranteeing the long-term maintenance of power is not violence in all the forms deployed by the dominant to control the dominated, but consent in all the forms in which the dominated acquiesce in their own domination." **Robert Frost**

"He who accepts evil without protesting against it is really cooperating with it." **Martin Luther King**

"Everybody wants something at the expense of everybody else and nobody thinks much of the other fellow." **Harry Truman,** after several months as President

Comment: The attitude of someone inflicted with an alpha complex is, "I know how things are supposed to be, and how both you and I are supposed to act, and your role is to accept my story. In other words, I dominate, you submit. Mutual respect is absent. As I try to impose my views on you, I may not even realize that they are not reality. In so doing I violate your personal boundary by extending myself (in the form of my thoughts, my feelings, my actions) into your personal space. If a person's tactics are clever enough, he or she can make you feel and respond as if he or she is better and you are worse without you ever quite realizing what's happening. Messages that you are "less than" can be communicated by the choice of a word or the tone of voice. They can be communicated nonverbally without a single word, by a contemptuous curl of the lip, a listlessly disinterested glance, or a particular way of holding and moving one's body. In either case the message is that *we are unequal and you are not as good as I am.* And often enough, *that I will damage you severely unless you buckle under to my wishes.* An alpha complex can take any of many forms:

> *"I can punch you out."*
> *"I'm smarter than you."*
> *"My car is better than yours."*
> *"My racial group is cleaner and more industrious than yours."*
> *"My country is better than your country,"*
> *"My religion is true and yours is false."*
> *"I have a diamond ring and you don't."*
> *"My _____ is bigger than yours."*
> Or ultimately,
> *"Our army can annihilate your army."*

It's all basically one up, one down. As for "my football team is better than yours"— that's expected.. Just don't take it too terribly seriously---such by giving yourself high blood pressure about it or attacking an opposing team's fans.

Actually the entire "I AM BETTER THAN YOU" and "mine is better than yours" put-down pattern is a small-minded manifestation of a shriveled state of mind and heart. **One-upmanship is inherently one-down consciousness. It is a craving to dominate stirred by the self-centered ego.**

The essence of the alpha complex is wanting to be Number One so badly that you are willing to hurt and humiliate others to reach that goal. There is no light of shared joy and happiness at the end of that tunnel. If you have an alpha complex, even your friends will be on guard against becoming your victim. Fortunately, the alpha complex does not have to be a terminal condition. I have seen people who suffer from it make the leap into a greater, wiser stage of understanding—in short, into relationships genuinely based on mutual respect.

Childhood roots of an alpha complex usually lie in either (1) overcompensation for feeling inferior due to put-downs from others; (2) emotional neglect by parents who were too busy or disinterested to pay enough attention to their child; (3) physical or emotional abuse; (4) being "spoiled" –i.e. getting almost everything you want without having to do anything or take any responsibility to get it. Hotshot businesspersons and politicians often justify stepping on others in order to "come out on top," by Darwin and Wallace's theory of evolution: "Survival of the fittest." This is a major misunderstanding. Neither Darwin nor

Wallace ever used the term "survival of the fittest"—it was coined and popularized by sociologist Herbert Spencer, who failed to understand Darwin and Wallace and put his own views and words in their mouths. Darwin and Wallace emphasized adaptation, which in practical terms means finding an "econiche" in your biological or social environment in which you can survive. It does not require pushing others down or humiliating them so that you can feel superior.

An alpha complex has especially damaging effects in political and economic affairs when leaders of one country or company try to dominate others. In politics, often enough it rips a nation in two as the more powerful impose their will and send young men and women out to die in wars to fulfill their pathological craving to dominate. There will never be social harmony or international peace as long as we elect people driven by alpha complexes to power, or let them seize power.

There is also **the Piggy Complex**, drawing on George Orwell's *Animal Farm* in which the pigs take power. (Although ostensibly written as a spoof of communism, Orwell remarked that he also intended it as commentary on much of what he saw in England of his day.) Like one-upmanship, it is a sub-category of the alpha complex. For some people, more is just never enough. They are always trying to get as much as possible. This may mean material things or power over other people. In our day, advertising agencies and demagogues are constantly trying to take control of your brain and induce a piggy complex, so that you will endlessly crave ever more of what they want you to want.

Some people say, "Oh, we can't really improve, because most people are basically aggressive and evil. Look at how children fight! We have to be aggressive in return to protect ourselves."

Of course most people have an aggressive side. They also have a loving and caring side, which appears even before the aggression. An infant is content and loving in Mama's arms long before aggressive inclinations surface. Which tendency becomes stronger, and how we direct each of them, depends on what we teach our children, and what they learn from other sources. A person can learn to be appropriately aggressive for self-protection, yet also become a basically loving, caring, capable person who does not suffer from any alpha complex.

<<<>>>

SOLUTIONS

- **Actively remind yourself to relate to others without comparison, meeting them as one person to another, on the same level, on common ground. Then be with them in a respectful way, whatever their station in life, and yours. The relationship becomes one of mutual respect, in which antagonism, dislike, conflict and violence all become less likely.**

- **Work diligently to develop an inward awareness in which you consciously and consistently notice, or ask yourself, "Who is being helped and who is being harmed, and how, by my words or actions?"**

- **Step out of power struggles. If you feel locked into a power struggle with another, ask yourself, "Do I truly care enough about that to have to "win?" If not, step into "the better angel of your nature" and let go.**

- **When you meet another person whose words or actions put you down, *shift the spotlight onto his or her behavior* by saying something like: "You're not being** very nice this morning. Are you always this way or have you just had a bad day?" Spotlighting the other person's behavior often derails his or her aggressiveness.

- Avoid an "I told you so" attitude. It's just another way of saying, "I'm better than you" and putting the other down.

- You can consciously step out of materialistic evaluation to avoid making an "I've got more than you" statement.

- If you make major progress in shrinking your alpha complex, beware of the egotism game that often pops up next: one-upmanship in the form of conceit: "My consciousness is more advanced than yours."

* * *

29. From Misguided Agendas to
"Crown thy Good with Brotherhood [and Sisterhood]"

Throughout history leaders, saints, and sages have offered wise counsel about acting with kindness and compassion toward our neighbors next door and across the tracks, and near and distant neighbor nations around the world. And throughout history liars and sociopaths have used similar words to cover schemes of extortion, aggression, and political and economic imperialism. Such political atrocities and economic exploitation have made it clear that good words alone are not enough to meet even the challenges we face today, much less the far greater ones that lie just over the horizon.

So is the world situation hopeless? Are we doomed to muddle long lying to each other, bilking each other, passing laws that make our government force some people to live as others decree, and resorting to guns and drones when we don't get our way?

As things stand now, both in the United States and elsewhere, prospects for peace, prosperity, liberty, justice, and equality appear at least a little grim. True, in some ways there has been great progress as history has unfolded. True too, within the U.S., for the most part we settle our grievances with words and courts and elections rather than guns and bombs. But in the past few decades we seem to have fallen into habits that challenge our integrity as a nation.

During the mid-twentieth century there was a genuine ethos of corporate responsibility in the executive suites of many our nation's companies. Then the misguided writings of Milton Friedman and Ludwig von Mises became influential. International corporate competition intensified, and this, combined with the Friedman-von Mises ideology of "get all you can and forget the other poor schmucks" hammered the concept of a corporate social conscience. And in the 1980s those trends combined with another dating far back in the nation's history to form a black hole that is disfiguring our national conscience.

When the progressive government of Theodore Roosevelt gained power, the holders of great wealth whose agenda was to attain power greater than the government's ability to temper it did not vanish from the scene. Nor did the corporate and other monied interests that controlled the country during the Roaring Twenties disappear when Franklin D. Roosevelt came forward as a champion of the 99% in the 1930s. They just bided their time and went underground. During and after the era when FDR, Truman, Eisenhower, Kennedy, and Lyndon Johnson held power, an era when middle class and working people were becoming more prosperous, the plutocrats set about quietly plotting to take over the country again. That goal became easier to attain when LBJ signed the Civil Rights Act of 1965, which ended segregation. Almost everybody wants to have somebody to look down on, and many in the South resented the new laws which provided that black Americans whose ancestors had been slaves could now sit anywhere on the bus, eat at the same lunch counters, and use the same drinking fountains and restrooms and swimming pools as they themselves. It was almost too easy for the power elite to tell Southerners, "Okay, white folks, the Democrats ended segregation and we know you don't like it. Vote with us and we'll do our best to keep you on top. Those who said, "Count me in" were not bad people – they were just carrying on an attitude of racial superiority that had been passed down from their grandparents, for whom it served to justify slavery. The stroke of a president's pen couldn't change their attitudes overnight. So the South swung over to become massively Republican. Few of the swingers read between the lines, where they would have discovered that the right-wing agenda they were snookered into supporting would pick their pockets, steal some of their important rights, give those at the top of the social heap in their very own states even more power, and leave them powerless and maybe even jobless. The small print in the contract was not what they thought they bargained for.

Meanwhile, there arose right-wing think tanks inhabited by pawns of the plutocracy, a development that in their wildest dreams the founding fathers never imagined—or at least never mentioned imagining. Today these include the Heritage Foundation, the American Enterprise Institute, the notorious Koch Brothers' Cato Institute, ALEC (The American Legislative Exchange Council), the Center for Security Policy, and many other equally exciting architects of oligarchy. (You doubt it? Just check out their websites.) Agendas include such items as ending public education and using taxpayer money to pay private and parochial schools; reshaping health care in ways designed entirely to boost corporate profits, and above all, to "privatize" services that government agencies perform perfectly well, such as Social Security and public water systems

The American Small Business Chamber of Commerce, by contrast, is a different kind of being entirely. Its website states, "Over the last two decades, more and more large firms took jobs (once held in America) off-shore, employed un-American tax strategies to prevent paying their fair share to support our country, and poured millions upon millions of dollars into the pockets of political lobbyists and campaign coffers reaping more and more undue privileges, government contracts and handouts. The growing big business domination catapulted to the next tier of supremacy during the recent, abrupt downturn in the American economy. Billions of dollars and bailouts went into the hands of big business -- who simply continued to escalate their dominance, reaping profits and further market-share gains off the backs of hard working American tax payers.. . . Small business owners care about their workers and their communities. We know how families are impacted by jobs sent overseas, and feel the frustration every day as consumer demand stagnates, unemployment grows, and capital readily available for business lending is held aside exclusively for our big-business competitors."

The "Small Business Imperative" is this: "We must level the playing field by stopping anti-American business practices, tax havens and tax evasion, greatly increase access to affordable capital for small businesses, stop big-corporate give always and unwarranted privileges, raise the federal mandate for contracting with small businesses . . . and put small business owners at the leadership table in Washington and all across our country."

"Is there some evidence that privatization is a good idea? It's just something that you repeat because it's drilled into your head. . . . There are experiences. For example, we can look at Mexico. What privatization did was rapidly increase the number of millionaires, accelerate the decline of real wages and social conditions. Did it make things better? Well, yes, for 24 billionaires. . . .{Now] lets take England. . . Under Thatcher they privatized the water system. It was a public utility. So now it's private. What happened . . . is, profits have gone through the roof, prices have gone way up, and service has gone way down. . . . A private corporation is not in the business of being humanitarian. It's in the business of increasing profit and market share. Doing that . . . may make some numbers look good. It may create what's called an 'economic miracle,' meaning great for investors and murderous for the population. . . . Sometimes private industry has been efficient, and sometimes even helpful to people. . . and many times it hasn't. It depends on the circumstances. . . . But the idea that somehow privatization automatically improves things is absurd." **Noam Chomsky**

> **Comment:** I'm guessing that Jefferson would have nodded in approval of the lines just above. Think again of the real 1773 tea party protest, which was against the British government-enforced corporate monopoly on tea. There is absolutely nothing wrong with big business *per se*. It has done many good things for us. I am deeply indebted to Steve Jobs and the personal computer on which I am writing this. I love the internet and thank the military for developing it, and thank Yahoo and Google for their search engines, and others like Alta Vista that laid the groundwork. The problem comes when maximizing profit eclipses other vital values—just as Adam Smith stated in *The Theory of Moral Sentiments*. (See the section devoted to his views in Part II above.)

Today part of the agenda of the Radical Wrong element of the corporate sector is rampant "privatization" to take over anything owned by the people from which a profit might be made (such as public water systems), and spin off onto the government anything that might cause them a loss (such as cleanup of their air and water pollution, and earthquake insurance—which in California the insurance companies all dropped, leaving the State government to start up a public earthquake insurance agency because insurance companies all abandoned such coverage.

A CASE STUDY OF THE PRIVATIZATION ZEALOTS AT WORK: THEY'RE EVEN TRYING TO KILL THE POSTAL SERVICE. When the Constitution was adopted, establishing post offices was one of its *enumerated powers*. The U.S. Constitution reads,

"Article 1 – The Legislative Branch . . .

"Section 8 – Powers of Congress . . .

"To establish post offices and post roads"

The Postmaster was a cabinet position and the final position in the presidential line of succession. Even before the Revolution and the Constitution, the 1775 Continental Congress asked Benjamin Franklin to organize a postal service for the nation, and he became its first Postmaster General. The government is now proposing to close 3,700 Post Offices (maybe the one you use) and 487 regional mail processing centers. Haven't our communities been torn apart enough already? We don't have to take an ax to the Postal Service so FedEx can pick up more business.

The bottom line is that your local post office may be shut down, your regional distribution center may be consolidated into another one far away, (which will delay your mail delivery by an extra day or two), and everybody who now picks up their mail at your post office will have to drive or take the bus to a distant one, meaning hundreds or thousands of extra round-trips a day, along with the dramatic spike in gasoline use needed to make the, (instead of one truck making one convenient delivery each day to your local post office which is located near its users homes). If your Post Office is one of those 3,700, you'll lose not only mail service, but one of the main places for chatting and connecting with others in your community. (I meet people there whom I seldom see elsewhere.)

Here's a touching detail: One of the locations to be shut down is the historic Franklin Post Office in Philadelphia, located right on the site of Ben's own house in Franklin square, next door to the U.S. Postal Service Museum. How patriotic! Next we could melt down the Liberty Bell and sell it for scrap, and I'll bet we could get a *premium* price for the Statue of Liberty from one of the world's multibillionaires. (It would look so nice on his private island.) Are you "conservative?" If so, I'm guessing that you'd like to conserve the postal service you have now. Are you "progressive?" Well, then you might want to progress toward a Post Office that offers even more useful services and products than yours does today.

Those who want to close down the post offices say that the Postal Service is "unprofitable," costs "taxpayers" billions of dollars a year in losses, and is plunging into "bankruptcy."

Publisher and former Texas Agricultural Commissioner **Jim Hightower** and **Phillip Frazer** reply, "UNPROFITABLE. So what? When has the Pentagon ever made a profit? Never. . .nor do [the] Centers for Disease Control . . . etc. Producing a profit is not the purpose of government—its purpose is service. . . . But Nixon shattered the public service model by imposing a bottom-line profit mentality on the agency. . . The cabinet-level Post Office Department that was overseen by Congress was transformed into today's Postal

Service, overseen by a Board of Governors and funded by postage sales. . . . Until last year, for example, one of its [board's] most influential members was James Miller III. . . a longtime proponent of totally privatizing mail service. He's a product of such right-wing Koch-funded outfits as the American Enterprise Institute and Citizens for a Sound Economy (now called Americans for Prosperity) that are ardent pushers of postal privatization.

"TAXPAYERS. . . Since 1971, the Postal Service has not taken a dime from taxpayers. All its operations. . . are paid for by peddling stamps and other products. . . . The Postal Service is NOT broke. Indeed, in [the last] four years of loudly deplored 'losses,' the Service actually produce a $700 million operational profit."

What's going on here? Right-wing sabotage of USPS financing. . . . the Bush White House and Congress whacked the post office with [legislation that makes it] PRE-PAY the health care benefits of . . . all employees who'll retire during the next 75 years. . . Imagine the shrieks of outrage if Congress tried to slap FedEx or other private firms with such an onerous requirement," write Hightower and Frazer. "Also . . . the federal Office of Personnel Management has overcharged the post office by as much as $80 billion for payments into the Civil Service Retirement System. Restore the agency's access to its own postage money and the impending "collapse" goes away. . . . FedEx CEO Fredrick Smith (a former board member of the Koch boys' Cato Institute) has been the leading corporate champion for "closing down the USPS." (See "Hightower Lowdown" in References)

The plot unfolds: Close down the government service so FedEx (and their Kinko's stores) can pick up the profits. Similar scenarios are being played out on other stages. You read about taxpayer-funded private prisons (Corrections Corporation of America, etc.) in an earlier chapter, with the deal they offered if state governments would "agree to keep the prisons mostly full." I think that's sick! And big corporations are aggressively buying up public water systems all around the world, converting them into private systems, and jacking up customer prices and their profits. Other companies are trying to get everyone to drink bottled water. Major players in the U.S. and elsewhere include Vivendi, Perrier, Suez, Bechtel, Nestle, and Monsanto. T. Boone Pickens has bought up a farm over the rapidly dropping Oglalla aquifer with the idea of pumping the water out and selling it to cities far away.

In a very few places water privatization makes senses. It most it does not. If all this sounds grim, well, it does to me too. As I write, I'm trying to find some way to be at least a little upbeat about it all, but it's not easy.

Wait, a flash of inspiration just came! **I'VE GOT IT!** All we have do to is make the "Let big business privatize everything" agenda into a Feelgood Scenario. We could just conclude that democracy was basically a failed experiment, that its new slogan is "Forget it" and that the wave of the future is --***Yes folks, you've been waiting for it and now here it is—CORPOCRACY!*** LET'S HAVE A BIG ROUND OF APPLAUSE FOR THE "CORPOCRATIC STATES OF AMERICA." Come on, now, everybody, lets cheer together: WE LOVE CORPOCRACY, CORPORCRACY IS TRUE DEMOCRACY! CORPOCRACY UBER ALLES! First thing tomorrow, I will ask my Congressperson to introduce a bill in Congress to replace the 50 stars on the American flag with 50 corporate logos, with the spaces for them sold to the highest bidders. Space for brief messages in red letters on the white stripes will be sold to major banks and brokerage houses. And the elephant and donkey are so – *yesterday*— as political symbols. We really need only one party, which will be a great economy for corporations that now pay off lawmakers of both parties. To achieve that economy, the Republicans and Democrats can simply merge. And what better symbol could there possibly be for the new **Corpocratic Party** than a red, white, and blue **DOLLAR SIGN**? Gosh, I'm feeling so much better already, aren't you?

Or maybe not. Maybe you're an old-fashioned stick-in-the-mud who is not quite ready to accept that glorious scenario. There is an alternative. Even now it may not be too late for us to sincerely ask, "How can we reverse directions and begin moving toward a nation that exists for its people again? Toward a government dedicated to public service rather than ensuring generous corporate profits? And toward a natural environment that is becoming healthier and more alive instead of dying a little more every year?"

For openers, we need to break through the passivity of feeling helpless to change the oligarchic agenda that the right-wing think tanks and ideological zealots are planning for us. The time has come for a dramatic change in direction. A crucial step in that, which few people in politics have been talking about, is that as a society, we need to bring about a transformation such that *the entire culture encourages the ongoing development of greater consciousness, awareness, and well-being of all its people.* This includes our politics, our production and allocation of goods and services, our schools, and even our religious institutions. That goal needs to become the lodestar of our culture, and indeed, the world.

Big job.

But essential. Families and schools need to move toward bringing up children in ways that open their minds rather than closing them. Workplaces, churches, colleges, community groups, all need to work together so that we help each other to become kinder, more loving and more compassionate beings who truly care about each other and about our living planet. I think Jesus, Buddha, Muhammad, Hillel, Lao-Tzu, Confucius, and the great Hindu saints and yogis would all agree. By my reckoning, on a scale of 1 to 10, the average level of human consciousness today is about a 5.5. I have met a few nines and tens in my lifetime; most ones and twos are in jail. The remarkable group who founded our nation, who lived during what was called "The Age of Enlightenment" probably ranged from 7 to 10. "Seven" got killed in a duel. Had he been an 8 he might have refused the challenge.

If we each strive to boost our personal consciousness up a notch, we may have a real chance to "crown our good with brotherhood -- and sisterhood." If we make it a cultural ideal, our liberty, our democracy, and the entire world may have a decent chance to survive.

The Founding Fathers, along with Abraham Lincoln, are incredible role models. I believe that those who are much quoted in this book can well be regarded as spiritual as well as political teachers. Of course we can't all be, for example, a Benjamin Franklin, but we can do our best to emulate those among his qualities that are within our reach.

"Of all the representatives sent abroad by the Congress . . . no one has equaled Benjamin Franklin in ability, tact, common sense, diplomacy and reputation that was national as well as worldwide. . . He began as a printer, became a publisher, founded papers [and] served as editor and reporter. . . His wise sayings and maxims show an unusual common sense philosophy. He established in Philadelphia better plans of transportation and also aided throughout Pennsylvania and improved communication. He helped save property from destruction and aided insurance plans against fire. He [invented] the Franklin Stove and started the pioneer work to harness electricity. . . . He also founded one of the great universities of the world. In . . . France . . . he came as a man of maturity, brilliance, ability, and as a world statesman." **Charles Williams Heathcote**

While he was ambassador to France, **Benjamin Franklin** wrote, "It is a common observation here [in Paris] that our cause is the cause of all mankind, and that we are fighting for their liberty in defending our own." Just before signing the Declaration of Independence in 1776, he declared, "We must, indeed, all hang together or most assuredly we will all hang separately." On another occasion Franklin added, "A few years of peace will improve, will restore and increase our strength; but our future will depend on our union and our virtue. Let us, therefore, beware of being lulled into a dangerous security; and of being both enervated and impoverished by luxury; of being weakened by internal contentions and divisions."

"Cherish. . . the spirit of our people, and keep alive their attention. Do not be too severe upon their errors, but reclaim them by enlightening them." **Thomas Jefferson**

"Many circumstances hath, and will arise, which are not local, but universal, and through which the principles of all Lovers of Mankind are affected, and in the Event of which, their Affections are interested." **Thomas Paine**

"Too much and too long, we seem to have surrendered community excellence and community values in the mere accumulation of material things. Our gross national product ... if we should judge America by that – counts air pollution and cigarette advertising, and ambulances to clear our highways of carnage. It counts special locks for our doors and the jails for those who break them. It counts the destruction of our redwoods and the loss of our natural wonder in chaotic sprawl. It counts napalm and the cost of a nuclear warhead, and armored cars for police who fight riots in our streets. It counts . . . the television programs which glorify violence in order to sell toys to our children.

"Yet the gross national product does not allow for the health of our children, the quality of their education, or the joy of their play. It does not include the beauty of our poetry or the strength of our marriages; the intelligence of our public debate or the integrity of our public officials. It measures neither our wit nor our courage; neither our wisdom nor our learning; neither our compassion nor our devotion to our country; it measures everything, in short, except that which makes life worthwhile. And it tells us everything about America except why we are proud that we are Americans." **Robert F. Kennedy**

BOB MARLEY

"I only have one thing I really like to see happen. I like to see mankind live together - black, white, Chinese, everyone - that's all." **Bob Marley**

A shift toward greater consciousness can only occur if it includes movement from trying to dominate and conquer to trying to cooperate and find synergies with others.

Comment: We all know that today's world is far more interconnected and "smaller," as measured by communication, transportation, and trade than it was in the late 1700s. Except in the minds of "neocons" and today's anachronistic economic imperialists, at this point in history it borders on mindlessness to think only in terms of America's interests. To improve our chances for a better tomorrow, we need,

. . . to look carefully at how our nation's and corporations' actions affect other countries and cultures and their peoples as well as how they affect us.

. . . to listen to people all around the world tell us how they experience our actions toward them, and integrate all those perspectives into a new kind of global and multicultural understanding.

. . . to truly acknowledge that we all live together on the same planet, which is not so very large relative to our impacts on it.

. . . to plan seriously about how to keep our planet's life-systems healthy for the infinite future—and stop exploiting and shooting each other for control of resources

"Do not act toward others as you would not have them act toward you," advised Confucius. "Do unto others as you would have them do unto you," declared Jesus, going even farther.

Within this present century, the scope of the environmental challenges that face us will become too apparent to deny. We live in an extraordinarily dangerous time. Our chances for global survival will increase when we realize that we are now all citizens of a single world and a single ecosphere.

<<<>>>

SOLUTIONS

- **One of the universal principles to which Thomas Paine refers is that we have a capacity to move toward relating, governing, and doing business from an inner place of greater consciousness, more compassion, and large-heartedness. Very few people, groups, or countries enjoy being stepped on, or shoved around, or cheated. A shift toward greater consciousness throughout our culture will only occur if it includes movement from an inclination toward domination and conquest to an attitude of cooperation, partnership, and mutual respect. Movement from demanding that others submit to us to finding synergies with others' needs. Movement from impervious selfishness to helping others get what they want too. In that polarity is written much of the history of the world and of America. In how we handle it today will be written the character of tomorrow.**

* * *

30. Clear and Present Danger

The hour is late. Today, democracy in the United States is like a rope burned halfway through, with pyromaniacs waiting nearby. In our own country, the forces arrayed against democracy are strong. The Introduction to this book states that right wing extremists are right in about 15% of their program. Much of that 15% is in areas where the radical left agrees with them. One major point of agreement is that the government snoops into citizens' affairs too much, and asserts too much control over our lives (with the major exception that some right-wing radicals want to control women's lives even more — (Why not just change the Pledge of Allegiance to "with Liberty and Justice for Men"?) "Right wing" folks who live out in the woods with a cache of guns to protect against the government and "left wing" citizens who are equally afraid of oppressive measures that have been taken in our country are pretty similar in their feelings about trends in the U.S. since the turn of the century. It is prudent to beware of excessive power by our government. It is also only prudent to beware of power exercised by the Wall Street financial oligarchy.

Nonetheless, despite irregularities like the stolen presidential elections of 2000 and 2004 (See Chapter 5), many Americans still think of our country as one of the world's most democratic. In contrast to many other countries that treat their citizens much worse, this is still more or less true. But as you will see, steps taken by Congress and the Executive Branch of Government in recent decades have created a situation in which even the semi-democracy that most of us take for granted is now in danger.

We have arrived at a watershed moment that may determine whether we remember our common heritage and move forward as a people or disintegrate into warring camps ruled by a coalition of plutocrats and inflexible ideologues. Sadly, some people make noises about the good of the nation, but when it comes to action, they act only to benefit themselves and their cadres of think-alike companions. Until now, most of us have been so thoroughly indoctrinated in the power structure's dominant narrative that we are prisoners of both their Machiavellian calculations and their shared delusions. The founding fathers foresaw this possibility.

"Single acts of tyranny may be ascribed to the accidental opinion of a day, but a series of oppressions, begun at a distinguished period and pursued unalterably through every change of ministers, too plainly prove a deliberate, systematic plan of reducing [a people] to slavery." **Thomas Jefferson**

"The dominion which the banking institutions have obtained over the minds of our citizens . . . must be broken, or it will break us." **Thomas Jefferson**

"Allow me to issue and control a nation's currency, and I care not who makes its laws." **Banker Mayer Rothschild, in 1791**

"It shall not be lawful to employ any part of the Army of the United States, as a posse comitatus, or otherwise, for the purpose of executing the laws, except [as] expressly authorized by the Constitution or by act of Congress." **The Posse Comitatus Act of 1878, 10 U.S.C. (United States Code) 375**

After World War I the following provisions were passed to clarify the Posse Comitatus Act: "The Secretary of Defense shall prescribe such regulations as may be necessary to ensure that any activity. . . under this chapter does not include or permit direct participation by a member of the Army, Navy, Air Force, or Marine Corps in a search, seizure, arrest, or other similar activity unless [otherwise] authorized by law. **(18 U.S.C. 1385).**

"Fascism should more appropriately be called corporatism because it is a merger of state and corporate power." **Italian philosopher Giovanni Gentile**

"The Fascist state . . . takes over all the forms of the moral and intellectual life of man. . . Fascism. . . requires discipline and authority that can enter into the spirits of men and there govern unopposed." **Benito Mussolini**

"Individual rights are only recognized in so far as they are implied in the rights of the state." **Mussolini's minister of justice Alfredo Rocco.**

"By the skillful and sustained use of propaganda, one can make a people see even heaven as hell or an extremely wretched life as paradise. . . . How fortunate for governments that the people they administer don't think. . . . I use emotion for the many and reserve reason for the few." **Adolf Hitler**

"With a fascist the problem is . . how best to use the news to deceive the public into giving the fascist and his group more money or more power. American fascism will not be really dangerous until there is a purposeful coalition among the cartelists, the deliberate poisoners of public information. . . . They claim to be super-patriots, but they would destroy every liberty guaranteed by the Constitution." **Vice President Henry Wallace**

"The liberty of a democracy is not safe if the people tolerate the growth of private power to a point where it becomes stronger than their democratic state itself. That, in essence, is fascism—ownership of government by an individual, by a group, or by any controlling private power." **Franklin D. Roosevelt**

"Do you realize that since 2001, there has been a 47 percent increase in American workers classified as security guards. . . . A? That's a culture increasingly based on fear. . . Since the dawn of the new millennium, our democracy has eroded to the point where it's hanging on by a bare thread. You can trace this directly to the times that George W. Bush and his cronies stole the 2000 and 2004 Presidential elections from their opponents, and also to the tragic events of 9/11 that unleashed their assault on our freedoms in the name of protecting them." **Jesse Ventura**

> **Comment:** During the 1930s there was a well-organized plot by big business leaders to overthrow the U.S. government and turn our country into a corporate-controlled fascist state. (How odd that I never heard about it in the many U.S. history courses that I took in school.) There was an attempt to assassinate Franklin D. Roosevelt a week before his inauguration, but the perpetrators were never discovered. After he was in office, the cabal that opposed him decided to try another tack to get rid of him. The "American Liberty League" founded in 1934 set out "to combat radicalism, to teach the necessity for the rights of persons and property, and generally to foster free private enterprise." The Rockefellers, Mellons, Pews, and the lawyer for the Morgan bank John W. Davis were part of this, all described in Jules Archer's *The Plot to Seize the White House*.
>
> Marine Corps General Smedley Butler was probably the most admired general in the nation during the 1920s and 1930s. After helping to rig elections in Nicaragua, and assisting American business interests in extracting their pound of flesh from other Latin American countries, he retired from the Marine Corps at the age of 50 and began to reflect on what he had been doing. When disgruntled World War I veterans who had never been paid the bonuses that were promised to them set up a tent city in Washington after the war, Butler showed up to support them. He told veterans that war was "largely a matter of money. Bankers lend money to foreign countries and when they cannot repay, the President sends Marines to get it. I know—I've been in eleven of these expeditions."

The "American Liberty League" viewed Butler as a military hero whom the nation would rally around and whom they thought they could manipulate. One of their group, Butler's old marine companion Robert S. Clark, heir to the Singer Sewing Machine fortune, approached Butler on behalf of the League and offered him the chance to be the front man in taking over the country.

They chose badly. Butler was committed to democracy. He held his tongue, brought in a reporter to document the plot, and in November of 1934 detailed what was going on to a committee of the House of Representatives. The next day the New York Times ran a headline: Gen. Butler Bares 'Fascist Plot' to Seize Government by Force." Nonetheless, the article was heavily biased. It consisted largely of denials from those involved in the plot, while Butler's charges themselves were buried deep in the article. *Time* magazine ran a piece that essentially ridiculed Butler. But the plot was dead. Jules Archer later interviewed John McCormack, Speaker of the House when the events took place. McCormack, said, "The plotters . . . were going to make it all sound constitutional, of course, with a high-sounding name for the dictator and a plan to make it all sound like a good American program. A well-organized minority can always outmaneuver an unorganized majority, as Adolf Hitler did. . . . The people were in a very confused state of mind. . . . Mass frustration could bring about anything." In the House hearings, the Veterans of Foreign Wars Commander said that he had also been approached by "agents of Wall Street" to head up a fascist dictatorship.

Now fast-forward to the present, skipping over the activities of one prominent political family that was involved in the perpetration of and profitmaking from World War I, World War II (on the Nazi side), and both Iraq Wars. (See Kevin Phillips' *American Dynasty* for details.) Today there exist detailed official plans to suspend the Constitution and eliminate democratic government that are far more extensive than the primitive plot against the Roosevelt administration. We can be grateful to Jesse Ventura for gathering all this information, described in chilling detail in the last chapter of his book, *American Conspiracies.*

"Military Action might encompass making arrests, seizing documents or other property, searching persons or places or keeping them under surveillance, intercepting electronic or wireless communications, setting up roadblocks, interviewing witnesses or searching for suspects." **U.S. Justice Department Document**

"In October 2001, [the Administration was] trying to construct a legal regime that would basically have allowed for the imposition of martial law." Director for Center for National Security Studies **Kate Martin**

"The [Justice Department] memos . . . lay the groundwork for a massive military takeover of the United States in cahoots with the president. And if that's not a coup d'etat then nothing is." Constitutional scholar **Michael Ratner**

The possibility of a coup d'etat by whatever party and administration holds power at a given time has been made far more salient by a variety of "continuity of government" acts and Presidential Executive Orders issued since Richard Nixon's Executive Order 11490 in 1969. Such an Executive Order becomes law simply by its publication in the Federal Registry, bypassing Congress. During the Cold War luxurious survival facilities for top government officials were built under Pennsylvania's Raven Rock Mountain and Virginia's Weather Mountain, later supplemented by other deeply buried "hardened" sites in Colorado, Nevada, and elsewhere. A long series of subsequent Executive Orders by both Republican and Democratic presidents allow the government to take over all air, rail, sea, and highway transportation, to seize and control the communication media, to take over all fuel and power production and distribution, to mobilize civilians into work brigades under government supervision, and so on. These are on the books, waiting to be used if and when the people will stand for it. Will you?

The so-called "Patriot Act," authored by the Bush-Cheney administration and passed by Congress just a month after the 9/11 attack (although it is so incredibly detailed that it must have been prepared long before 9/11) makes it a crime for you, me, or Aunt Nellie to give money or material support to any group on the Terror Watch List. This is a *watch list* of groups that *may or may not* have any connection with terrorists. *Anybody connected with national security can put any group on that list,* with no evidence that their suspicion is correct, since it's just a "watch list." *They can put any group you belong to on the list.* The Act also lets the FBI record discussions between attorneys and clients, which were formerly privileged. It opened the door for surveillance of our mail and e-mail (and probably contributed to opening the door for the internet corporations that now do the same thing with e-mail). It even lets the FBI order librarians to turn over information about what books or magazines people read. It was not a long step from there to the Bush Administration's widespread *illegal* wiretapping. The National Security Agency headquarters set up shop to tap into AT&T's fiber optic cables that also happen to be connected to all other networks, which provided "a complete copy of the data stream." The Obama Administration has not moved to rescind these steps.

This whole approach, however, is crude and heavy handed. Despite the inevitable trappings of glorious words about "protecting our precious heritage of freedom" that would doubtless surround it, the perpetrators would probably be remembered as the most despicable scum in our nation's history, and I imagine that few but the most power-hungry political and corporate leaders are eager to be remembered as worse than Benedict Arnold. Now the oligarchy has hit on a subtler way to accomplish the same end, neatly summarized in the title of Greg Palast's book, *"The Best Democracy Money Can Buy."* The strategy is simple: Remove all limits on how much money any corporation, wealthy donor, or other organization can give candidates and spend on elections, and permit all that to be done secretly so that citizens have no way to know whose money is buying, for instance, a political TV ad. The "Citizens United" ruling is part of that agenda.

Fascism with a capital "F" was a creature of 1930s and early 1940s Italy and Spain. In Germany Fascists were called Nazis. With a small "f," fascism is the appropriate description for any regime that is authoritarian, punitive, and controlled by a dictator or oligarchy (that may or may not start out as plutocratic, but almost always becomes so as it rakes off the nation's riches for itself.) Fascist governments are usually ultra-nationalistic, wrapping themselves in the flag, whipping their people into a patriotic frenzy, and implying that criticism of the government (or with capitalist fascism, the corporations that support it) is unpatriotic. Stalin's Soviet Union and Mao Zedong's China were fascist regimes in communist drag. In today's United States, many who stridently accuse others of being "Hitlers" or "Communists" show fascist tendencies in their own words and actions.

In today's America, driven energetically by right-wing extremist parties, groups and think-tanks, dollar-driven fascism appears to pose a greater danger than almost anyone imagines. It is a far greater danger than socialism or communism. In Europe, contemporary socialist parties support political democracy and are still a force, but In the United States today, socialism is politically dead with the lid to the coffin nailed shut. Calling something or someone "socialist," however, serves as a red-herring scare tactic that some use to distract attention from the darker aspects of their own policies and actions. Communism, which had some influence in the U.S. in the early 20th Century, attracts people who are starving and desperate. In reality, everywhere it has gotten stuck in the "dictatorship of the proletariat," which is based on Mao Zedong's dictum that "political power grows out of the barrel of a gun." A new totalitarian "state capitalist" oligarchy run by Party members replaces the old capitalist oligarchy. Today in the U.S., Communism exists only in history books, but calling someone or something "Communist" still serves as a bogeyman tactic for those who are dense enough to get taken in by it."

On the international stage. 9-11 was an example of the broader phenomenon called "blowback." People in some countries view the United States as an imperialistic, militaristic power that has been beggaring them and installing dictators who serve U.S. interests. The CIA invented the word blowback to describe reprisals against Americans for covert operations against other countries, and other aspects of U.S foreign policy that harm other peoples in diverse ways. This may range from killing leaders our administration dislikes to imposing economic policies that cause severe poverty. The word blowback first surfaced in a CIA report on its 1953 overthrow of the Iranian government. In 2000 the *New York Times* wrote in "The ABCs of Coups" that the word "has since come into use as shorthand for the unintended consequences of covert operations." Chalmers Johnson, president of the Japan Policy Research Institute, wrote in the spring of 2000, "World politics in the twenty-first century will in all likelihood be driven primarily by blowback from the second half of the twentieth century—that is, from . . . the crucial American decision to maintain a Cold War posture in a post-Cold War world."

Johnson continues, "Actions that generate blowback are normally kept totally secret from the American public and from most of their representatives in Congress. This means that when innocent civilians become victims of a retaliatory strike, they are at first unable to put it in context or to understand the sequence of events that led up to it. . . . The American people may not know what is done in their name, but those on the receiving end surely do." Patrick Henry, Thomas Paine, Benjamin Franklin, George Washington, Thomas Jefferson, John Adams, James Madison, and Abram Lincoln would not be pleased about U.S. foreign policies of the last half-century.

Today clandestine mini-wars are carried out by the CIA without ever appearing in the military budget. Chalmers Johnson's incisive books (cited in "References") describe many of these actions and reveal, for example, that beginning in 1984, Osama Bin Laden was on the CIA payroll for at least a decade before he turned against the United States. The CIA still carries out assassinations and drone strikes against suspected enemies in various countries. This removes short-term threats, but guarantees continuation of a long-term threat, since the craving for revenge is a motive that can last a lifetime: "I will even the score against those bastards who murdered my family and friends even if I myself die doing so."

Meanwhile, the neocons of both major parties and our clandestine agencies lovingly stroke their Darth Vader masks and plot "our" next exciting round of operations. Instead, our nation needs to develop a foreign policy in which we find ways to live together peacefully with the rest of the world for mutual advantage instead of one that will ensure an endless cycle of violence and continued loss of our personal freedoms. Without such a fundamental transformation, the vision of our founding fathers will be gone forever. Are we willing to resurrect that vision and care for it?

31. The Tasks Ahead

It is time to step out of the trance induced by the power structure and the strident cries of right-wing extremists. It is time to reclaim the dreams that animated those who wrote the Declaration of Independence and the Constitution and brought our nation into being. It is time to advance the visions of those who struggled to end the restriction of the right to vote and hold office to those who owned property, and struggled to end slavery and segregation, and struggled to grant women and all adult citizens the right to vote. It is time to reconfigure our communities, our education, and our economy so that everyone can find or create a livelihood. It is time to seek ways to live in peace with the rest of the world instead of imagining ourselves to be the overlords of a latter-day Roman Empire. And it is time to realize that in a larger sense, each one of us is a citizen of the world. As we learn to see the one-sided narratives that so many of us have long accepted for the fictions that they are, previously ignored alternatives begin to be visible.

Financing campaigns in a way that almost forces politicians into lapping up the swill from lobbyists and other special interests was no part of Paine, Franklin, Washington, Jefferson, Madison and Lincoln's vision for our nation. Now almost all previous limits on how much money the corporate elite can spend to buy elections are gone. Meanwhile, self–righteous true believers who are convinced that the principles espoused by their religion should be put into laws that bind us all are making headway in state legislatures across the land, while alleged libertarians roll their eyeballs and look the other way.

As all that goes on, those on the side of the Radical Wrong ridicule environmentalists and laud the G.W. Bush cancellation of Superfund pollution cleanups. They pooh-pooh present pollution and try to ramp up resource extraction to unprecedented levels, while the ecosystems of the natural world are slowly unraveling. The Earth itself is sending warning messages in the form of unprecedented storms and droughts and heat and cold waves. But who listens? The mindless mantra of "Drill, Baby, Drill" seems to be the only answer from the endless echo-chamber of the far right. When the phone rings with nature's latest warning, no one picks it up. It is truly bizarre that not even Hurricane Katrina and the British Petroleum Deepwater Horizon Gulf of Mexico oil spill got through to those people, companies, and agencies that are committed to looking the other way no matter what the warning signs. These are not just a dead canary in the coal mine, but flocks of dead canaries falling from the sky.

Patrick Henry said, "The battle, sir, is not to the strong alone; it is to the vigilant, the active, the brave."

"For Jefferson . . . man as he is had to be restrained from his overwhelming tendencies toward oppression, injustice, greed, and tyranny. And there had to be room. . . for human beings to exercise their freedom to think – and this meant to think together, in community; to exchange with each other in the realm of ideas and perception. There had to be space for human beings to become improved and perfected by the process of free inquiry and by the natural obligations of living on the earth and carrying out their natural, human responsibilities. . . . The community, the nation, is, or can be, the conduit for the force that elevates humanity through the dual power of education of the mind and the engagement of heart and body in honest work – all undertaken within the milieu of a free exchange of thought and communal inquiry in search of truth."
Jacob Needleman

Have we fallen so far that we are willing to abandon the principles pursued by Abraham Lincoln to protect our pursuit of the latest Lincoln limousine?

"The fiery trial through which we pass will light us down in honor or dishonor to the last generation. . . . You cannot escape the responsibility of tomorrow by evading it today." **Abraham Lincoln**

"The Chinese use two brush strokes to write the word 'crisis.' One brush stroke stands for danger; the other for opportunity. In a crisis, be aware of the danger – but recognize the opportunity." **John F. Kennedy**

"We must join together-the people of the neighborhood, government, private enterprise, foundations, and universities-in an effort of unprecedented scope. The future of our nation demands that." **Robert F. Kennedy**

I can conceive of a community, to-day . . . where a couple of hundred best men and women, of ordinary worldly status, have by luck been drawn together, with nothing extra of genius or wealth, but virtuous, chaste, industrious, cheerful, resolute, friendly, and devout. I can conceived such a community organized in running order, powers judiciously delegated – farming, building, trade, courts, mails, schools, elections, all attended to; and then the rest of life, the main thing, freely branching and blossoming in each individual, and being golden fruit. I can see there in every young and old man, after his kind, and in every woman after hers, a true personality, develop'd, exercised proportionately in body, mind, and spirit. . . perhaps unsung, undramatized, unput in essays or biographies --- perhaps even some such community already exists." **Walt Whitman**

WALT WHITMAN

"We cannot seek achievement for ourselves and forget about progress and prosperity for our community... Our ambitions must be broad enough to include the aspirations and needs of others, for their sakes and for our own. . . From the depth of need and despair, people can work together, can organize themselves to solve their own problems and fill their own needs with dignity and strength." **Caesar Chavez**

"We are tied together in the single garment of destiny. . . I can never be what I ought to be until you are what you ought to be. And you can never be what you ought to be until I am what I ought to be." *Martin Luther King*

"We are called to play the Good Samaritan on life's roadside, but . . . one day we must come to see that the whole Jericho Road must be transformed so that men and women will not be constantly beaten and robbed as they make their journey on life's highway. True compassion is more than flinging a coin to a beggar. It comes to see that an edifice which produces beggars needs restructuring." **Martin Luther King**

King also said, "Freedom is not something that is voluntarily given by the oppressor. It is something that must be demanded by the oppressed. Freedom is not some lavish dish that the power structure. . . will voluntarily hand out on a silver platter. . . If we are going to get equality, if we are going to get adequate wages, we are going to have to struggle for it."

"Where there is a sufficient social movement of self-reliant communities, there can be political change. . . . We have to restore power to the family, to the neighborhood, and the community with a . . . principle of equality, of charity, of let's-take-care-of-one-another. That's the creative challenge. . . . When the farmer can sell directly to the consumer, it is a more active process. There's more contact. The consumer can know, who am I buying this from? What's their name? Do they have a face? . . . We have to deal with where we are. We have to create cooperatives, we have to create intentional communities, we have to work for local cooperation where we are." California Governor **Jerry Brown**

And don't forget **Gerald Ford's** astute observation that, "Things are more like today than they have ever been before."

Let us dream and work together as we step into the dawn of the next stage of geohistory. Let us walk hand in hand in the immense adventure of creating the emerging new civilization that will be needed to cope with the tomorrow's world.

There is another path than the one the Radical Wrong has been trying to impose on our nation. It is a path of joining with our fellow citizens of every class and party and religious orientation to meet the challenges of this day and the days and decades to come. On that path we actively and wholeheartedly seek ways to release narrow-minded attitudes that turn us against each other or cause us to try to legislate how others think and live. For better or worse, a new age is coming. As of now we can only see dim glimpses of it through momentary openings in the clouds of time. Resurrecting the ideals and dreams of our nation's founders can help us navigate it wisely.

One aspect of this is a point on which the "Tea Party" platform very nearly gets things almost right. It reads: "Promote Civic Responsibility – Citizen involvement at the grassroots level allows the voice of the American people to be heard and directs the political behaviors of our representatives at both the local and national level so they, in turn, may be most effective in working to preserve the life, liberty, and pursuit of happiness of this country's citizens."

The statement is good. It falls short in just three ways. First, the "Tea Party's" history to date make it obvious that two unwritten words in the statement are " happiness of **some of** this country's citizens." The words should be explicit, and should read **all of** this country's citizens." Another is that in practice, it "directs the political behaviors of our representatives" in an imperiously authoritarian manner that leaves little room to for them to think for themselves. Third, in another sense the statement does not go far enough. Throughout this great land, citizens ought not just organize to be heard and to influence representatives, but to create local civic and economic facilities and institutions to encourage the exchange of ideas, abilities, goods, and services within and between local communities. For example, creating an inviting farmer's market encourages local farming and right livelihood. It has a strong impact on the environment that makes as powerful a statement as sending a "NO

GMO CROPS" message to Congress (carried by a representative who may be bought off by a big-time chemical agribusiness company that wants no competition from local small farmers.)

No one alive today—no one---has all the answers. But unless we release our white-knuckled grip on the idea that we are always right and those who think differently are always wrong, we will remain prisoners of our delusions.

Klaus Schwab, executive chairman of the World Economic Forum in Davos, Switzerland, a favorite gathering of the world's corporate rich and powerful, declared in January of 2012, "Capitalism, in its current form, no longer fits the world around us. We have failed to learn the lessons from the financial crisis of 2009." Events like that annual gathering in Davos, and Google's annual Zeitgeist conference, consist of members of the power elite conversing among themselves, developing narratives for the rest of society. They have yet to open their doors of forums so that the elite, the middle class, the working class, and the dispossessed (to say nothing of scientists and fundamentalist preachers) engage in genuine dialogue.

In *Only the Rich Can Save Us,* Ralph Nader has crafted a tale in which investor Warren Buffet enlists seventeen aging ultra-billionaires who have grown bored with merely being rich to use their billions and brains in a grand undertaking to move the nation from its present polarized path onto a new one. It's an entertaining and informative tale. Could such a movement succeed in real life? Maybe or maybe not. But now it is becoming clear that even though most people don't realize it yet, the very survival of humankind and our planet's life-systems are endangered. Confronting the threats the world now faces may be a challenge large enough to unite people of all income levels in common cause. If the ultra-rich do not join in, with their immense potential influence in whatever direction they choose to throw it, the cause is almost surely lost. In that sense Nader's title is right: Only the rich can save us because without their help, homo sapiens could become just one more species on the extinction list.

<<<>>>

SOLUTIONS

PART 1: GENERAL PRINCIPLES.

We need to abandon rigid, throw-everything-into-the-stew ideologies that confuse us as much as they help us. We need to abandon attitudes that severely damage our ability to accomplish essential goals by filling our neural networks with a win-or-lose, dominate-or-submit mindset. That's fine for ball games, but leads to disaster in politics and economics. We just can't afford poor policy any longer. Rather, we need to transform obsolete "liberal vs. conservative" ideologies into constructive, productive new approaches. How? With each question that faces us, we can ask:

- *What do we want to conserve or preserve?* **This includes comfortable and customary habits of thought and action that still serve us well. It also includes real things in the constructed and natural worlds. For some, it includes differences of wealth and power about which there are likely to be large differences of opinion, and in regard to which the viable answers may be** different from any of our old ones.

- *What do we want to liberalize or liberate?* Are there customs or policies in our community, state or nation that restrict us unnecessarily, even though our actions harm no one or nothing? Are there ways in which our lives are circumscribed and determined by the corporations that are part of our community, state or nation in ways that they ought not to (and that may have the support of government behind them)?

- *What do we want to go back to? ("Reactionary" is not necessarily a bad word.)* What have we lost in community and family life, and customs and circumstances of times gone by? What have we lost to the scattered, fragmented growth of our cities, the lack of public transportation, the disintegration of community life, and care and support for children and families? How can we reconstruct our communities and culture in ways that restore good things of yesteryear that we value?

- *What do we want to progress toward?* For example, which ideals of our Constitution, with its amendments, are yet unrealized? Which of its provisions are being systematically violated, and how can we restore our culture's integrity in adhering to them? What kind of a future do we hope for, and what can we do to bring it into being?

- *What do we face that we do not yet fully understand, and have not yet developed ways to cope with?* At present both our nation and the world as a whole are being overwhelmed by a rapidly rising tide of population as a result of excessive immigration, high birthrates, or both. Around the world, ecosystems are deteriorating or dying. And each year we move farther into potentially apocalyptic environmental catastrophes. Sticking our heads in the sand like ostriches is unwise.

- Since techniques of propaganda and manipulation are being constantly refined by advertisers, media, political parties, and government agencies, we need to ask *"How can we outflank them?"* and develop creative, imaginative ways to do that.

When we follow old outlooks that throw all these questions into two pots of stew labeled "liberal" and "conservative," all we can be sure of is that we're (a) sure to be conflicted or confused, and (b) likely to end up with antagonistic, hostile attitudes toward some of our fellow citizens who want to achieve many of the same goals we do. This is not necessary. Jefferson and Hamilton differed in some of their views: Jefferson was agrarian and libertarian, while Hamilton was big business and strong central-government and central-bank oriented. Washington and Adams were somewhere in between. Even in their day they were frustrated by some of these differences. But when we read them all, there is an overall outlook that emerges, like a sunrise that spreads its shining light over all the land. They were able to agree on a Declaration of Independence and a Constitution that guides us still. I strongly doubt that the luminaries of today's Congress could equal it. But those are all generalities. Now let's look at some specifics.

SOLUTIONS PART II: SPECIFIC STEPS. You have encountered most of these in previous chapters. I bring them together here because they seem to me essential starting points.

They are not, taken all together, nearly as imposing as they might look at first glance, because many of them are things that many of us already know we should be doing.

Protect our security – against assaults of every kind from small time criminals who use knives and guns, and big time criminals who employ financial shell games and pricey lawyers. Personal security includes help in coping for the costs and care of illness and injury, in the most efficient and economical way possible. We also need to protect against breakdowns in our infrastructure, such as by moving to cellular power grids that remain largely intact when one part is damaged. And against resource exhaustion, by giving efficiency-driven reductions in demand a high priority. Against environmental damage, by protecting and restoring the lungs of our world—its seas and forests--and by both prevention of and preparation for climate-related catastrophes. Protecting our security may sometimes include helping other nations when they are threatened or attacked, but starting wars in other countries is in direct conflict with our traditions and opposed to our national interest.

a. *Protect our personal freedom* – from oppressive and intrusive government, oppressive and intrusive big business, religious imperialists (whether Christian, Muslim, or any other variety) who seek to impose their views and prescriptions for behavior on the rest of us, and from any other people or organizations that would threaten it. This includes protection against abuses by our own legislatures, the executive branches of state and local government, and the criminal justice system and judiciary.

b. *Protect and care for the great tree of democracy, which many are now chopping away at, and give it a chance to live and grow and thrive again.* Demand that Congress, Administration and Judiciary act in behalf of the *entire* preamble of the Constitution—not just the clauses that suit their interests. Encourage all citizens to vote, and remove all obstacles that make it harder for those who are entitled to vote to do so. Abolish the anachronistic electoral college that people in every other nation in the world can see is a farce. Take money out of politics with complete and total public financing of elections at every level, and prohibit every currently legal form of public bribery. Pass national legislation that ensures fair and unbiased elections and vote counting. This includes multipartisan supervision of all elections, state-of-the art monitoring of computer tallies by skilled neutral persons, a paper trail for all voting and an electronic trail or sequestering for all chips, drives, and devices used in vote counting.

c. *Acknowledge that everyone needs a source of livelihood and that it is better to earn it for themselves with the sense of contribution to society that goes along with that than to be on the dole.* "The dole" can be welfare payments to the poor or subsidies and other handouts to the rich. Yet there are times when everyone needs a helping hand (whether from government or their community or their church) to get back on their feet. Providing jobs for all who can work, from the local level to the national and even the international levels, will require going far beyond the limiting ideologies and limited imaginations of today's parties and factions. We will need multiple forums and dialogues, all around the world and involving people from all strata of society, to develop multimodal economic approaches that fit diverse people and circumstances. Join with others to organize your neighborhood, your town, and your city to create useful undertakings and enterprises that provide work and livelihood for those who need it, and diversion and joy for those who don't, because neither big business nor state and national governments can or will do it all. How? That's another whole story that many of us must take part in composing.

d. *Truly prize equality of being and equality of opportunity.* This includes moving from an attitude of trying to dominate others and be "on top" to an attitude of mutual respect and appreciation for the unique qualities of people of both genders and all races, ethnic groups, religions and nations. This means embracing a lifestyle that includes moving toward greater cooperation in most areas of life.

e. *Make government as local, community-based and community-focused as we can.* Larger units of government can reasonably step in when local, county, or state governments violate people's rights, freedoms, and safety.

f. *Keep the people fully informed about government activities.* Facilitate and protect the free flow of information through diverse media. This most especially includes transparency, representation, and accountability in multinational organizations like the World Bank, the International Monetary Fund, and the Trilateral Commission. Any political or economic treaty agreed to by the national government must not restrict any city, county, state, or our nation's ability to protect the people's rights and the natural environment. (This provision may require a Constitutional Amendment.)

g. *Balance these principles*: On one hand, almost everyone prefers lower taxes to higher taxes. On the other hand, taxes adequate to provide needed and widely desired public services are better than taxes that are not. Those who are most able to pay should pay more than those least able to pay, but even those least able to pay who receive government assistance for their survival should pay a token sum.

h. *Whether a utility, transportation agency or company, or any other service is better owned and run by the government, private owners, or some form of a public or private cooperative is an empirical question.* Who provides better service and runs it most efficiently at least expense? Can ownership by the people, like North Dakota's State Bank, provide better service and also reduce taxes for everyone? The answers will differ in different places with different peoples and circumstances. One size does not fit all.

i. *Establish an iron-clad principle that no company or agency or other organization is a "person."* Each is a separate kind of real and legal entity, and the laws, regulations, and customs that fit each are unique. The provisions of the Constitution were written to apply to actual living individual human beings, not to organizations.

j. *Unless the nation is attacked or has gone to the aid of another nation that has been attacked from outside, Congress shall abide by the Constitution and not authorize any debt to pay for military expenses that requires more than two years to pay off.* (I imagine that a period of transition from today's procurement contracts paid for by deficit financing will be needed).

    k. *A procedure should be established to enable a president and both houses of Congress together to overrule a Supreme Court decision or to impeach a Justice at any level for specifically defined instances of lack of good behavior (such as not recusing oneself from a case that involves a conflict of interest.)*

Energy expert Amory Lovins of the Rocky Mountain Institute points out that when Dwight D. Eisenhower ran into an apparently insoluble problem, his response was often to "make the problem bigger." That is, expand the boundaries of the situation that we are taking into account. Gestalt psychologists refer to the "field" which includes all the elements, connections, and configurations of the situation we are concerned about.

As we see that larger picture, new options emerge. Instead of reacting with old mental, emotional, and behavioral conditioned responses, new ways of handling the situation become possible. In years and decades ahead, we are likely to need those expanded capacities more than most people begin to imagine. The time is overdue for letting go of the same old scripts and stories that, with only minor variations and clever cosmetic cover, have been prescriptions for advancing the interests of the 1% at the expense of the 99% at least since the Civil War.

The shopworn stories of the Radical Wrong offer no suggestions for avoiding a decaying national fabric, a poorly educated public, and a poisoned, polluted planet. They offer no strategies for handling the transition from the age of oil and mountaintop demolition coal mining. They leave us driving a Model T Ford with a set of Calvin Coolidge Tires on the Green Technology and Trade Racetrack while Europe, Japan, China, India, and Brazil zoom ahead with tomorrow's advanced plug-in hybrids. They say very little about how to sail into the storm winds of tomorrow's environmental crises.

Never before has civilization had such an overwhelming impact on Earth's land and rivers and seas and skies. It is up to us to find a new balance in which humans and nature exist in a mutually supportive relationship.

Of course we need to honor and follow old traditions and practices that are of real value in our present situation, and even recapture valuable old ways from the past that we erroneously abandoned. "Reactionary" sounds pretty good when it means doing that -- such as, for example, saving heritage seeds, eating organic food, and encouraging independent family farming rather than helplessly letting industrial agribusiness chart our food and farming agendas.

At the same time, we can vigilantly notice when our ego-attachment to old opinions brings a constricting stagnation of our visionary energies, and be willing to let go of such attachments. We can combine childlike curiosity with independent, resourceful adult analysis instead of accepting what any authority tells us. We can articulate high ideals, and honor them in practice. We can chart our way through this new era's complex community of nations with imagination, tact, and diplomacy. We can offer prizes and incentives for individuals and companies to develop inspired original solutions to the many challenges that we and the world are facing. And we can put our best analysis, our most creative thinking, and our most innovative energies into the great adventure of coping with all these challenges and opportunities.

And we must. For never before has the combination of modern medical science and labor-saving machinery opened the way for human population to explode like water in a huge lake suddenly rushing through a broken dam. Never have there been the kinds of threats to the whole interconnected fabric of life on earth posed by nuclear bombs and the reactor disasters at Three Mile Island, Chernobyl, and Fukushima. Nature is striking back at human rapaciousness and neglect now, with fiercer typhoons and hurricanes from warmer ocean waters, and more devastating storm winds howling across the lands as hot air from the tropics and cold air from the poles change places faster. It is up to us to help create a new balance in which humans and nature live in a mutually supportive relationship.

These dilemmas are monumental. Can we really change course fast enough to protect ourselves and future generations from the scourge of greed, injustice, indifference, ignorance, and all the negative ego-centered activities that we, the human family, have undertaken in the name of progress and survival? Or are we, like lemmings, hell bent on rushing over the cliff to self-annihilation?

Sadly, at the present moment, we seem to be more of a gridlocked republic comprised of battling special interest groups than the beacon of liberty and freedom that that once was admired the world over. In near and distant tomorrows, will the words and work of our nation's founders and great later thinkers still mean anything at all? Or will they just be fancy words that echo through the years as if bouncing off the walls of a deserted warehouse, as though they were still relevant, long after we have given up on them, long after we have left them to become empty symbols, standing like abandoned tombstones in the landscape of our history? We may be wise to let science fiction writer Frank Herbert's words reverberate in our minds: "If you think of yourselves as helpless and ineffectual, it is certain that you will create a despotic government to be your master." Leaders of other countries see our present struggle with greater clarity than we do ourselves. "Do not lecture us about democracy," they say. "Stop trying to impose your multinational banks and political systems on us, when you do not even come close to following your own ideals. We can handle our own affairs better than you can, in our own interest rather than in yours."

In past times of crises, America has usually risen to the challenge, and met its moral responsibilities as a world power. So the question is: Are we merely an empire in decline now, like ancient Rome in its latter days, or can we still be the New Atlantis that the great idealistic souls who founded our nation once envisioned? Dick Gregory says, "In America with all its evils and faults, you can still reach through the forest and see the sun. But we don't know yet whether that sun is rising or setting for our country." Poet Langston Hughes replies: "Let America be America again. Let it be the dream it used to be." In this new age of global consciousness, I believe America must lead and inspire by example, and not merely pay lip service to tired old platitudes that no longer ring true at home or abroad.

How can we do this? The steps described just above are the ones that make most sense to me now. Some have been identified more often with the political right, some with the political left, many with the political center but with little commitment to them, and some from "none of the above." I think of them as an agenda that means, *Let us actually act on the inspiring thoughts and sentiments from our yesterdays that fit the present and emerging realities of today and tomorrow.* You may disagree with some of them. But we can start by identifying those on which we agree, and begin there.

Like a phoenix rising from the ashes, it is time for us to again exemplify the highest ideals of our nation's founding fathers. It is also time for us to remember these words from John F. Kennedy, in a different context from the one in which he uttered them: "We stand today on the edge of a new frontier. . . But the New Frontier of which I speak is not a set of promises – it is a set of challenges. It sums up not what I intend to offer the American people, but what I intend to ask of them." Much will be asked of us as we face the new geo-historical era that we are already moving into. We will be asked not only to behave in new and different ways, but to transform our consciousness in ways that allow us to see and hear more clearly, act more effectively, and relate to one another and to other nations on a basis of mutual respect rather than one of trying to force others to do as we wish them to.

Destiny is in our hands. We may not be able to "save the world," but with our best effort and a little luck we can at least avoid destroying it. If it is our will to do so, we can even help make it incredibly beautiful. The choice is ours. But those are the opening lines of another story, and it is time for this one to end. And so I am borrowing a closing line from Gabriel García Márquez: **"A true friend is one who holds your hand and touches your heart."** May the tides and currents of our national life come to reflect his words. May those of us who have opposed one another now confront the challenging task of learning how to listen deeply to each other, and to be friends. Our destiny is beckoning, waiting for us to give it form. Will we take that next step up in consciousness?

* * *

ACKNOWLEDGMENTS

I will be forever indebted to the towering figures whose remarkable minds formulated the visions and spoke or penned the words that are the central feature of this work. Since I have quoted them repeatedly, I need not repeat their names here. Of the many colleagues and friends whose conversations have influenced this book, a few deserve special mention. Bob Silverstein of Quicksilver Books Literary Agency has been a remarkable source of inspiration and support. (I have even borrowed some of his good words verbatim in these pages.) I appreciate philosopher Jacob Needleman's excellent work several years ago, *The American Soul—Rediscovering the Wisdom of the Founders,* that treats the same subject as this one, and I may have quoted him a just bit in excess of the "fair use" rule. Interviews with my colleagues – especially anthropologist Margaret, philosopher Stan, and social psychologist Heather all had their influence on these pages. Psychologist Charlie and research director Lew read the manuscript and suggested important changes. Sociologist Peter of *Project Censored* critiqued the section on Freedom of Speech and the Media, and lawyer Anthony made valuable suggestions on the Constitution and Justice sections. My incomparable wife, who completed two books of her own while I was writing this, worked diligently as copy editor for the entire manuscript. Nikola at BookBaby was a great help. And finally, I thank Griffin for his artistic rendering of the cover picture.

ABOUT THE AUTHOR

Victor Daniels is Professor Emeritus of the California State University, where after earning a Ph.D. in psychology from UCLA, he taught for 40 years and also served as Psychology Department Chair. Later he trained in Gestalt Therapy. Outraged by directions our nation has taken in the last half-century, he felt compelled to write this book to dispel widespread misconceptions about the views of the U.S. founding fathers and what has happened since their time. Married for 34 years, with two adult children, he now spends his time writing, tending a small orchard, and carrying out ongoing woodsman's and erosion control projects along the creek that flows near his home. Born in a small mining town in northwestern Utah, he grew up in Utah, Nebraska, Florida, California, and on and around Army posts and Air Force bases in Germany, France, and England where his parents worked during the period after World War II. As a result of spending his childhood in four countries, he developed a sense of perspective that is hard to come by when you grow up in just one. After completing his Ph.D., he was a Peace Corps Volunteer in Chile during the term of President Eduardo Frei Montalva, the president who preceded Salvador Allende, before the fascist General Pinochet murdered the latter and set up a terror-based dictatorship to replace Chile's democracy (which has since been restored). He has previously written *Matrix Meditations* (with K.N. Daniels); *Tarot d'Amour*, (also with K.N. Daniels); *Being & Caring: A Psychology for Living* (with L.J. Horowitz); and numerous online articles on Gestalt Therapy.

For free downloads of choice selections from *The Radical Wrong* that you can send your friends, see <http://radicalwrong.com>

If you liked Part III of *The Radical Wrong*, you'll probably also like *Matrix Meditations* by Victor Daniels & Kooch N. Daniels. See <http://www.matrixmeditations.info/>

REFERENCES

Much of the research for this work was done online. The quotation sites I used most are Brainyquote.com and ThinkExist.com, but I used numerous others related to specific topics or people. I used Wikipedia extensively. Except for the hardcopy books listed below, I have not cited sources for statements by American presidents and other well-known figures (such as Benjamin Franklin) because they are all readily available in online searches. And for the most part I have not cited other online sources, because search engines have improved so remarkably that now you can usually get the material faster with a search than by typing in the url. Therefore most of the references below are actual books that I held in my hands. There are many more books in this list than are mentioned in the text, for they provide background and context. The list is also a door you can step through into a world of experiences and ideas that are at once strange and disturbing, and also deeply informative.

- - - - - - - -

Abu Ghraib photographs: http://endthiswar.org/abughraib.htm Accessed on 9/24/10.
Allport, Gordon W. *The Nature of Prejudice, 25th Anniversary Edition*. New York: Perseus/Basic Books, 1979.
Anderson, Alfred. *Liberating the Early American Dream,* Tom Paine Institute, 1985, pp. 161-74.
Anderson, Walter Truett. All Connected Now: Life in the First Global Civilization. New York: Perseus Wesstview, 2001.
Anonymous. *Imperial Hubris: Why the West is Losing the War on Terror*. Washington, D.C.: Brassey's Inc, 2004.
Archer, Jules. *The Plot to Seize the White House: The Shocking True Story of the Conspiracy to Overthrow FDR*. New York: Skyhorse Publishing, 1973, 2007.
Avlon, John. *How the Lunatic Fringe is Hijacking America*. New York: Beast, 2010.
Babiak, Paul & Robert D. Hare. *Snakes in Suits: When Psychopaths Go to Work*. New York: HarperCollins, 2006.
Bacevich, Andrew J. *The New American Militarism: How Americans Are Seduced by War*. Oxford University Press, 2005.
Bacevich, Andrew J. *Washington Rules: America's Path to Permanent War*. New York: Henry Holt, 2010.
Bacevich, Andrew. J. *The Limits of Power: The End of American Exceptionalism*. Henry Holt, 2009.
Bagdikian, Ben H. *The New Media Monopoly*. Boston: Beacon, 2004.
Baker, Russ. *Family of Secrets: The Bush Dynasty, America's Invisible Governmet, and the Hidden History of the Last Fifty Years*. New York: Bloomsbury, 2009.
Ball, Terrence and Richard Dagger. *Ideals and Ideologies, a Reader, 6th ed*. New York: Pearson, 2006.
Barnet, Richard J. and John Cavanagh. *Global Dreams: Imperial Corporations and the New World Order*. Simon & Schuster Touchstone, 1994.
Beck, Aaron. *Prisoners of Hate. The Cognitive Basis of Anger, Hostility, and Violence*. New York: HarperCollins, 2000.
Begley, Sharon. (2007) *Train Your Mind, Change Your Brain: How a New*
Berry, Thomas. *The Great Work: Our Way Into the Future*. New York: Bell Tower, 1999.
Blumenthal, Max. *Republican Gomorrah: Inside the Movement that Shattered the Party*. New York: Nation Books, 2009.
Boorstein, Daniel J. *The Image: A Guide to Pseudo-Events in America*. New York: Random House Vintage, 1961, 1987.
Brehm, Jack W., and Arthur R. Cohen. (1962) *Explorations in Cognitive Dissonance.*-New York: Wiley, 1962, p. 77.
Brock, David. *The Republican Noise Machine: Right-Wing Media and How it Corrupts Democracy.* New York: Crown, 2004.
Brock, David. *Blinded by the Right: The Conscience of an Ex-Conservative*. New York: Three Rivers, 2002.
Brown, Lester. *World on the Edge: How to Prevent Economic and Environmental Collapse*. New York: Norton, 2011.

Cavanagh, John and Jerry Mander, eds. *Alternatives to Economic Globalization*. San Francisco: Berrett-Kohler, 2004.

Chiniquy, Charles. *Fifty Years in the Church of Rome* Readaclassiconline, 2011.

Chomsky, Noam. *Class Warfare: Interviews with David Barsamian*. Monroe, Maine: Common Courage Press, 1996.

Chomsky, Noam. *Deterring Democracy*. New York: Hill & Wang, 1992.

Chomsky, Noam. *Media Control, 2nd ed. The Spectacular Achievements of Propaganda*. Open Media Books, 2001.

Chomsky, Noam. *Powers & Prospects: Reflections on Human Nature and the Social Order*. Boston: South End Press, 1996.

Chomsky, Noam. *Secrets, Lies, and Democracy*. Tucson: Odonian Press, 1994

Chossudovsky, Michel. *The Globalization of Poverty and the New World Order*. Ontario, Canada: Global Outlook, 2003.

Cooper, Mark N., ed. *The Case Against Media Consolidation. Evidence on Concentration, Localism, and Diversity*. Stanford, CA: Creative Commons, 2007.

Coser, Lewis A. *Masters of Sociological Thought: Ideas in Historical and Social Context*. Long Grove, Ill: Waveland Press, 1977.

Daniels, Victor & Horowitz, Laurence J. *Being and Caring: A Psychology for Living, 2nd ed*. Long Grove, Ill: Waveland Press, 1999.

Daniels, Victor & Kooch N. Daniels. *Matrix Meditations: A 16-Week Program for Developing the Mind-Heart Connection*. Inner Traditions, 2009.

De Toqueville, Alexis. *Democracy in America*. (1838) New York: Pocket Books, 1964.

Dean, John W. *Conservatives Without Conscience*. New York: Penguin, 2007.

Domhoff, G. William. *Who Rules America? Challenges to Corporate and Class Dominance, 6th ed*. McGraw-Hill, 2010.

Drucker, Peter F. *Post-Capitalist Society*. New York: HarperCollins, 1993.

Durant, Will and Ariel. *The Lessons of History*, p. 61. New York: Simon & Schuster, 1968.

Festinger, Leon. *A Theory of Cognitive Dissonance*. Palo Alto: Stanford University Press, 1957.

Founding Fathers. *Words of our Fathers: Declarations of Freedom* (Contains some of our countries most important documents) (Kindle Locations 993-995). Uplifting Publications. Kindle Edition, 2009.

Frank, Thomas. *The Wrecking Crew: How Conservatives Ruined Government, Enriched Themselves, and Beggared the Nation*. New York: Holt, 2008.

Franken, Al. *Lies and the Lying Liars Who Tell Them: A Fair and Balanced Look at the Right*. New York: Penguin, 2003.

Franken, Al. *The Truth* (with jokes.) New York: Dutton, 2005.

Freeden, Michael. *Ideology: A Very Short Introduction*. New York: Oxford, 2003.

Freeland, Chrystia. "The Rise of the New Global Elite." *The Atlantic,* January/February 2011, p. 44.

Freire, Paolo. *Pedagogy of the Oppressed*. New York: Seabury, 1974.

Friedman, John S. *The Secret Histories: An Anthology. Hidden Truths that Challenged the Past and Changed the World*. New York: Picador, 2005.

Funderburk, Charles & Robert G. Thobaben. Political Ideologies, 2nd ed. HarperCollins, 1994.

Goldwater, Barry, *The Conscience of a Conservative*. Shepardsville, KY: Victor Publishing, 1960.

Goleman, Daniel. "*Vital Lies, Simple Truths*. New York: Simon & Schuster/Touchstone, 1985.

Goodman, Paul & Taylor Stoehr. The Paul Goodman Reader. PM Press, 2011.

Griffin, G. Edward. *The Creature From Jekyll Island: A Second Look at the Federal Reserve*. Appleton, Wis.: American Opinion Publishing, 1994.

Hacker, Jacob S. & Paul Pierson. *Winner-Take-All Politics. How Washington Made the Rich Richer and Turned its Back on the Middle Class*. New York: Simon & Schuster, 2010.

Hardin, Garrett. "The Cybernetics of Competition." In: Shepard, Paul and Daniel McKinley: *The Subversive Science: Essays Toward an Ecology of Man*, p. 278. Boston: Houghton Mifflin, 1964.

Hartmann, Thom. *The Last Hours of Ancient Sunlight: The Fate of the World and What We Can Do About It*. New York: Three Rivers, 2004.

Hartmann, Thom. *What Would Jefferson Do? A Return to Democracy*. New York: Three Rivers, 2004.

Hartmann, Thom. *Rebooting the American Dream: 11 Ways to Rebuild Our Country*. San Francisco: Berrett-Kohler, 2010.

Hartmann, Thom. *Screwed: The Undeclared War Against the Middle Class.* San Francisco: Berrett-Kohler, 2006, 2007.
Hartmann, Thom. *Unequal Protetion: How Corporations Became 'People' – and How You Can Fight Back.* San Francisco: Berrett-Kohler, 2010.
Hawken, Paul, Amory Lovins, & L. Hunter Lovins. *Natural Capitalism: Creating the Next Industrial Revolution.* New York: Harper, 1999.
Heilbronner, Robert L. *The Essential Adam Smith.* New York: Norton, 1986.
Henderson, Hazel. *Building a Win-Win World: Life Beyond Global Economic Warfare.* San Francisco: Berrett-Kohler, 1997.
Henderson, Hazel. *Ethical Markets: Growing the Green Economy.* Vermont: Chelsea Green, 2006.
Henderson, Hazel. *Politics of the Solar Age: Alternatives to Economics.* Garden City: Doubleday Anchor, 1981.
Hersh, Seymour M. "The General's Report: How Antonio Taguba, who investigated the Abu Ghraib scandal, . became one of its casualties. *The New Yorker," June 25, 2007.*
Hightower Lowdown. Hardcopy and online. See www.hightowerlowdown.org/
Hopkirk, Peter. *The Great Game: The Struggle for Empire in Central Asia.* John Murray Publishers, 1990.
Huff, Mickey and Project Censored. *Censored 2012: The Top Censored Stories and Media Analysis of 2010-2011.* New York: Seven Stories Press.
Huff, Mickey, Peter Phillips and Project Censored. *Censored 2011: The Top 25 Censored Stories of 2009-10.* New York: Seven Stories Press.
Huffington, Arianna. *Pigs at the Trough: How Corporate Greed and Political Corruption are Undermining America.* New York: Three Rivers, 2003.
Huffington, Arianna. *Third World America: How Our Politicians are Abandoning the Middle Class and Betraying the American Dream.* New York: Crown, 2010.
Huxley, Aldous. *Brave New World Revisited.* New York: Harper & Row, 1958.
Huxley, Aldous. *Brave New World.* New York: Harper, 1932, 1998.
Jamieson, Kathleen Hall. *Dirty Politics: Deception, Distraction, and Democracy.* Oxford University Press, 1992.
Jarecki, Eugene. *The American Way of War: Guided Missiles, Misguided Men, and a Republic in Peril.* New York: Free Press, 2008.
Jay, Antony. *Oxford Dictionary of Political Quotations.* New York: Oxford, 2001.
Jensen, Carl (ed). *Censored: The News that Didn't Make the News—And Why: The 1993 Project Censored Yearbook.* Chapel Hill, N.C.: Shelburne Press
Jensen, Carl (ed). *Censored: The News that Didn't Make the News—And Why. The 1994 and 1995 Project Censored Yearbooks.* New York: Four Walls, Eight Windows Press.
Jensen, Carl (ed). *Censored: The News That Didn't Make the News—And Why. The 1996 Project Censored Yearbook, 20th Anniversary Edition.* New York: Seven Stories Press.
Johnson, Alan G. *The Gender Knot: Unraveling our Patriarchal Legacy.* Philadelphia: Temple University Press, 1997.
Johnson, Chalmers. *Blowback: The Costs and Consequences of American Empire.* New York: Holt, 2001 & 2004.
Johnson, Chalmers. *Nemesis: the Last Days of the American Republic.* New York: Holt, 2006.
Johnson, Chalmers. *The Sorrows of Empire: Militarism, Secrecy, and the End of the Republic.* New York: Holt, 2004.
Keen, Sam. *Faces of the Enemy: Reflections of the Hostile Imagination.* San Francisco: Harper & Row, 1986.
King, Martin Luther, Jr. *Where Do We Go From Here: Chaos or Community*? Boston: Beacon, 1968, 1986.
King, Martin Luther, Jr. (Ed. By Clayborne Carson) *The Autobiography of Martin Luther King, Jr.* New York: IPM & Grand Central Publishing, 1998.
King, Martin Luther, Jr. *Strength to Love.* Philadelphia: Fortress Press, 1963, 1981.
Kinzer, Stephen. *Overthrow: America's Century of Regime Change from Hawaii to Iraq.* New York: Henry Holt, 2006.
Klein, Ezra. "Tax Cutters for Truth." *Newsweek,* Dec. 20, 1010, p. 18.
Korten, David. *The Post-Corporate World: Life After Capitalism.* Bloomfield, Ct: Kumarian Press, & San Francisco: Berett-Kohler, 1999.

Korten, David. *The Great Turning: From Empire to Earth Community*. Bloomfield, Ct.: Kormarian Press, & San Francisco: Berrett-Kohler, 2006.

Korten, David. *When Corporations Rule the World*. Bloomfield, Ct.: Kumarian Press, & San Francisco: Berrett-Kohler, 1991.

Kristol, Irving. "The Neoconservative Persuasion: What it was, and what it is." *The Weekly Standard*, 8, no. 47 (August 2003) 23-25.]

Lakoff, George. *Don't Think of an Elephant: Know Your Values and Frame the Debate*. Vemont: Chelsea Green, 2004.

Lakoff, George. *Moral Politics: How Liberals and Conservatives Think, 2nd ed*. Chicago: University of Chicago Press, 2002.

Lakoff, George. *The Political Mind: A Cognitive Scientist's Guide to Your Brain and Its Politics*. New York: Penguin, 2009.

Lakoff, George. *Thinking Points: Communicating Our American Values and Vision*. New York: Farrar, Straus & Giroux, 2006.

Lakoff, George. *Whose Freedom? The Battle Over America's Most Important Idea*. Picador: 2006.

Lappé, Frances Moore. *Democracy's Edge: Choosing to Save Our Country by Bringing Democracy to Life*. San Francisco: Jossey Bass, 2006.

Leopold, Aldo. *A Sand County Almanac*. New York: Ballantine, 1966.

Lewis, Sinclair. *The Millennium: A Comedy of the Year 2000*. New York: Seven Stories Press, 1907, 2000.

Lewis, Sinclair. *It Can't Happen Here*. Signet: 1935, 2005.

Lichtenberg, Philip. *Community & Confluence: Undoing the Clinch of Oppression*. Cambridge, MA: GestaltPress, 1990.

Lichtenberg, Philip, Janneke van Beusekom, and Dorothy Gibbons. *Encountering Bigotry: Befriending Projecting Persons in Everyday Life*. Cambridge, Mass: GestaltPress, 1997.

Lindner, Robert. *Prescription for Rebellion*. New York: Grove Press, 1952, 1962.

Lipton, Bruce H. and Steve Bhaerman. (2009) *Spontaneous Evolution: Our Positive Future (and a Way to Get There From Here)*. Carlsbad, CA. and New York: Hay House, p. 117.

Lovelock, James. *Gaia: A New Look at Life on Earth*. Oxford Univ. Press, 1979, 1987.

Lovelock, James. *The Revenge of Gaia: Earth's Climate Crisis & the Fate of Humanity*. New York: Perseus, 2006.

Lovelock, James. *The Vanishing Face of Gaia: A Final Warning*. New York: Perseus, 2009.

Lovins, Amory. *Reinventing Fire: Bold Business Solutions For the New Energy Era*. Rocky Mountain Institute, 2011.

Malone, Dumas. *Jefferson and His Time: The Sage of Monticello*. Boston: Little, Brown, 1981.

McKibben, Bill. *Deep Economy: The Wealth of Communities and the Durable Future*. New York: Holt, 2007.

McKibben, Bill. *Eaarth: Making a Life on a Tough New Planet*. New York: Holt, 2010.

Meadows, Donella H. *Thinking in Systems*. Vermont: Chelsea Green, 2008.

Mill, John Stuart. *Three Essays: On Liberty, Representative Government, The Subjugation of Women*. New York: Oxford, 1975, pp. 1-9.

Mondale, Walter. Quoted in Dunford, Kara and Ashley Larkin. *"At SMPA,   MondaleTalks Politics."*

Moore, Michael. *Stupid White Men . . . and Other Sorry Excuses for the State of the Nation*. New York: HarperCollins 2001.

Moore, Michael. Capitalism: *A Love Story* (film, DVD). Anchor Bay.

Moore, Michael. *Dude, Where's My Country*. New York: Warner Books, 2003.

Munves, James. *Thomas Jefferson and the Declaration of Independence*. New York: Scribners, 1976.

Nader, Ralph. *The Ralph Nader Reader*. New York: Seven Stories Press, 2000.

Naomi Klein. The Shock Doctrine: The Rise of Disaster Capitalism. New York: Henry Holt, 2007.

Needleman, Jacob. *The American Soul: Rediscovering the Wisdom of the Founders*. New York: Tarcher/Penguin, 2003.

Neiwert, David. *The Eliminationists: How Hate Talk Radicalized the American Right*. Sausalito: PoliPoint Press, 2009.

Oakeshott, Michael. "On Being Conservative." In Love, Nancy S. *Dogmas and Dreams: A Reader in Modern Political Ideologies, 3rd ed*. Washington, D.C.: Congressional Quarterly Press, 2006.

Oakley, Barbara A. (2007) *Evil Genes: Why Rome Fell, Hitler Rose, Enron Failed, and My Sister Stole My Mother's Boyfriend*. Amherst, N.Y: Prometheus Books, P. 89.

Orwell, George. *1984*. Harcourt/Penguin Plume, 1949, 1983.

Orwell, George. *Animal Farm.* Harcourt/Penguin Plume, 1946, 2003.
Pacem In Terris: Encyclical of Pope John XXIII on Establishing Universal Peace in Truth, Justice, Charity, and Liberty. April 11, 1963.
Palast, Greg: "George Bush's favorite vultures: How financial birds of prey are seizing Africa's AIDS medicine." *Dollars and Sense* (newsletter), Thomson Gale, March 22, 2007, Issue 270, p. 8
Palast, Greg. *Armed Madhouse.* New York: Penguin, 2006.
Palast, Greg. *The Best Democracy Money Can Buy: The Truth About Corporate Cons, Globalization, and High-Finance Fraudsters.* New York: Penguin Plume, 2004.
Parenti, Michael. *Inventing Reality: The Politics of News Media, 2nd ed.* Belmont: Wadsworth, 1993.
Parenti, Michael. *Against Empire.* San Francsco: City Lights, 1995.
Parenti, Michael. *History as Mystery.* San Francisco: City Lights, 1999.
Paul, Ron. *A Foreign Policy of Freedom: Peace, Commerce, and Honest Friendship.* New York: Rosetta Books electronic edition, 2010.
Pearce, Fred. *When the Rivers Run Dry: The Defining Crisis of the Twenty-First Century.* Boston: Beacon Press, 2006.
Pearl, Austin. *Bipolar Nation: Will the REAL Majority Please Stand Up?* Washington and New York: Lido Press, 2010.
Perkins, John. *Confessions of an Economic Hit Man.* New York: Penguin Plume, 2004.
Perkins, John. *The Secret History of the American Empire: The Truth About Economic Hit Men, Jackals, and How to Change the World.* New York: Penguin Plume, 2007.
Phillips, Kevin. American Theocracy: *The Peril and Politics of Radical Religion, Oil, and Borrowed Money in the 21st Century.* New York: Viking, 2006.
Phillips, Kevin. *Wealth and Democracy: A Political History of the American Rich.* New York: Broadway Books, 2002.
Phillips, Peter (ed) & Project Censored. *Censored 1997: The News That Didn't Make the News.* (And all intervening years through 2007.) New York: Seven Stories Press.
Phillips, Peter & Andrew Roths (eds) with Project Censored. *Censored 2008: The Top 25 Censored Stories of 2007-2007* (and Censored 2009—same editors). New York: Seven Stories Press
Phillips, Peter & Dennis Loo. *Impeach the President: The Case Against Bush and Cheney.* New York: Seven Stories Press, 2006.
Phillips, Peter & Mickey Huff with Project Censored. *Censored 2010: The Top 25 Censored Stories of 2008-9* (and Censored 2011—same editors.)
Polster, Erving. Uncommon Ground: *Humanizing Psychotherapy & Community to Enhance Everyday Living.* Phoenix: Zeig, Tucker, & Thiesen, 2006.
Press, Bill. *Toxic Talk: How the Radical Right Has Poisoned America's Airwaves.* New York: St Martin's, 2010.
Prouty, L. Fletcher. *The Secret Team: The CIA and Its Allies in Control of the United States and the World.* New York: Skyhorse, 2011.
Rand, Ayn. *Anthem.* New York: Penguin Signet, 1961, 1995.
Rand, Ayn. *The Fountainhead.* Penguin Signet, 143, 1999.
Reich, Robert B. *Aftershock: The Next Economy & America's Future.* New York: Viking, 2011.
Religious Coalition for Reproductive Choice. http://www.nmrcrc.org/action.php
Roberts, Paul Craig and Lawrence Stratton. *The Tyranny of Good Intentions: How Prosecutors and Law Enforcement are Trampling the Constitution in the Name of Justice.* New York: Three Rivers Press, 2008.
Rokeach, Milton . *The Open and Closed Mind.* New York: Basic Books, 1960.
Romm, Joseph. *Hell and High Water: Global Warming—the Solution and the Politics—and What We Should Do.* New York: William Morrow, 2007.
Safire, William. "Inside a Republican Brain." *New York Times,* July 21, 2004Scheuer, Michael. *Marching Toward Hell: America and Islam After Iraq.* New York: Free Press, 2008.
Schmidt, Hans. *Maverick Marine: General Smedley D. Butler and the Contradictions of American History.* University Press of Kentucky, 1987.
Schumacher, E.F. *Small is Beautiful: Economics as if People Mattered.* New York: Harper & Row, 1973.
Shils, E.A. (1954) *Authoritarianism: "Right" and "left."* In R. Christie and M. Jahoda (Eds.) Studies in the scope and method of "The Authoritarian Personality." New York: Free Press.
Siegel, Daniel J. *Mindsight: The New Science of Personal Transformation.* New York: Bantam, 2010.

Silk, Leonard & Mark Silk. *The American Establishment*. New York: Avon, 1980.

Simpson, Alan. Quoted in Kosova, Weston. "Alan Simpson: 'No One Forgives Anyone," *Newsweek,* April 22, 2010, p. 35.

Smith, Adam. See also Heilbronner, R.L., ed.

Smith, Adam. *The Theory of Moral Sentiments*. Edinburgh, Scotland, Kindle edition.

Solomon, Norman. *Made Love, Got War: Close Encounters With America's Warfare State*. Sausalito: PoliPoint, 2007.

Solomon, Norman. *War Made Easy: How Presidents and Pundits Keep Spinning Us to Death*. New Jersey: Wiley, 2005.

Steinem, Gloria. *Moving Beyond Words*. New York: Simon & Schuster, 1994.

Steiner, Rudolf. *Polarities in the Evolution of Mankind*. New York: Anthroposophic Press, 1987.

Stout, Martha. *The Sociopath Next Door*. New York: Broadway Books, 2005.

Taibibi, Matt. *The Great Derangement: A Terrifying, True Story of War, Politics, and Religion*. New York: Spiegel & Grau, 2008.

The "Taguba Report" On Treatment Of Abu Ghraib Prisoners In Iraq. ARTICLE 15-6 INVESTIGATION OF THE 800th MILITARY POLICE BRIGADE. SECRET / NO FOREIGN DISSEMINATION http://news.findlaw.com/hdocs/docs/iraq/tagubarpt.html

Tye, Larry. *The Father of Spin. Edward L. Bernays and the Birth of Public Relations*. New York: Henry Holt, 2001.

Ventura, Jesse, with Dick Russell. *Don't Start the Revolution Without Me*. New York: Skyhorse Publishing, 2008.

Ventura, Jesse, with Dick Russell. *63 Documents the Government Doesn't Want You to Read*. Delaware: Skyhorse Publishing, 2011.

Ventura, Jesse. *I Ain't Got Time to Bleed: Reworking the Body Politic From the Bottom Up*. New York: Signet, 2000.

Ventura, Jesse. *American Conspiracies*. New York: Skyhorse, 2011.

Watterson, Karen (1995). *Not by the Sword: How the Love of a Cantor and His Family Transformed a Klansman*. New York: Simon & Schuster

Wells, H.G. The Shape of Things to Come: The Ultimate Revolution. London & New York, 1933, 2005.

Wheeler, Gordon. *Beyond Individualism: Toward a New Understanding of Self, Relationship, and Experience*. Cambridge, MA: GestaltPress, 2000.

Wills, Gary. *Confessions of a Conservative*. New York: Doubleday, 1979.

Works of Thomas Jefferson from Mobile Reference. Mobile Reference, 2003-2009.

Works of Thomas Paine. Mobile Reference, 2003- 2009.

Zaitchik, Alexander. *Common Nonsense: Glenn Beck and the Triumph of Ignorance*. New Jersey: Wiley, 2010.

Zimbardo, Philip. (2008) *The Lucifer Effect: Understanding How Good People Turn Evil*. New York: Random House.

Zinn, Howard. *A People's History of the United States*. New York: Harper, 1995/

Zinn, Howard. A Power Governments Cannot Suppress. San Francisco: City Lights, 2007.

Zinn, Howard. *The Twentieth Century*. New York: HarperCollins Perennial, 2003.

* * *

www.ingramcontent.com/pod-product-compliance
Lightning Source LLC
Chambersburg PA
CBHW070001300526
45794CB00001B/136